# ST. MAXIMILIAN KOLBE

## APOSTLE OF OUR DIFFICULT AGE

Translated and adapted
by the
**Daughters of St. Paul**
from the Italian biography
*Beato Massimiliano Maria Kolbe*
by
**Rev. Antonio Ricciardi, O.F.M. Conv.**

**BOOKS & MEDIA**

BOSTON

NIHIL OBSTAT:
   Rev. Richard V. Lawlor, S.J.
   *Censor*

IMPRIMATUR:
   ✠ Humberto Cardinal Medeiros
   *Archbishop of Boston*

Library of Congress Cataloging in Publication Data

Ricciardi, A., adapted by the Daughters of St. Paul
   St. Maximilian Kolbe, apostle of our difficult age.

   1. Kolbe, Maximilian, Saint, 1894-1941.
2. Christian saints—Poland—Biography. I. Title.
BX4700.K55R53     1982     282'.092'4 [B]          82-18316

ISBN  0-8198-6838-8 cloth
      0-8198-6837-X paper

Printed and published by Pauline Books & Media, 50 St. Paul's
Avenue, Boston, MA 02130.

Pauline Books & Media is the publishing house of the Daughters of
St. Paul, an international congregation of women religious serving
the Church with the communications media.

3 4 5 6 7 8 9   99 98 97 96

*To our beloved Holy Father,*

*POPE JOHN PAUL II.*

*The whole world is grateful
for Your Holiness' having elevated
to the honor of the altars the heroic
Father Maximilian Kolbe,
who "voluntarily offered himself
for death in the starvation bunker
for a brother, and so won
a spiritual victory like that
of Christ Himself."*

*The Daughters of St. Paul*

# Contents

# Introduction

The life of the Church has been enriched with a new glory—Maximilian Mary Kolbe, O.F.M. Conv., a saint of today, so close to our generation, to the events that we ourselves have experienced, that his figure is familiar to many of us. Since 1941, when he died at the age of forty-seven in the starvation bunker at Auschwitz, he has touched our hearts and filled us with deep emotion. By the sacrifice of his life, which he lovingly offered to take the place of an unknown prisoner—the father of a family, who had been condemned to die in reprisal for the escape of another prisoner—he exemplified the redemptive love of Christ. "There is no greater love than this: to lay down one's life for one's friends" (Jn. 15:13).

At his death the fame of Kolbe spread rapidly and captured the world's attention and admiration. He has been called "the saint of the Second World War," "the holy prisoner," "the saint of the concentration camps," "the saint of the press," "the saint of aviation," "the saint of progress," "the saint of the poor." Rarely has a person of our times enjoyed such a universal reputation for holiness!

The cause of Father Kolbe's beatification was promoted and officially opened on March 16, 1960, with a decree of the Sacred Congregation of Rites. Few other processes have been supported by such a wealth of information. His beatification, which occurred on October 17, 1971, aroused in the print and electronic media the same wave of explosive enthusiasm as when the details of his heroic death were first made known.

Subsequently, the cause of his canonization was speedily undertaken, culminating in the solemn declaration of October 10, 1982, by which His Holiness John Paul II proclaimed this humble Franciscan priest a saint of the Church.

Although the best-known circumstances of St. Maximilian Kolbe's life are those of his martyrdom, they have not obscured his great apostolic achievements. Rather, the nature of his death has shed new light and aroused an ever-increasing interest in his work which, in the words of Cardinal A. G. Piazza, "has the charm of a novel and the dimensions of a miracle."

Throughout his life Father Kolbe was committed to the promotion and diffusion of the *Militia Immaculatae,* or *Knights of the Immaculata Movement,* * which he founded on October 16, 1917, in the Roman seminary where he was stationed. This movement, which from its inception aimed at the evangelization and sanctification of both individuals and vast multitudes through the Immaculate Virgin, was implemented through *The Knight of the Immaculata,* a little blue magazine which by 1939 had 800,000 subscribers in Poland alone. Gradually the programs of the "M.I." developed in the "City of the Immaculata" *(Niepokalanow)* in Poland, which before the tragic conflagration of the Second World War housed nearly 650 religious and over 180 aspirants. Today native vocations flourish in its Japanese counterpart, also called "Garden of the Immaculata" *(Mugenzai No Sono),* which Father Kolbe established in Nagasaki before the war.

---

*We no longer use the name Militia of the Immaculate or Immaculata in the U.S. as it does not accurately translate the Latin name *Militia Immaculatae.* The Latin word *militia* literally means "forces" or "troops," while the English word designates a civilian force or army that is called out only in emergencies. Kolbe's *Militia* is a permanent, full-time force that is always active and on-duty, striving for the victory of Mary's cause.                    —Fr. B.M.G.
National Director of the M.I.

Father Kolbe's zeal for souls knew no bounds, but spurred him always onwards to the foundation of other cities of the Immaculata all over the world. On his journey to the Far East in 1930, he was dreaming of a network of foundations embracing India and all the countries of the Arab world. In an exuberance of enthusiasm he exclaimed: "It is necessary that every country have its own city of the Immaculata; we have to establish *The Knight of the Immaculata* in every corner of the earth with a circulation of millions of copies."

Not even violence and death could stop him. He confidently proclaimed that he would "use both hands" to continue his conquests from heaven.

St. Maximilian Kolbe was not only a Marian apostle, but also a writer and promoter of a Marian spirituality which emerges from the doctrinal contribution of the Order of Conventual Franciscans to which he belonged. This doctrine, which he himself lived, is reflected in his numerous writings contained in various publications centering around his person and work. The original collection of his writings, which was approved on May 12, 1955, by the Sacred Congregation of Rites, comprises the *Treatise on the Immaculata* (incomplete), letters, conferences and various other writings.

A particularly interesting study of Father Kolbe's Mariology available in English is the *Immaculate Conception and the Holy Spirit,* by Father H. M. Manteau-Bonamy, O.P., a consultant at the Second Vatican Council who closely followed all conciliar discussions concerning Marian teaching. This work shows that Father Kolbe's grasp of the mystery of Mary made him a real precursor of Vatican II's Marian theology. It also explains his fundamental insight into the Immaculate Mary's place in God's plan: she is the chief visible manifestation of the Holy Spirit's presence in the Church and the universal instrument of the Spirit's mission to unite all men to Christ our Savior. This Marian aspect of the sanctity of St. Kolbe ranks him—as Pope Paul VI stated in his beatification homily—"among the

very great saints and farsighted visionaries who understood, venerated and sang the mystery of Mary." Maximilian Kolbe's Marian spirituality wholly permeated
his apostolate, open to all forms of activity, to all the
needs of souls, to all the resources of technology, to all
the latest conquests of progress, to all the most modern
means of communication.

The fear that Father Kolbe's enthusiasm for devotion to Mary overshadows his Christological and eccle-
siological doctrine is groundless. In Kolbe's thought,
Christ holds not only the first place, but also the only
place necessary and sufficient, absolutely speaking, in
the economy of salvation; nor is the love of the Church
and of her mission undermined in the doctrine and apostolate of the saint. Kolbe views Mary in salvation history
as the Servant of the Lord, the chosen one through
whose cooperation God gradually and firmly carried
out and continues His saving designs. Mary is the one
through whom men reach Jesus, and the one through
whom Jesus reaches men.

St. Maximilian Kolbe was a person of incredible daring and extraordinary organizational genius, but his
activity did not weaken or diminish his interior life.
Rather, his apostolic effectiveness came from prayer,
from divine help, from the fidelity of the apostolic
worker to his intimacy with God. In this he was absolutely unyielding: he would prefer that all his numerous
apostolic achievements be destroyed rather than that
laxity in religious observance take root in his communities.

The primacy of God and of interior life are repeatedly
affirmed throughout his writings with a force which
allows no yielding, with an insistence which gives no
respite.

Now, from the glory of Bernini, the figure of this man
of God, of this apostle, of this martyr, towers even higher,
and the mission he began on earth is completed and
perfected and continues bringing abundant fruits.

Today, Catholics strongly believe that the surprising vitality of the Church in Poland—a Church which is hampered, humiliated and persecuted—can be explained only in the light of the many anonymous martyrs who have drawn from the spiritual doctrine of Father Kolbe the strength to withstand any attack and the grace to forgive, to love, and to pray for their executioners.

—*The Translator*

A. Mari

*"I am here today as a pilgrim. It is well known that I have been here many times. So many times! And many times I have gone down to Maximilian Kolbe's death cell and stopped in front of the execution wall and passed among the ruins of the cremation furnaces of Brzezinka. It was impossible for me not to come here as Pope."*
Pope John Paul II

# The Kolbe Family

A native son of Poland, Maximilian (baptized Raymond) was born when his country was still divided and subject to Russian and Austrian power. His mother, Maria Dabrowska, was the daughter of a humble weaver of Zdunska-Wola; his father, Jules Kolbe, was also a weaver, the son of a workman from Rosomyls, in the same district.

Life in Zdunska-Wola was poor. The inhabitants, like those of nearby villages, would obtain their raw materials from the neighboring city of Lodz. Then, in their homes, men and women alike would work from morning to evening, bent over the looms without counting the hours, producing as much as they were able. At the end of the week, they would bring the cloth back to the merchants of Lodz and receive their meager wages.

Father Maximilian's parents shared the common lot of their fellow-townsmen. They were poor, but rich in that refreshing faith which views hardships as a necessary means for gaining eternal life.

Father Kolbe always had a singular esteem for his parents, a reverence that shines through his letters to his mother, which she carefully preserved. It seems as though she foresaw that one day those letters would be useful.

As an adolescent, Maria Dabrowska prayed to the Lord with all the fervor of her young heart: "I would rather die than reach the age of marriage." In spite of the prevailing custom which viewed marriage as an obligatory step for a girl of her social standing, Maria longed for the religious life, so as to enjoy paradise, as she said, together with pure souls. When she must have become convinced that it was impossible for her to enter a convent because she had no dowry, she began to storm heaven in another way:

"Nevertheless, O Lord, I do not want to impose my will on You, If Your designs are different, Give me, at least, a husband who does not curse, who does not drink, who does not go to the tavern to enjoy himself. This, O Lord, I ask You unconditionally!"

God answered the prayer of Maria Dabrowska. On October 5, 1891, at the age of twenty-one, she married Jules Kolbe, who was a year younger, but truly a man according to her desires. "He was a fervent Catholic," a contemporary testified, "who diligently attended church and went to Holy Communion every Sunday. He belonged to the Third Order of the Franciscans, of which he was also the leader."

The young couple had a modest dwelling and a little workshop for weaving. In Zdunska-Wola they rented a big room. In one corner they set up the kitchen and the looms in another. Behind a curtain, they placed beds and two cabinets. Between these, according to the custom of good Polish families, was an altar with a picture of the Madonna and other sacred images.

In this workroom on July 25, 1892, Francis, the first son, was born, followed on January 8, 1894, by Raymond —Father Maximilian. On January 29, 1896, at Lodz, a third son, Joseph, was born, followed on November 2, 1897, at Jutrzkowice, by Valentine, who died as an infant.

As the children grew, the narrowness of the house and scarcity of means convinced Jules Kolbe that he should move to Pabianice, a nearby village which was more populated. Here he rented a little house near the cemetery, to which he transferred the workshop. He even hired a worker, and Mrs. Kolbe opened a small store in which neighbors could find a little of everything. Meanwhile, Mr. Kolbe tried to supplement the family's income by cultivating three rented vegetable gardens. Here in Pabiance on May 19, 1900, was born Anthony, who died at the age of four.

At Pabianice, after a few years of great sacrifice, the economic condition of the Kolbe family improved somewhat, and they were able to move into a better house. Jules Kolbe kept the workshop and the store, which he enlarged; he also took on the management of a small, rented factory. Meanwhile, Maria occupied herself as a midwife—as was the custom in the villages—certainly not because she had a diploma, but because of her experience.

# His First Education

In his photographs, Father Kolbe is characterized by a kindly appearance. Those who knew him attest to his goodness and gentleness. These qualities earned him the nickname "marmalade."

But the boy Raymond actually possessed a lively, and even fiery, temperament. He was quick to react and sometimes quite obstinate. Undoubtedly, he had to work much to overcome himself and acquire full control over his character. The good education he received at home helped him very much in this.

As a good mother, Maria observed the virtues and defects in her son, and wisely sought to correct the latter in order to cultivate the former. Here is how she describes young Raymond for us:

"He was a boy who was very lively, quick and a bit spiteful. But of my three sons he was the most obedient to us, his parents. I had in him a real help when I went to work with my husband. Raymond would take care of the kitchen, and would keep the house spic and span, hurrying to do all the duties. He distinguished himself from his brothers even in receiving punishment for some harmless prank. He himself would bring the switch used for punishment, and without hesitating he would lie down on the bench; after having received the punishment, he would thank us and unperturbed put the switch back in its place."

Mr. Kolbe collaborated with his wife in Raymond's sound education, which today we would consider almost severe. One of Raymond's friends testified:

"The father saw to it that his sons also grew up physically healthy. Therefore, as soon as the first snow had fallen, he would take them with him into the garden for a barefoot race. He kept watch lest they took part in any amusements that were too noisy."

## The Story of the Two Crowns

Raymond was about ten years old when the most important and extraordinary episode of his childhood took place. It was a tender, motherly apparition of the Virgin, which he would never forget. This apparition became a continual incentive in his love for the Immaculata and in the fatigue of the apostolate which he later carried out. Although Father Kolbe exchanged countless confidences with his confreres, he never let slip the least hint of this great grace. It was his mother who revealed the event to Father Maximilian's fellow religious after her son's death. The letter is dated October 12, 1941.

"I knew right from the beginning, following the extraordinary event that happened to Father Maximilian in the years of his childhood, that he would die a martyr. I just do not remember whether the event took place after or before his first confession. Once I was not pleased with something he had done and I said to him, 'Raymond, who knows what will become of you?' Afterwards I did not think of it any more, but I noticed a complete change in him.

"We had a small, hidden altar where he often went to pray without letting anyone notice. As he prayed he would cry.

"Generally he acted in a manner older than his age, being always recollected and serious. He would pray with tears in his eyes.

"I was concerned that he might perhaps be sick, so I asked him: 'What is the matter with you?' And I began to insist, 'You must tell everything to your mother.'

"Trembling with emotion and with tears in his eyes, he told me: 'When you scolded me, Mama, I prayed very much to the Madonna to tell me what would become of me. And later, in church, I prayed to her again. Then the Madonna appeared to me, holding two crowns in her hands: one white and one red. She looked on me with affection and asked me if I wanted those two crowns. The white one meant that I would remain pure, and the red, that I would be a martyr. I told her I accepted them. Then the Madonna looked at me sweetly and disappeared.'

"The extraordinary change that took place in the boy testified to the reality of the vision. He was always fully aware of it, and on every occasion, with his face radiant, he would mention his desired death of martyrdom. And so I was prepared, as the Madonna was after the prophecy of Simeon."

We do not know whether Maria in turn confided her son's secret to his father. Certainly the vision was well understood by Raymond and no less by his mother, who years later still had a lively remembrance of it. Nevertheless, nothing changed in the plans of Mr. and Mrs. Kolbe for their sons.

Ordinarily it was their custom to make an annual pilgrimage to the sanctuary at Czestochowa. In one of the years preceding Raymond's vision, with a generous act of faith, the Kolbes had offered their firstborn son, Francis, to the Lord, promising the Madonna that they would make every sacrifice so that the boy could become a priest. Raymond, instead, would have to help out at home and plan to continue in his father's footsteps.

Even after the apparition of the Virgin, the Kolbes continued to hold to these plans. Apprehension and doubts, however, caused them many sleepless nights.

The simplest solution would have been to keep Raymond in school, too. But how could they do it? It was impossible, as we know from this confidence of his mother:

"He (Raymond) had finished elementary school, and in the Kingdom of Poland, under Russian domination, high school was rare and very expensive. We, instead, were not rich and did not want to become rich, being convinced that wealth is a great obstacle to perfection and therefore to salvation. And God protected us from such evils. We had decided that our oldest son should be educated, and that little Raymond, that is, Father Maximilian, would help us at home. This he accepted willingly, helping me very carefully in everything. He did this to such an extent that he even sought to surprise me at times with some new dish. Even though he was a little boy, he already knew how to provide different satisfactions for his mother...."

In view of these circumstances, one can better appreciate the dispositions of the ten-year-old boy. He always let himself be guided by the voice of obedience, or in the absence of this, by external events, which he regarded with faith as signs of the will of God. Notwithstanding the fact that he had been favored with a vision of Mary, he knew that at his age he had only one duty: to obey his parents. He applied himself to the task with all the generosity and simplicity of his good heart.

Mr. Francis Pisalski, a neighbor, described Raymond at this stage of his life, as follows:

"He was of a happy character: very lively. He told me that he was full of joy, as St. Francis had been, and that he would have liked to talk to the birds. Nevertheless, in church he was recollected, gentle and absorbed in prayer. From his youngest years, he served Mass. He went to church willingly. He avoided noisy entertainments, and he did not even attend family weddings. He was obedient to his parents and disciplined."

# His Attraction to the Franciscans

Raymond had read the life of St. Francis, given to
him by his father, a Franciscan Tertiary. He had developed an admiration for the great saint of Assisi and also
for the Franciscan friars. He was particularly attracted
by a friary located a short distance from Lodz, a little
outside the village of Kagiewniki, and hidden among the
trees of the forest. Throughout the year the church
there, dedicated to St. Anthony of Padua, was the goal
of local pilgrimages. After having venerated the holy
wonderworker, the faithful would go into the crypt to
pray at the tomb of Venerable Father Raphael Chylinski, a religious of the Conventual Franciscans.

The life of this Servant of God, formerly an officer of
the Polish army, was a marvelous example of love for
the most holy Virgin. During the years of war and epi-
demics which afflicted Poland at his time, he had
displayed the most heroic charity in behalf of the victims. For this reason the Catholics of Poland have held
him in great veneration, as the many votive offerings
given throughout the ages bear witness.

Raymond was held spellbound by the story of this
noble officer who, like Brother Angelo Tancredi, companion of St. Francis, had exchanged the sword for the
sacred habit. Visiting the tomb of this holy priest, recalling Father Chylinski's examples and reflecting on his
own vision of the two crowns, the boy asked for greater
recollection in his prayer life.

The apparition of the Madonna had constituted a
turning point in Raymond's life, and it spurred him to an
ever greater devotion to the Immaculata. Most probably
this was the period in his life that Father Kolbe was
referring to when he confided: "I remember that as a
boy I bought a little statue of the Immaculata which cost
me five kopiejki."

Undoubtedly Raymond had a bright mind which
could not pass unobserved. One day he was sent
by his mother to the drugstore to buy a medicine for

one of her patients. The knowledge of Latin that the boy displayed, even though rudimentary, must have impressed Mr. Kotowski, the good pharmacist of Pabianice, because he offered to tutor Raymond. Mr. and Mrs. Kolbe seized the opportunity given by Mr. Kotowski's generous offer and allowed their son to continue his studies. To spare Raymond for those few months of school, even if no expenses were involved, was a sacrifice for the family, but they made it willingly, even more so as they clearly saw the intervention of Providence.

Here is a more detailed account given by his mother:

"I was a midwife. One day I was taking care of a sick woman, to whom I needed to apply a packing. So I sent my little Raymond to the pharmacy to get the necessary powder. When he asked for *Vencon greca,* the pharmacist asked him, 'How do you know it is called *Vencon greca?'* And he answered, 'That is its name in Latin.'

"'And how do you know that it has a Latin name?'

"'Because we go to learn Latin from the priest.'

"The pharmacist continued to question him, asking his name, where he lived and what school he went to. Little Raymond told him that his brother went to the high school and was in the first class of business, because at that time there was in Pabianice the Higher Business School, and he added that if the good God permitted it, 'my brother will be a priest, while I must stay at home. My parents cannot let both of us be educated, since they are not rich enough, and much money is needed.'

"Then the pharmacist said, 'My boy, it is a pity to leave you like this. Come to me and I will give you lessons, so that at the end of the year, you will have caught up to your brother, and after the examinations you can both be promoted to the second class.'

"He therefore established the hours for the sessions. After this, my little Raymond came to me, as though borne on wings, and with great joy he told me of the great fortune he had met with. Indeed, from that day on, he went to the pharmacist for lessons, and this fine and providential man prepared him in such a way that he did reach the level which his older brother had attained, and both were promoted together."

Thus, together with his older brother, Raymond began attending business school.

A step had been taken, although not in the right direction. The Kolbe parents themselves seemed convinced that their son was not cut out to be a businessman, as this episode, recalled by Father Maximilian in 1919, reveals:

On the eve of the exams for admission, Raymond's mother said to him: "When you are a merchant, I will be a queen."

"And I will be a bishop," his father added.

It was to be a period of expectation.... They continued to have faith.... Providence would again show the way with clearer and more definite signs.

# The Religious Formation

The religious formation of Friar Maximilian took place from the time of his entrance into the Order of Friars Minor Conventual until his ordination to the priesthood and the completion of his theological studies. Under the guidance and inspiration of intelligent, prayerful and zealous teachers, the future founder of the Knights of the Immaculata grew day by day in wisdom and sanctity. The excellent preparation he received and to which he corresponded in such a quiet yet exemplary way formed a strong foundation for the apostolate to which he was called by God through the voice of obedience.

## In the Minor Seminary of Lwów

Northern Poland was under Russian domination. In 1864, after the religious orders had been suppressed, only two friaries of the Order of Friars Minor Conventual in the north were left open—those of Kalisz and Grodno. There the older Fathers were allowed by the Russian authorities to retire "to die." In Galicia, the southern part of Poland, on the other hand, which was united to the Austro-Hungarian Empire, the friaries of the Order were experiencing a spiritual revival. Galicia constituted the sole Polish province of the Order and included the two northern monasteries of Kalisz and Grodno.

In the early 1900's, however, a new political order arose in Poland. The superiors in Galicia felt it was a favorable time to undertake initiatives for reopening the monasteries in the north. This desire was shared by the other members of the community and spread through the province like a breath of fresh hope.

In preparation for Easter, 1907, a mission was preached by two Franciscan Fathers from Galicia. At the end of the preaching, one of the two missionaries, Father Peregrine Haczela, announced from the pulpit the opening of a new seminary in Lwów (at that time Lemberg). All young men willing to consecrate themselves to the Lord in the Franciscan Order were welcome. Young Raymond Kolbe, spellbound by the words coming from the pulpit, felt a mysterious inner joy. The voice of the missionary echoed in his heart, and he accepted the invitation. He had read about the generous, heroic life of St. Francis, and seemed to see in the Franciscan Order the reflection of the two crowns of chastity and martyrdom, which the Blessed Virgin had offered him.

So it was that Raymond and his brother Francis asked the missionary Father how to go about entering the order.

The missionaries, however, wanted them to finish out the year at the business school they were attending. They entrusted Rev. Vladimir Jakowski, who was already teaching Latin to Francis, with the task of helping the two boys enter the seminary of Lwów at the beginning of the new school year.

In October, 1907, with the help of their pastor, Francis and Raymond left their family to enter the peaceful atmosphere of the Franciscan community. Their father accompanied them as far as Krakow; then they proceeded alone toward Lwów.

In the three years that followed, Raymond completed his studies of the humanities. The few pieces of testimony we possess about this period in his life unanimously bear witness to his intelligence and goodness, to his progress in studies, and to his prayerfulness.

Mr. Gruchala, a professor of mathematics at the minor seminary, expressed his thought this way: "It is a pity that this young man, so richly gifted, should become a priest."

Father Cornelius Czupryk, who was a few years ahead of Father Kolbe in his studies, synthesizes his impressions thus:

"His schoolmates knew that Maximilian (at that time his name was still Raymond) was among the most diligent. He was well known for his firm grasp of science and mathematics. Even his older companions turned to him for the solution of the most difficult problems."

Finally, Father Felice Wilk, who entered the seminary of Lwów at the same time as the Kolbe brothers, gives this more complete account:

"Diligent and conscientious in carrying out his duties, he was especially gifted in mathematics. He was obedient to his instructors. To his companions, he was serviceable and courteous. Smiling and happy, he possessed a balanced character. He fulfilled his religious duties with admirable recollection and without any singularity. I remember just one incident that deeply impressed me. During free time I found him in the hall alone, kneeling before a large crucifix, absorbed in prayer."

After three years of study and prayer, Raymond reached the stage which demanded a more serious commitment: the year of novitiate.

The Fathers who had the task of accepting the new candidates to the novitiate found no difficulty in admitting Raymond Kolbe. During his postulancy they had observed in him an ever-increasing attachment to religious discipline, a great love for virtue, a quick and versatile mind, and above all, an uncommon enthusiasm.

Although from childhood he had experienced the maternal benevolence of Mary Immaculate, he was not spared temptations. Soon enough, enticing voices wrenched his heart and threatened his very vocation.

On the eve of his religious investiture, Raymond was overcome by doubts and uncertainties. He was tormented by a temptation that was especially dangerous because it was clothed in persuasive arguments presented by holy intentions.

In a memoir written at the request of his superiors, for the purpose of manifesting the hand of God in all his work, Father Maximilian later confessed that his life was to be wholly consecrated to the Immaculata. For this reason he prayed unceasingly to his "Mamina" (as he affectionately invoked her) to let him know on what battlefield he would earn the two crowns she had shown him previously. From another confession, made in Japan in 1935, we know that one day in the chapel of the seminary of Lwów, bowing his face to the floor before the altar of the Immaculata during Mass one day he promised her that he would fight for her. Although at that time he did not know how he was to do this, he thought of his "battle" as a material and bloody one. The military life and career, for which he had an obvious inclination, appeared to him to be in perfect harmony with that of a knight devoted to his Lady.

From a testimony of Father Czupryk we know that at this time Maximilian "suffered from scruples." It is possible, therefore, that this spiritual disease lay at the heart of his inner struggle. Perhaps under its influence the youth considered himself unfit for religious life and so decided to refuse the religious habit. He even tried to convince his brother Francis, who had been his companion in the postulancy, to do the same. Fortunately the wise counsel of Father Dionysius Sowiak, the novice master, who was expert in guiding young vocations, and the providential intervention of Mrs. Kolbe were able to prevent him from taking this step.

At the critical point of Raymond's inner struggle, Mama Maria, who was living in Lwów with the Sisters of St. Benedict,* came to visit him, and with her loving words she saved her son's vocation.

---

* For note, refer to page 39.

It is not known what Mama Maria said to her son, but as she finished speaking, Raymond felt a renewed confidence and all the darkness of uncertainty vanished.

Left alone, Raymond hurried to his superior and asked for the religious habit, which he received on the evening of September 4, 1910, assuming the name of Friar Maximilian.

All his life, Fr. Maximilian remembered this episode with immense gratitude to his mother. In 1919, after having received the news that his brother Francis had left the Order, he spoke of it again to his mother in a letter from Rome:

"As my mother can imagine, I read with joy and with sorrow the letter of February 23.

"Poor Francis!... He cannot understand the mercy of God toward us. He was the first to ask for reception into the Order. Together we received First Communion and Confirmation. Together we went to school. We were together in the novitiate and together we made simple vows.

"Before the novitiate, I did not want to ask for the habit and I also wanted to persuade him to do the same,...but how can I forget that moment, when Francis and I were about to go to present ourselves to the Father Provincial to tell him that we did not want to enter the Order, and we heard the door bell? In that critical moment, Providence, in infinite mercy through the Immaculata, sent Mama. Nine years have already passed since that day.... I think of it with fear and gratitude to the Immaculata. What would have happened if she had not sustained me with her hand...? He, Francis, with his example drew me to this door of salvation. I, instead, wanted to leave and to convince him to leave the novitiate also.... And now! Every day I make a memento to the Immaculata for him, and I hope that Mama also implores the divine mercy."

Finally, on September 5, 1911, Maximilian made his simple profession, vowing himself to the practice of the virtues of poverty, chastity and obedience according to the rule of Saint Francis and the Constitutions of the Friars Minor Conventual.

# From Lwów to Rome

After taking their vows, the newly professed usually left the novitiate house to live in a "professed house." There the young religious completed their formation, continuing the philosophical and theological studies.

The Province of Galicia had its "professed house" for clerics at Krakow, and this seminary would normally have been the residence of Friar Maximilian after the novitiate. Instead, he remained for another year in the seminary of Lwów, which was separate from the novitiate house, to complete his studies in the humanities. At the end of the school year, on July 4, 1912, he went from the seminary of Lwów to Kalwaria Paclawska, the summer residence for all the professed clerics. In autumn, when the other young men returned to the seminary of Krakow, Friar Maximilian joined them. Upon his arrival there he was surprised to discover that he was one of the seven candidates chosen to pursue academic degrees in philosophy and theology at the International Seraphic College in Rome.

At first, Maximilian hesitated because of the difficulties caused by his poor health. He spoke to his superiors and was so convincing in expressing the fear of not being able to complete his studies far from his native climate that his name was removed from the list of the candidates for Rome. Later in the day, however, Friar Maximilian was worried that he might have hindered the will of God expressed by his superiors. He went therefore to the Provincial, declaring: "Father, do with me as you wish."

The answer was: "Well, son, you will go to Rome."

Thus on October 28, 1912, Friar Maximilian set out for the Eternal City, where he remained for seven years. About his Roman sojourn he could repeat with Lacordaire: "In Rome I saw nothing but the Pope; all the rest was foreign to me." This does not mean that he failed to contemplate and admire Rome's historical beauties. But, disgusted by the anticlerical movements of those troubled years, he fixed his glance on Vatican hill and received from it light which enlivened his apostolic zeal, already nourished by his great love for the Immaculate Virgin.

Friar Maximilian studied philosophy for three years and on November 22, 1915, obtained his degree at the Pontifical Gregorian University. From 1915 to 1919, he continued studies at the Pontifical Theological Faculty, near the International Seraphic College, and obtained his doctorate on July 22, 1919.

Meanwhile, on November 1, 1914, after three years of temporary vows, Friar Maximilian made his perpetual and solemn profession in the hands of the Vicar General of the Order. On that very important day of his total and perpetual consecration to God, he wanted the name Mary to be added to his religious name of Friar Maximilian, as an expression of the dominant note of his spirituality.

After solemn profession, there began the steps from minor to major orders, climaxing in the great moment of the priestly ordination on April 28, 1918, in the Church of S. Andrea della Valle. On the following day, Father Maximilian said his first Mass with edifying devotion in the Church of S. Andrea della Fratte, at the altar of the miracle recalling the apparition of the Immaculate Virgin to the Convert Alphonse Ratisbonne. Father Maximilian would return to this altar in the most important and decisive moments of his life.

Two documents which refer to his priestly ordination give an idea of Father Maximilian's sentiments on that beautiful day. The first is in his handwriting on the front page of the book of daily Mass intentions.

"By the mercy of God—through the Immaculata—on April 28, 1918, on the feast of St. Paul of the Cross,

Fourth Sunday after Easter—in Rome, in the Church of S. Andrea della Valle—I was ordained a priest of Our Lord Jesus Christ—by His Eminence, the Cardinal Vicar, Basil Pompili."

The second document is a letter to his mother in which he shares with her the moment of his priestly ordination. The letter is dated from September 1918, that is, five months after his ordination had taken place. Father Kolbe was not able to send news sooner because of World War I, which interrupted all communication with Poland. This letter to his mother fills three sheets; we give only the most significant passages:

"On September 26 in Amelia, where I spent the summer vacation with Bishop Berti, the Franciscan Bishop, I received my mother's letter of September 11. I considered it a gift of divine Providence through the Immaculata, and on my knees I immediately thanked and recommended to her mercy all the members of my family and each one in particular. On that day I had celebrated my fifty-second holy Mass. For me, ordination to the priesthood had come suddenly. Last April 9, the Father Rector had told me to prepare myself for the examination before the Vicariate for Ordination.... On April 28, after the prayers recited in common in chapel, I went out together with others who were to be ordained....

"We were more than one hundred.... There was even an Indian who was to be ordained and another among those attending at the altar. What a beautiful sight! We were all united, despite the differences, with the bond of the Catholic religion and the charity of Jesus Christ.... After the ordination, together with the Cardinal we pronounced, besides other prayers, the formula of consecration. I recognize, with gratitude, everything to be a gift obtained through the Immaculata, our common Mother.

"How many times in life and in the most important moments I have had a special protection of the Immaculata. For this reason, glory be to the most Sacred Heart of Jesus through the Immaculata, who in the hands of Divine Mercy is the instrument to dispense every grace. For the future, therefore, I place all my trust in her.

"As for myself there would be much to tell. If God wills it, if I live, I will tell it by word of mouth. I only repeat that in everything I recognize a particular benevolence of the Immaculate Mother....

"I recommend myself fervently to the prayers of my mother, so that I may correspond worthily to such great graces and to such a great dignity. Always and sincerely, most affectionately, your son," *Father Maximilian*

## Disciple of Father Stephen Ignudi

At the Roman International College, Father Maximilian had as rector Father Dominic Tavani, who left the College in 1913, to assume the government of the whole Order; Father Louis Bondini, who was later elected Provincial of the Orient and afterwards titular Archbishop of Perge in Pamphilia and Apostolic Visitor of the Armenian Patriarchate; and finally in 1916, Father Stephen Ignudi.

Father Ignudi possessed eminent qualities of mind and heart which won the admiration and respect of others and made them desire to imitate him. Always serene, always amiable, always complete master of himself in joy and sorrows, sincere in his judgments, thoughtful in speech, and rich in deeds, he was certainly an example for his students.

Father Ignudi had a great impact on Friar Maximilian. In his unreserved love for the Pope and his unwavering defense of the moral and material rights of the Church, in a spirit of opposition to the Masons, he certainly aided the development of the spirit and future work of Father Kolbe.

Although Father Kolbe must be considered the "father" of the entire work of his Marian apostolate, Father Ignudi fostered in him noble and holy ideals. He knew how to read the heart of Father Maximilian and his companions, provide fertile ground for their growth in the spiritual life, and inspire them to apostolic activity.

A testimony of His Excellency, Most Reverend Joseph Palatucci, Bishop of Salerno, who was a contemporary and companion of Father Maximilian at the Seraphic College in Rome, underscores the tremendous impact exercised by Father Ignudi on Maximilian Kolbe:

"Father Master Stephen Ignudi was appointed for two terms as Rector of our International College at Rome. He developed in the students an eminently Roman spirit, a great attachment to the Pope and a spirit of struggle against evil, especially against Masonry. This explains why Father Maximilian directed his activity and his work in devotion to the Immaculata and in promoting the *Militia* for the conversion of all the enemies of the Church, and in particular the Masons."

# Love Without Limits

The only extant letter from Friar Maximilian's years in college is addressed to his younger brother Joseph —in religion, Father Alphonse. The letter is dated from April 21, 1919. In it he exhorts Alphonse to the practice of religious obedience and outlines an enthusiastic apostolic program. He aims at stirring him to renewed fervor to persevere in the work of his own sanctification, their common ideal.

"Dear brother, Mama sent me the letter you wrote to her on February 13. May God be thanked and the Immaculata glorified for all the graces that they shower upon us despite our unworthiness. I am most happy to learn that you feel enthused to procure the glory of God. In our days, the worst poison is indifference, which finds victims not only among the people, but even among religious—it is understood, to different degrees. And yet to God is due infinite glory. We finite creatures cannot give

God infinite glory; therefore, let us apply ourselves as much as we can to procure for Him the greatest glory possible.

"As you already know from ethics, the glory of God consists in the salvation of souls. The salvation of souls therefore and the perfect sanctification of them, already redeemed at a great price by Jesus with His death on the cross, begins naturally from one's own salvation. It is our *noble ideal*. With it we can show our gratitude to the most Sacred Heart of Jesus.

"But how can we procure the greater glory of God and sanctify a greater number of souls?

"Without doubt, only God fully knows 'this way.' He is infinitely omniscient, infinitely wise.... He and only He knows what we can do to procure His greater glory.

"Only from God can we and must we learn what we have to do. But how will this come about? Through His representatives on earth.

"Obedience, therefore—only holy obedience will securely manifest to us the will of God.

"The superiors can make mistakes, but we in obeying can never make a mistake. There is only one exception: if a superior should ever command a thing clearly *evident* to be a sin, even the smallest sin. This is a thing that does not happen in practice. In such a case the superior would not be the representative of God, and we would not be obliged to obey him. Apart from the superiors we cannot trust our reason, which can make a mistake. Only God, only He, infallible, most holy, most loving, He is our Lord, Father, Creator, End, Reason, Strength, Love...our Everything!

"Anything that is not God has value only if it refers to Him, Creator of the universe, Savior of all men, final end of creation.

"It is He, therefore, who through His representatives on earth manifests to us His adorable will, drawing us to Himself. And through us He wants to draw to Himself the greatest number of souls possible.

"Dear brother, think of how great our collaboration with the Divine Mercy can be. Through our obedience we can raise ourselves beyond our nothingness and we can act, without exaggeration, according to an infinite wisdom, according to the wisdom of God.... God gives us His infinite wisdom and His prudence so that our actions may be well directed. What greatness!...

"It is not enough. Through obedience we become infinitely powerful. Who can oppose the will of God?

"Behold, dear brother, the only way of true wisdom, of prudence and of the capability of giving greater glory to God.

"If there were a different way, Jesus would have pointed it out to us. Sacred Scripture says it clearly: for thirty years of His hidden life, *'He was obedient to them.'* At the same time we read in regard to His entire life, that He had come to fulfill the will of the Heavenly Father. You know these things very well; but the more they are meditated, the more their greatness is discovered.

"Love, then, love without limits for our Heavenly Father, love that must become concrete in obedience and which must be shown by doing especially that which is not pleasing to us.

"The most beautiful and secure book from which you can deepen this love so as to imitate it is the crucifix. Everything then is easily obtained by imploring it of the Immaculate Mother, since God has entrusted to her the economy of His mercy, reserving for Himself only justice, as St. Bernard says."

This letter witnesses to what heights of religious perfection Father Maximilian had already reached at the age of twenty-five. It portrays a well-balanced and reflective Father Maximilian, endowed with that supernatural wisdom which refers everything to man's last end: God. This characteristic can be found in all his writings, sermons and exhortations. But when he spoke or wrote of the Immaculate Virgin, his words and his pen became enthusiastic and revealed the sincere love of a son for his "Mother," of a knight for his "Queen."

Among the resolutions which Father Maximilian made in 1915, after the annual retreat at the Seraphic College in Rome, we read:

"Remind yourself often of obedience, each time that you make the Sign of the holy Cross.

"In pronouncing the words, *in the name of the Father,* remember that you intend to consecrate your *judgment* to the Heavenly Father.

"At the words, *of the Son,* you will consecrate your will and heart to Jesus.

"At the words, *of the Holy Spirit,* you will consecrate your *shoulders* to bear the burden for the glory of God, for the good of the Order and of the Church and for the salvation of souls.

"In joining your hands and pronouncing the word, *Amen,* you will remember to love your neighbor supernaturally in thought, word and actions.

"If you have worked in this way, you will win heaven; otherwise, hell will be reserved for you.

"Life is short. Even sufferings are brief.

"Heaven, heaven, heaven!

"Courage!

"Conform yourself to the divine Will. Observe the laws of God and the Rule. Be obedient and patient. Take up your cross and follow Jesus."

In the practice of the religious vows, Father Maximilian did not know compromise. The following episode testifies to his delicacy of conscience in regard to observance.

During his stay in Zagarolo (Rome) in the Friary of Santa Maria delle Grazie, Father Maximilian went for a walk in the country together with three of his confreres. Besides the food supply necessary for a full day, they had taken a quart of wine. After they had had their meal, there was half a quart left. One of the brothers proposed giving the remainder to a farmer, but Friar Maximilian intervened: "We cannot dispose of it, because we have made the vow of poverty and cannot give anything away without the permission of the superior." Thus the wine that was left over was brought back to the friary.

Father Joseph Pal, a confrere who lived with him for some time during his college years in Rome, offers this testimony:

"From 1913 until our separation toward the end of August 1919, I was persuaded that he was truly a saint in the precise meaning of the word. He was humble and meek in everything and with everyone, even in the most difficult moments. These two virtues represented a victory which with great effort he had won over himself from the time of his novitiate. This was the testimony of the Polish religious who were novices with him.

"His chastity was most spotless and protected by a profound modesty of his whole person, especially his eyes.

"Love for his fellow religious was truly evangelical. When the discourse fell upon the faulty observance of the Rule, he invited me to pray with him for the transgressors. I never heard him say anything more about this, even though he suffered much in seeing that some religious were not wholly obedient to the Rule of the Order. He was most observant, even in the most minute details of the Rule. At the first summons of the superior or the sound of the monastery bell, he would immediately impose silence on himself. He would cut his word in half and take leave of anyone who was speaking with him, even a distinguished person as he once did with His Excellency, Bishop Dominic Jaquet, Titular Archbishop of Salamina.

"As for his piety, love for Jesus in the Most Blessed Sacrament was deeply rooted in his heart. He had enrolled himself in perpetual adoration at the monastery of the Franciscan Sisters outside Porta Pia. He visited the Blessed Sacrament every hour: before and after each period of class or recreation, he would go to the chapel to make a visit to Jesus in the tabernacle. At night he would remain there, almost always the last one. On his face, which appeared angelically radiant, was reflected something of the interior ardor which lit up his features even exteriorly.

"The devotion that he had for the Madonna was sincere and filial. During the walk, he would exhort me to say the rosary and other prayers with him, especially the *Memorare* and the *Sub tuum praesidium.* He often did the same in free periods when we were in the courtyard of the college. To the Madonna he always gave the sweet name: *Mama mia.*

"I remember the night before the novena in preparation for the feast of the Immaculata. We were returning together from the Basilica of the Holy Apostles when we met four young rowdies returning from work. They were blaspheming the holy Virgin. All of a sudden I no longer saw Father Maximilian beside me. He had stationed himself in the middle of the street to get close to those thoughtless men and to ask them why they were blaspheming against the august Mother of the Lord. At the end he wept so bitterly that the men, attempting to excuse themselves, said that they had done it out of a bad habit, ignorant as they were, and in an outburst of anger. I called to him; but he insisted to such a point that, finally, the four men submitted and said that they were sorry.

"Never in my life have I met anyone who loved the Madonna more than Father Maximilian.

"He was a true son of Mary most holy."

Father Ignudi summarized the life of Father Maximilian with these few but eloquent words:

"Maximilian Kolbe from the province of Galicia. Entered on October 29, 1912. Ordained on April 28, 1918. Made doctor of philosophy at the Pontifical Gregorian University. Received doctorate of theology in this College on July 22, 1919. Left for Poland on July 23, 1919. Holy youth."

NOTE

Not long after her three sons had left home—Joseph, too, having entered the Franciscan Order—Maria again felt in her heart the desire to consecrate herself to God in the religious life. With the permission of her husband, she went to Lwów, where her sons were first stationed, and lived temporarily with the Benedictine Sisters. Thus she could follow the life of her sons from a short distance.

However, Maria was a "Franciscan" at heart. When her sons were transferred to Krakow, she followed them and there entered the Felician Sisters, who were Franciscan Tertiaries.

Among the proceedings for the beatification of Father Maximilian is found the following report from Sr. Mary Bronislaus Brzezinska, Provincial Superior, regarding the stay of Maria Kolbe in the congregation at Krakow:

"Maria Dabrowska Kolbe, born on February 25, 1870, mother of Father Maximilian and Father Alphonse of the Franciscan Order, was accepted into our congregation in 1913, as a tertiary to perform services outside of the cloister, at the request of P.M. Sobolewski, the Provincial Superior of the Franciscans in Poland. She lived in the Motherhouse of Krakow, on Smolensk Street, until her death on March 17, 1946.

"She carried out the affairs of the congregation with much spirit of sacrifice. She took care of the payments for the light, water and so on, with the communal offices of Krakow. She provided medicines for the house, took care of sending out the mail and was in charge of the funerals of the sisters.... In all of these duties she was very useful for our congregation.

"She was a person of eminent virtue and she edified everyone who came in contact with her. She had a particular devotion for the Immaculata and in her room she had two small altars to the Immaculata, which she adorned with fresh flowers. Late at night she would sing religious hymns softly. In the morning she would rise at 4:00 in order to have more time to dedicate to prayer.

"She was most mortified and never asked anything from the congregation, so much so that the superiors had to watch to see that she was not missing anything necessary.

"After her death, a discipline was found in her bed, and a plank between the sheet and the mattress. In such a way, this elderly woman of seventy-six knew how to mortify herself.

"She practiced religious poverty in an uncommon way and helped the poor. When she received the money that the superior had destined for her needs, she returned it right away to have a Mass celebrated. From daily Holy Communion, she drew strength for the sorrows caused by the death of her son Father Alphonse and the martyrdom of Father Maximilian. During her agony, she probably saw this last son, because she pronounced these words: 'My son.' Inexplicably, she had to bear with patience a calumny made by a servant, the falsity of which was known only after her death. She spent all free moments in adoration before the most Blessed Sacrament. She had predicted that one day she would fall on the street, and this is what happened."

After Maria's departure, Jules Kolbe sold his business and entered the Franciscan monastery at Krakow as a lay brother. Because of his age, however, he could not accustom himself to the religious life and therefore was advised to leave the monastery. He moved to Czestochowa where he opened a religious gift shop. He also cooperated with the movement for the liberation of Poland from the Russian yoke. In August, 1914, at the outbreak of World War I, he enlisted among the volunteers and left for the Russian front. Captured in the neighborhood of Oklusz, and found in possession of a Russian passport, he was sentenced to be hanged. Thus he gave his life for the freedom of his country.

At the outbreak of war (1914-18), Francis Kolbe, Raymond's older brother, could not resist the call from legions of volunteers rebelling against foreign oppression. For three years he fought heroically and was wounded several times. After his last recovery, he asked the competent superiors to readmit him into the Franciscan Order. But it was impossible to grant this request: he was declared unfit for the religious life because of his injuries.

In 1917, Francis married Irene Tribling (d. 1945). They had one daughter named Amelia.

Francis' patriotism inspired him to join those who conspired against the Nazis during the Second World War (1939-45). In 1943, he was discovered and arrested. At first it was believed that he had been sent to Auschwitz to die, but further investigations have ascertained that he died in the concentration camp at Buchenwald.

# The Foundation of the Militia of the Immaculata*

The seven years that Friar Maximilian spent in
Rome nourished in him three loves: the Eucharist, the
Madonna and the Pope. In defense of the Pope and the
Church, he conceived and founded a movement of
prayer and evangelism under the protection of the
Immaculata. "At first," as a confrere from college
revealed it, "he seemed to want to found the *Militia* in
Poland," in behalf of his people, ruled and oppressed by
the Russians. Little by little, however, the awareness of
a worldwide power working against the well-being of
the people broadened his horizons. The development of
events in the world made Father Kolbe realize that a
more widespread renewal was needed. Guided by the
Spirit of God, maternally and visibly assisted by the
heavenly Queen, he set for himself the task of conquering the world for the Immaculata.

Anti-Catholic forces, with Masons in the foreground,
were on the move, and they were especially strong in
Rome, the center of Christianity and the seat of the
Vicar of Christ.

Sectarian propaganda on the part of government
representatives was directed against the Marian sanctuary of Pompei, which in those years had been built
through the work of the Servant of God, Bartolo Longo.
Attacks were being made against the Popes, from Pius IX
to Benedict XV.

Friar Maximilian did not see these events as casual
happenings prompted by the political needs and crises

---

* International abbreviation—M.I.

of historical periods, but as evidence of a deep-rooted program against Christ and His Church. He reflected on the struggle foretold at the beginning of man's history, the struggle between the offspring of the "Woman"— Mary—and the offspring of Eve (Gn. 3:15), and he recognized attacks on the Church's life and teaching as part of this endless conflict. In Mary—who would overcome Satan in her Immaculate Conception—Friar Maximilian saw the heavenly standard bearer who would lead the ranks of new apostles to final victory. Certainly the education Friar Maximilian received in the Franciscan Order, noted for its zealous defense of the dogma of Mary's Immaculate Conception, had a special impact on the development of his Marian apostolate. As a Franciscan he went to the source of the ideal of St. Francis. He was not a reformer, like other eminent Franciscan figures of the past; he was a "renewer." For him the Franciscan life was not only to be a life of personal sanctity lived within the walls of the friary. For him, as for St. Francis, the Franciscan vocation was the dedication of one who was called to bring Christ to all classes of society. This ideal is clearly reflected in a letter he wrote on February 25, 1933, from Nagasaki to the Polish provincialate:

"For seven centuries we fought for the recognition of the truth of the Immaculate Conception. This struggle was crowned with the proclamation of the dogma and with the apparitions of the Immaculata at Lourdes. It is now time for us to start the second part of the history: to implant this truth in souls, cultivate its growth and help it produce fruits of holiness. And this in all the souls that exist now and who will exist up to the end of the world. The first part of this history, that is, the first seven centuries, were only a preparation, the formation of the plan, and of the password; but now we proceed to the fulfillment, that is, to make this truth tangible and visible, to reveal the Immaculata to souls, to introduce her into souls with all her beneficent effects."

As this ideal grew more clear and more concrete, it was only natural that young Friar Maximilian would reveal it day by day to a few confidants, chosen from among the most fervent of his confreres. Regarding this, we have the following account by Father Quirico Pignalberi, one of the first members of the M.I.:

"And so, after his project had matured, he manifested it to his closest companions, who shared his ideas. Some meetings were held in which the nature and the objectives of the *Militia* were outlined. The principal aim was to obstruct the overflow of ever-widening godlessness and those ever-growing movements hostile to the Church. Although, after the retreat of the soldiers at Caporetto, the war had reached its most painful phase, nevertheless the hostility, more than against political enemies, seemed to be directed against religion, as open and public anti-religious demonstrations showed.

"This prompted Friar Maximilian to make this reflection:

"'Is it possible that our enemies must be so active as to have the upper hand, while we remain passive, limiting ourselves to some prayer? Do we not, perhaps have more powerful arms, the protection of heaven and of the Immaculate Virgin? The "sinless one," conqueror and destroyer of all heresies, will never yield to the enemy who raises his head. If she finds faithful servants, docile to her command, she will win new victories, greater than those that we can ever imagine.

"'Certainly,' continued Friar Maximilian with profound modesty, 'the Madonna does not need us, but she deigns to make use of us to give us the merit and to make the victories more stupendous by employing poor persons and means as totally inadequate by worldly standards as the spiritual arms that the world derides and despises.

"'It is necessary that we place ourselves into her hands as docile instruments, using all lawful means, working ourselves in with the word, with the diffusion of the Marian press and Miraculous Medal, strengthening action with prayer and with good example.

"'Therefore the means of the Marian apostolate will be to enroll ourselves in the holy *Militia* disposed to fight under the banner of the Immaculata, wearing as an emblem the Miraculous Medal, saying each day the ejaculation in which, while we implore the protection of the Madonna over us, we particularly ask for the conversion of the Masons, who are the most numerous and most persistent enemies of the Church.'"

Father Joseph Pal adds:

"Friar Maximilian presented the dream which filled his mind and heart with such deep feeling and energy that the program he proposed to us seemed to him already in action. And truly, through the goodness of the Virgin, the fruits willed by God began to be obtained. The conversations of that day were intermingled, because of the holy fervor of hearts, with a song taught us by Father Glowinski. The song was: 'I Will Go To See Her One Day.' To the rhythm of that song, Friar Maximilian seemed to have become a child again. His whole being sparkled with smiles and almost with heavenly rapture. The sweetness of that name and love for the Mother of all so moved his heart that he showed it by asking a number of times that evening that the devout song be repeated."

Father Albert Arzilli, a former companion of Father Kolbe, completes the description with this revealing testimony:

"He *spoke* with ardor and passion of mission action. One day I saw him greatly moved and *excited* when I told him that the Knights of Mary Immaculate needed to be not only in *Poland,* but in *Europe, China, Japan* and in *the whole world.*"

## The Half Hour of Meditation

The above testimonies offer us a vivid picture of Friar Maximilian, the apostle of the Knights of the

Immaculata, in the midst of his confreres. In a brief summary, they also present a well-defined program which would be perfected within about ten months.

By following the events more closely and trying to penetrate the soul of the young religious, one is convinced that the work this apostle undertook was directly inspired and willed by the most holy Virgin, who prepared everything and made all converge toward an end.

Docility to holy inspiration was characteristic of the young friar. Simple episodes, insignificant to others, had particular meaning for him, as though they were signs from heaven inviting him to follow a determined course of action. Once he had become convinced, he would mobilize all his energies of mind and heart. Finally, some brief reflections made by the Rector of the College, Father Ignudi, during a morning meditation seemed to crystalize, focus and give direction to his aspirations in honor of the Immaculata.

At daybreak, on January 20, 1917, all the student friars of the college were gathered together in chapel, as was their custom, for common prayer. Friar Maximilian was in his place, recollected and unassuming, his manner revealing nothing of what was going on in his heart. That day would be one of the most solemn and decisive days of his life.

Father Rector read the meditation about the day's feast and commented on it with an appropriate thought. It was the anniversary of a famous victory of the Immaculata. With devout eloquence, Father Rector recounted to that youthful gathering the miraculous apparition of the Immaculate Virgin to the Hebrew Alphonse Ratisbonne in the Church of S. Andrea delle Fratte in Rome, and the conversion of this privileged son of Mary.

The seventy-fifth anniversary of the apparition was being celebrated in Rome that very day. The occurrence of this miracle was a new proof of the efficacy of the Miraculous Medal, which Ratisbonne was wearing almost by chance. On this very day Friar Maximilian—to whom the white-robed Virgin had appeared as she had appeared to St. Catherine Labouré —was inspired to found the *Militia Immaculatae,* or Knights of the Immaculata movement, and to choose the same Miraculous Medal as the shield and insignia of its Knights.

Let us listen to what Father Joseph Pal relates about the extraordinary happening:

"From that moment, Friar Maximilian remained so convinced and inspired about what he had to do, that he spoke to me with a radiant face, overflowing with joy at the power of the Madonna manifested in the conversion of Ratisbonne. And smiling, he told me that we must pray that the Madonna would destroy all heresies, especially Masonry. From January until the end of the vacations of the same year he often returned to the same subject. I, as the prefect of the college, since I was the only priest, and the older collegians spent the summer days at the *Vigna Antoniana* near the Baths of Caracalla. Instead, Friar Maximilian went to Amelia to Bishop Berti, who on July 16 ordained him sub-deacon. Returning to the Vigna, he told me more than once:

"'One of our bishops said that the Madonna will do great things through one of our priests. She will renew the religious spirit in many hearts, of our Order and of others. Moreover she will reawaken the Christian spirit among the faithful of many nations.'

"Since I now knew him and regarded him to be a holy soul, I was convinced that the religious—chosen instrument of the Madonna—was Friar Maximilian himself, and the said bishop, Bishop Berti. Being both somewhat sickly, we took walks to the Vigna during which we spoke often of the same topic."

From that day on, the beautiful Church of S. Andrea delle Fratte became most dear to Friar Maximilian, and the altar of the apparition his favorite place of prayer.

With the resolutions drawn from the meditation of January 20, 1917, the Knights of the Immaculata movement was not merely an idea, but almost a reality. What followed was only the preparation for the solemn, canonical erection with the approval of the ecclesiastical authorities.

Testimony about the beginnings is drawn from the confidences Friar Maximilian shared with six of the most exemplary student friars of the college. These six, in a sense, could be called the co-founders of the *Militia Immaculatae*. They were the first knights of Mary and therefore, the most zealous propagators of the new Marian institution.

*Father Joseph Peter M. Pal,* from Rumania, being an older priest, held the office of prefect of the college. He died as the Minister Provincial at Liuzi-Calugara on June 21, 1947, as a result of typhoid, which he contracted while caring for patients in the local hospital. Father Pal was the confidant of Father Maximilian and zealously propagated the M.I. in Rumania. The passages that he wrote in memory of Father Kolbe help us to know this priest who was a close friend of Father Maximilian in life and a most devoted admirer of his after his death. He was among the first of those inspired by Father Maximilian's ideals of a holy life spent in doing good.

*Father Quirico Pignalberi* was an Italian priest from the province of Rome. He enjoyed a particular esteem; in fact, for forty years he was the master of novices. Almost all of the religious of the Friars Minor Conventual from the Roman province and numerous other provinces owed to him a religious formation that inspired them to observe the Franciscan rule strictly and to follow the ideals of the M.I. He was the last of the original seven co-founders, dying at the age of 91 in Anzio, Italy, on July 18, 1982.

*Father Anthony Glowinski* was born in Rumania of a Polish father and a Rumanian mother. He died at Assisi on October 18, 1918, at a young age, having contracted influenza while visiting a camp of Rumanian refugees. Father Emil Norsa, a Jewish convert and a well-known musician, assiduously assisted Father Glowinski during his last illness. He confided afterwards to Father Maximilian that Father Glowinski had foretold the day of his death, having learned it from his guardian angel. Father Glowinski actually died on the day foretold.

*Friar Anthony Mansi,* of the province of Naples, was born in London of Italian parents from Ravello. He died of the "Spanish flu" as a young cleric on October 31, 1918. "During his illness, he asked Father Rector for permission to sing one of the little songs to the Immaculate Virgin which he had composed and put into music in his free time. Although certain that the young man would not be able to succeed because of his extreme weakness, Father Ignudi wished to satisfy his desire. To the wonder of those present, Friar Mansi sang with a most clear voice. Among the poems found after his death was one dedicated to Blessed Bonaventure of Potenza, a Conventual friar who was buried at Ravello. In it Friar Anthony asked the Blessed, who had been very devoted to the Immaculate Virgin, to obtain for him the grace of being able to sing the praises of Mary on his deathbed."

*Friar Henry Granata,* also from the province of Naples, was born at S. Antonio Abate on August 8, 1888.

He was at the Roman College together with Father Maximilian "from November, 1916, to the end of July, 1918," and after that "in 1919 at the friary at Ravello (Salerno)." He died in Rome on January 24, 1964.

Assigned to the ministry in his native province, at a distance from the other surviving co-founders, Friar Granata kept in continual contact with Father Maximilian. A zealous propagator of the Miraculous Medal and of the M.I., he always wore around his neck the Miraculous Medal he had received on the evening of the foundation of the M.I.

In recalling the two years of college at Rome, he has left among other things, the testimony of the following episode:

"After his priestly ordination Father Kolbe together with Bishop Berti was received in private audience by His Holiness Benedict XV. Father Kolbe asked the Pope for the faculty of blessing Miraculous Medals, using the expression, "the *papable* and *non-papable* faculty," meaning the reserved and non-reserved faculty! The expression pleased the Pope, who granted it saying: 'All right, *papable* and *non-papable.*'"

The recollection of this episode, passed over in silence by others and underlined by Father Granata, shows his cheerful and witty spirit, characteristic of his native land.

*Friar Jerome Biasi* was from the province of Padua. A truly beautiful soul, he died of consumption at Campo-sampiero (Padua) on June 20, 1929, after a most edifying life of patient suffering. He was the second confrere to whom Friar Maximilian, after the meditation of January 20, confided the idea and the program of the Knights of the Immaculata. Being very devoted to the Madonna, Friar Biasi was immediately enthused and from then on was an untiring propagator of the M.I.

Nine months after that momentous January 20, on the evening of October 16, 1917, these six first candidates to the new "Knighthood," guided by Friar Maximilian, knelt before the altar of the Immaculata in the chapel of the Franciscan College and consecrated themselves to Mary. The *Militia Immaculatae* was thus officially founded.

The description of this ceremony, which reminds one of the investiture of the ancient medieval knights, is given in the words of one who was the fortunate celebrant that evening, Father Joseph Pal:

"On the evening of October 16, 1917, in anticipation of October 17, the feast of St. Margaret Mary Alacoque, Friar Kolbe gathered us in the room next to that of Father Rector and read to us from a small sheet of paper the program he alone had traced out, the same one that is now known and published in the enrollment leaflet: *La Milizia di Maria Immacolata*. He asked us to approve it and to enroll ourselves in it. I was the first to do so, as a priest and as the oldest of the group. I think that Friar Maximilian was the last to sign it. I do not know whether this paper is now to be found at the headquarters of the *Militia*. It would be very interesting, for it showed how Friar Maximilian, unconcerned about external form, used an eighth of a sheet of paper to set up such a great work of apostolate and piety.

"From the room we all went into the chapel of the college and, without the knowledge of the other students, I blessed the medals and put them on the first Knights of the Immaculata, on myself and on Friar Maximilian. Having done that, secretively and silently, each of us went to his cell. Everything had been done in secret. Only the Father Rector, who was not present, knew about it. The foundation of the M.I. had been laid."

## The M.I. and Its Rule

The characteristic features of the new foundation are clearly outlined in the above reports by Friar Maximilian's confreres. Referring to this statute Father Pal wrote that "the eighth part of a sheet of paper set forth such a great work of apostolate and piety." It is interesting to know that years later this small slip, missing from the Archives of the Franciscan College, became the object of a passionate search until a happy occurrence brought it to light. A chance conversation with Father Quirico Pignalberi, one of the first seven, offered the clue that led to its discovery. This good father, who jealously saved as relics everything belonging to Father Maximilian, had preserved two precious, hand-written documents of his saintly confrere: the little piece of paper with the outline of the bylaws and a postcard on which Friar Maximilian had confirmed them. The plan shows the clear vision that Friar Maximilian had, from the very first day, of the Knights of the Immaculata movement and the spirit which, even at that time, would animate it.

The bylaws were drawn up in Latin, certainly for the sake of the co-founders, Father Pal and Father Glowinski. Parts of them were underlined in black and in red, revealing the mature reflection involved in their formulation.

In this first draft one finds all the details: the reasons for the movement, its end, conditions and means. These are presented in such a clear way that they do not need further clarification. The text is as follows:

"She will crush your head" (Gn. 3:15). "You alone have struck down every heresy in the world."

### I. Purpose of the Knights

Pursue the conversion of every person living in sin, heresy, schism and especially Freemasonry, and the growth in holiness of all persons, under the sponsorship of the B.V.M. Immaculate.

### II. Conditions for Membership

1. Make a voluntary and total oblation of oneself to the B.V.M. Immaculate as an instrument in her most holy hands.
2. Carry or wear the "Miraculous Medal."
3. Have one's name placed on the register of the Pious Union of Rome at the Primary Center or at some canonically erected Affiliated Center.

### III. Means of the Apostolate

1. Once a day if possible, beseech the Immaculata with the ejaculation: "O Mary, conceived without sin, pray for us who have recourse to you, and for all who do not have recourse to you, especially for the Freemasons."
2. Use all the legitimate means that one's particular state in life, condition, and varying oppor-

tunities make possible, the choice of which is left to the zeal and prudence of each member, and especially, propagate the "Miraculous Medal."

The same plan is repeated on the handwritten card given to Father Pignalberi on November 27, 1918. In addition, for the first time in the writings of Father Maximilian after the foundation of the M.I., there appears the explicit statement:

"After a year of expectation in the midst of doubts and uncertainty on our part, our Immaculate Sovereign has deigned to confirm the bylaws for her Knights."

To prevent any discouragement on the part of his friend Father Pignalberi, Father Maximilian added this decisive statement:

"Perhaps you may ask me how I know that our most lovable Sovereign wants this? How? From the most certain means enabling us to know the will of God, and as consequence that of our Lady and most tender Mother. From obedience in the *internal forum*. This is enough. From this very source I know also that the *Militia* must *spread out*."

Noteworthy is his reference to obedience in the *internal forum*. Most probably it refers to obedience to his confessor and spiritual director.

When Father Stephen Ignudi was Rector of the International Seraphic College of St. Theodore, the confessor and director was the Jesuit, Father Alexander Basile, from whom, in 1917, Father Kolbe received the first approval of the foundation of the M.I. This approval was followed by that of the Rector, Father Ignudi, who permitted the famous ceremony on the evening of October 16, 1917. Regarding this, Father Maximilian wrote: *"After having received permission on the part of holy obedience, I decided to proceed into action."*

Father Maximilian's procedure in the foundation of the M.I. consisted first in receiving the approval of the confessor, then that of his religious superiors and finally, that of the ecclesiastical authorities. This method would be constantly applied to all phases of his apostolate and to the further development and perfecting of the M.I. In revealing to his friend and confidant, Father Pignalberi, that for the moment things would be limited to the *internal forum,* he intended to remind him that his eventual cooperation in the extension of the M.I. would have to be supported by permission from the superiors of the Order and from the ecclesiastical authorities. The expansion of the M.I.'s sphere of action among the faithful could not be undertaken without the permission of Church authorities.

# The Degrees of Apostolate in the M.I.

The Knights of the Immaculata is an association that aims for the formation of more than one category of persons.

"It is," said Father Maximilian, "a movement that must draw the masses, snatch them from Satan. Only among these souls, already conquered for the Immaculata, can some be formed to the highest, even heroic, abandonment for the cause of spreading the Kingdom of God through the Immaculata.

"To the *Militia* can belong all religious orders, every congregation and every religious institute. Membership in the *Militia* enables the single members to give the best of themselves to the apostolate and thus to reach Christian perfection in their own state of life or profession."

It is no wonder that, with the passing of years, the *Militia Immaculatae* received from its Founder regulations regarding its purposes. This was required by the development of the apostolate according to the *zeal and prudence* of the members. With prudence and discernment, Father Maximilian realized that not all the members of the M.I. would be able to dedicate themselves, with equal activity, to the cause of the Immaculata.

According to the possibilities of apostolate within the M.I., he distinguished three degrees, corresponding to the zeal and the organizational capacity of the members.

In a lecture he specified them as follows:

*"In the first degree of the M.I.,* anyone may consecrate himself individually to the Immaculata and strive to carry out privately the end of the same *Militia* according to his own possibilities and prudence.

*"In the second degree of the M.I.,* particular bylaws and programs bind together in a union of strength the members who want to carry out the end more speedily.

*"In the third degree of the M.I.,* the consecration to the Immaculata is made *without limits.* Thus she can do with us everything that she wants and as she wants. We are entirely hers and she is ours. We do everything with her help; we live and work under her protection. When it concerns her cause, there does not exist any 'but'!... We always obey, even if she orders us to go to Moscow, to Spain, or to Mexico.

"We shall go.

"When she wants something, when we know that a thing is willed by her, when we shall be totally hers, every suffering will be endurable.

"Dear brothers!

"We believe in the Immaculata....

"We believe that she exists...that her glorification is necessary.

"We believe that she sees us and hears us...and that we depend totally on her, because we are hers.

"Jesus Christ as man is our Mediator with the Heavenly Father.

"His most holy Mother is mediatrix between us and Jesus Christ, through whom all graces come to us.

"She is constituted by Jesus as mediatrix and we firmly believe this.

"We receive graces from her and she brings us to the most Sacred Heart of Jesus.

"Our victory will be the salvation of souls...."

A further specification by Father Maximilian is contained in what follows:

"In the general bylaws the three degrees converge, and are distinguished only in expression, more precisely in the first part of the general bylaws: 'All the legitimate means that one's particular state in life, condition, and varying opportunities make possible, the choice of which is left to the zeal and prudence of each member....'

"And thus, the first degree is limited to *individual* action; the second adds *social* action, and the third, exceeding every limit, tends to *heroism.*"

# The Voice of the Superiors

After the evening of October 16, 1917, silence came upon the M.I. Consumed by the desire to lose no time and to work without rest for the glory of the Immaculata, Friar Maximilian had instead to patiently wait for the approval of his superiors. It seems that they saw in the conduct of the seven clerics nothing more than a desire for a more intense Marian piety within the framework of the spiritual life of the college. However, many difficulties arose which prevented the seven from developing their apostolate, as Friar Maximilian himself bears witness:

"That meeting (of October 16) was the first and last one of that time. A year of intense difficulties followed, for which reason no one dared to speak of it even among the friars who knew about it."

Most probably the difficulties mentioned by Friar Maximilian do not refer to problems created by World War I with the subsequent call to arms of many students, but to decisions of the superiors concerned about—if not forbidding, at least postponing—the new apostolate.

It was in October, 1918, after the death of Father Glowinski and of Friar Mansi, two of the first seven, that a certain reawakening took place, as we are informed by Friar Maximilian himself:

"These two brothers must have worked hard in heaven for the M.I., since after their death all the difficulties vanished. The Supreme Pontiff, through the instrumentality of Mons. Dominic Jaquet of the Friars Minor Conventual, Titular Archbishop of Salamis and professor of Church History at the Theological Faculty of the Seraphic College, on March 28, 1919, granted his blessing and encouragement. From that moment on, the number of the members began to increase."

Although one could not yet speak of a formal approval, there was the consoling fact that the M.I. found many supporters among the other students.

The definitive ecclesiastical approval was granted three years later, on January 2, 1922, with the decree of His Eminence, Basil Cardinal Pompili, Vicar General of His Holiness in Rome. By this decree the M.I. received the character and juridical constitution of "pious union." It could thus emerge from the Franciscan College and freely enroll the faithful everywhere. Father Maximilian began immediately in Poland, enrolling numerous followers at the center in Rome.

Later, His Holiness, Pius XI, with the brief of April 23, 1927, elevated the M.I. to the dignity of "primary pious union," thereby conferring on it the faculty to admit into the society other "daughter" centers.

On the twenty-fifth anniversary of the foundation of the M.I., its revised constitutions, required by its rapid diffusion throughout the world, were approved with the decree of Francis Cardinal Marchetti Selvaggiani, Vicar General of His Holiness (March 24, 1942). Around the same time, on the preceding March 12, His Holiness, Pius XII, with his letter of congratulations and blessing gave the *Militia Immaculatae* the seal of his supreme authority.

The concern of the Ministers General of the Franciscans merits special mention, in particular, the appreciation of Most Rev. Father M. Beda M. Hess (d. 1953). In a circular letter to all the members on the occasion of the twenty-fifth anniversary of the foundation, he definitively associated the M.I. with the centuries-old Franciscan Order, as a form of apostolate well in harmony with the glorious Marian traditions of its past.

On the occasion of anniversary celebrations or in commemoration of the founder, especially after his heroic death, eminent Cardinals, archbishops and bishops have expressed their approval of the foundation of other centers of the M.I.

# An Historical Parallel

In order to better understand the youth of Father Maximilian and the foundation of the Knights of the Immaculata, it is necessary to give some historical information. Without the M.I., we would not be able to understand Father Maximilian's youth. If his life as a student was a laborious intellectual preparation, it cannot be forgotten that his spiritual preparation consisted, uniquely and essentially, in fulfilling his ideal of apostolic activity for the Immaculata. His priesthood, which would be spent to the last instant for the cause of Mary, rested on a logical and precious foundation laid during his stay at college.

It is not difficult to see a providential and supernatural design in the work of Father Maximilian.

In the crucial year of 1917, when Friar Maximilian meditated on and began the foundation of the M.I., the heavenly Mother gave the three children of Fatima a mission which, in the mind of Father Kolbe, was and is the purpose of the M.I. In faraway Portugal, the Virgin Mary requested love, reparation and the consecration of the human race to her Immaculate Heart. In Rome, on a day consecrated to the victories of the Immaculata, Friar Maximilian conceived his work. On the eve of another day honoring the heroine of reparation, St. Margaret Mary Alacoque, he gave life to his work of love, of reparation and of consecration to Mary, as the first warrior of the new Marian crusade.

At Fatima the Virgin exhorted the simple hearts of the three little shepherds to believe, to hope and to love for those who do not believe, do not hope, and do not love. In Rome that same year, during the same months, on the same days, the first Knights of Mary Immaculate, the first platoon which would grow like the mustard seed of the Gospel, promised faith, hope and love to the Immaculata, pledging to recite daily:

"O Mary, conceived without sin, pray for us who have recourse to you and for those who do not have recourse to you, especially for the Masons and for those who are recommended to you."

# The Beginning
# of the Apostolate in Poland

From the autumn of 1919 to the summer of 1927, Father Maximilian was able to determine even better the character and aims of the *Militia Immaculatae* and he laid down the spiritual foundations for his great editorial work.

The events that occurred during this time can be outlined as follows:

In autumn, 1919, Father Maximilian was assigned to the college at Krakow, where he taught and established the first Marian "Focus Groups."

From August 11, 1920 to April 28, 1921, he was in the tuberculosis sanatorium in Zakopane, where he exercised an apostolate of suffering and religious instruction among Catholic and atheist patients.

From May 4 to November 2, 1921, he convalesced in the friary of Nieszawa.

In 1922, he returned to Krakow and began the publication of *The Knight of the Immaculata,* the first official bulletin of the M.I.

On October 20, 1922, together with the editorial office of *The Knight of the Immaculata,* Father Maximilian was transferred to the friary of Grodno, where he remained until December, 1925.

On September 18, 1926, he was sent a second time to the sanatorium in Zakopane; he was discharged on April 13, 1927.

His direct apostolate was thus reduced to only a little more than four years, interrupted by long, periodic returns to the hospital.

# At Krakow

Soon after his arrival at the friary in Krakow, Father Kolbe was appointed professor of philosophy, Sacred Scripture and Church history in the Franciscan scholasticate. After two months, however, his superiors had to remove him from teaching since his lung disease had weakened him to the point that his voice was hardly heard by his students. He was then entrusted with priestly duties—hearing confessions and doing some preaching. But because of the wretched state of his health, the long hours in the confessional tired him even more than teaching in the classroom.

Often he was seized by violent fevers, which raged mercilessly through his weak body. He bore his infirmities without uttering the slightest complaint, suffering silently and patiently for souls and for the success of the M.I. One time while confined to bed he invoked the name of Mary repeatedly and kept on pointing to something. His brother Alphonse, who was assisting him, finally succeeded in guessing his desire. Father Maximilian was looking for his eyeglasses and watch, which he wished to be placed at the foot of his statue of Mary. Later he explained the meaning of his request: "The glasses are the symbol of my eyes, the watch, of my time, both I have totally consecrated to her."

As a knight of Mary, he renewed daily his mystical consecration of October, 1917, and in his priestly ministry he saw nothing but the Immaculata; he did nothing except for the glory of Mary.

In fact, when his schedule and health permitted it, he endeavored to establish the M.I. in Poland, as he had already done in Rome. Father Kolbe regarded October 7, 1919, as the beginning of his Marian program in Poland, a program destined to reach bewildering proportions. Here is how the momentous date is marked in the diary of his personal recollections:

"October 7, 1919 (Tuesday), Our Lady of the Rosary.... This evening during recreation, six cleric friars, together with their teacher, Father Keller, signed their names in the book (which must serve for registration) of the M.I. They desired that I, too, as one already belonging to the M.I., sign my name at the top. My little Mother, I do not know where we will arrive with this undertaking, but deign to make use of me and of all of us as it pleases you for the greatest glory of God. I am yours, my beloved Immaculate Mother. You know how miserable I am, walking on the edge of the precipice, full of self love. If your immaculate hands stop supporting me, I will first fall into the most grievous sins and then into the abyss of hell. But if, however unworthy I be, you do not leave me, if you guide me, certainly I will not fall and I will become a great saint...."

For the moment, the enrollment of a few members did not constitute a new foundation in Poland, but only an enlistment waiting for the approval of the superiors. The approval was soon given. On October 2, the Minister Provincial, Father Louis Karwacki, approved and blessed the initiative. On December 4, accompanied by the recommendation card of Father Keller, Father Kolbe went to the bishop's house to inform His Excellency, Most Rev. Sapieha, of the foundation of the *Militia Immaculatae* in Rome, and of his new program in Poland, and to ask permission to print the bylaws. This permission arrived on the twentieth of the same month and was followed by a letter from the Provincial dated December 30, containing the written approval stated in these terms:

"I recommend the diffusion of M.I. and the publication of its bylaws with, it is understood, the permission of the local superior."

This sequence of dates is enough to provide us with a vivid picture of the unlimited faith, willpower and untiring activity displayed by Father Kolbe, on behalf of his Marian apostolate; and to fulfill the program of M.I. in order to conquer as many as possible, as quickly as possible, to the cause of the Immaculata.

Finally, on January 5, 1920, the inaugural meeting of the first gathering of lay members of the M.I. took place, with the blessing of the Archbishop.

But this was not all.

In October of 1917, the foundation of Marian focus groups was also seen as a means of apostolate. Father Maximilian began to promote them without delay among university students, among students of religious institutes for women, and among soldiers, to whose barracks he went weekly to hear confessions. He also organized instructions after regular school hours in a school for the mentally handicapped and for wayward young people, "giving for two years a valid contribution in the work of rehabilitation of these youngsters," as Father Alphonsus Bielenin, catechist of a school in Krakow, testified.

The necessity of keeping contact among the different focus groups and the first members of the M.I. paved the way for the second means of social apostolate already included in the act of foundation of the M.I.: the press.

The *Knight of the Immaculata,* the magazine which would bring the Immaculata into the hearts of all: a fruit of the yearning of Father Maximilian's soul and his priestly zeal, was envisioned from the first months of the Marian apostolate. It would come out after two long years of reflection and meditation by Mary's apostle, which included his first stay in the hospital.

# At Zakopane

As a seminarian, Father Maximilian, aware of his weak constitution, had asked not to be sent to Rome to study, giving his poor health as the reason. In Rome, during his stay in the International College, he was always sickly. Strong headaches accompanied him during his long years of philosophical and theological studies. In 1914, perhaps as a consequence of his anemic and lymphatic constitution, the index finger of his right hand became so gangrenous, that the doctor decided to amputate it. In such a case the priesthood would have been ruled out, except by apostolic dispensation.

Instead, Maximilian recovered without an operation, almost overnight, after having poured on the sore some drops of Lourdes water.

Back in Poland, it seemed at first that his native climate was beneficial to him. He was able to begin the hard work of forming his Knights of the Immaculata. But on August 11, 1920, he was sent to the sanatorium at Zakopane, definitely ill with tuberculosis of the lungs.

Confronted with the extraordinary activity of Father Kolbe in the following years, one might think that he had recovered completely from tuberculosis. In reality, this was not so. He derived some benefit from thorax treatment, but since both lungs were injured, he had frequent relapses, which required much attention and long stays in the sanatorium.

Would tuberculosis harm his zeal and his mission?

By no means! However surprising it may be, it was especially at this time, when Father Maximilian had to sacrifice his will to conform to that of the Immaculata, that the M.I. received its definitive physiognomy. Thus, once moderately recovered, Father Maximilian could continue his apostolate with renewed efforts and an ever greater commitment.

The conviction that personal sanctification must be at the basis of the apostolate prompted Father Kolbe to write in a promotional leaflet:

"It is only right that anyone who wants to dedicate himself to the sanctification of souls (the purpose of the *Militia Immaculatae)* begin with himself. Therefore, he, first of all, must draw closer to the Immaculata, to receive from her those graces through which, in every moment of life, he can more perfectly progress in the love of God. He draws close to Mary in a perfect way when he gives himself to her as her *project and property.* Here lies the first and essential condition: the total offering of oneself to the Immaculata."

He was only twenty-six years old, yet his highly developed supernatural spirit enabled him to conform himself to Christ in the way of the cross and in contradictions, in the immolation of his own will, in his total abandonment into the hands of Mary. With perfect supernatural intuition he saw in all this the sanctification of the M.I. Tried by thousands of contradictions hampering the fulfillment of his own plans, he wrote:

"In regard to the *Militia* we are in the hands of the Immaculata. We must therefore do whatever she desires and what obedience indicates for us.... Let us guard against doing more in the M.I. than obedience permits, because then we would not act as instruments of the Immaculata.

"The Immaculata can do with us what she wants and as she pleases, because I am her property and completely at her disposition."

# Among the Unbelievers

In the promotional leaflet mentioned above, Father Maximilian considered the apostolate as the expression and overflow of the love that burns in one's heart:

"When a Knight will have experienced the kind of strength that is given him in temptations and the comforts he enjoys in trials, he will strive to communicate to others his own happiness, to draw them all to Mary and to win their hearts for her. Seeing the great number of souls who do not even know the name of Mary, he will feel pain and will really want to conquer the whole world for her. He will desire that she enter every heart that lives and that will live on earth, so that she with her numerous graces may illumine and warm each with the flame of her maternal heart, enkindling ardent love for the most Sacred Heart of Jesus."

These words are the best commentary on his priestly ministry in the sanatorium.

At that time, in the well-equipped sanatorium of Zakopane, there were, in separate wards, many patients of every social rank. One ward of the hospital consisted almost entirely of intellectuals, Jewish, Protestant or anti-Catholic. Puffed up by their knowledge, academic degrees and achievements, most of them gave no thought to religion.

Soon enough Father Kolbe found his way among them, and when his illness allowed him to do so, he began to hold interesting and animated discussions with them, which gradually began to take root in the patients' hearts and to produce conversions.

Writing to his brother Alphonse about this time, he gave an enthusiastic report:

"We can thank the Immaculata because the most rabid adversary at Zakopane has gone to confession. I also baptized a Jewish student in danger of death. That was a motive of indignation on the part of the mother and brothers who came late, but it was *after the fact!* I beg you to ask the Heart of Jesus through the Immaculata for the conversion of all professors who are here. I have experienced that only prayer obtains the grace of conversion."

As time went by, the apostolate of Father Kolbe became so organized as to include periodic conferences and discussions in the ward of the university students. In his letters he refers to moving episodes, which, although not described, can be easily imagined by reading, for example, the following passage:

"I limit my activity to a brief writing because the Immaculata wants this.

"The Immaculata permitted me to approach other intellectuals who are here to have treatments. Now they often invite me to their ward so that I may enlighten them about religion. I therefore have held a series of conferences on apologetics with the opportunity and freedom of discussion. We have already spoken about the existence of God and the divinity of Jesus Christ. Many have obtained a New Testament, others the *Nights on Lake Leman* and *Apologetics* by Bartynowski.

"During these conferences many very beautiful things have happened but I do not have time to describe them."

Fr. Florian Koziura in the process for Father Kolbe's beatification refers to the following:

"When Father Kolbe was in Zakopane, he made the acquaintance of a certain intellectual. At every encounter he begged him: 'Sir make your confession.' But the man would answer: 'Father, I respect you, but I will not go to confession; perhaps another time....'

"After a few weeks, the gentleman was released from the sanatorium and went to say good-bye to Father Maximilian who warned him again: 'Sir, go to confession.'

"Once again the answer was: 'I beg your pardon, Father; I have no time. I have to rush to the station.'

"'Then at least accept this Miraculous Medal,' Father urged.

"The gentleman accepted it out of courtesy and left immediately for the station. Meanwhile Father Maximilian fell on his knees and implored from the Immaculata the conversion of the obstinate man.

"A moment later, a knock was heard. Still standing on the threshold, the same gentleman who had been in such a hurry exclaimed: 'Father, please hear my confession!'"

# A True Educator

Father Kolbe's apostolic undertakings were joined to a truly supernatural prudence which permeated his whole life. He developed it at the school of the spiritual childhood of St. Therese of the Child Jesus and of the mystical abandonment of St. Gemma Galgani. Reading their biographies, as he confessed, was a delight to him, and more spiritually enriching than a course of spiritual exercises. Under their influence he grew in the conviction that the M.I. was the direct work of the Virgin of whom he was only a humble and temporary instrument.

This inspired him to adopt a filial abandonment to the will of his heavenly Mother. In turn he took care to instill these same principles and the spirit of the M.I. in his brother Alphonse, who was studying for the priesthood in the college of Lwów.

Father Alphonse would be the spokesman and right arm of Father Maximilian, not because of human ties but because he let himself be guided and spiritually molded by his older brother while the latter was in the sanatorium.

The letters to Friar Alphonse that Father Maximilian wrote during his stay in Zakopane bear evidence that at the basis of their common sanctity, as well as the sanctification of every member of the M.I., were two essential conditions: a good theological education and the subordination of every activity to the scrupulous observance of the religious vows.

He foresaw that the M.I. would meet with many difficulties arising from the religious environment itself, in which it was developing. Often the superiors had to reconcile the daring apostolic programming of the members of the M.I. with the exigencies of community life and provide financial means according to the norms of an administrative prudence. Yet, Father Maximilian was totally convinced that overcoming difficulties depends not on human shrewdness but on that supernatural prudence which rests on the will of God. This is reflected in the following consideration:

"The intellect is above the senses, and faith is above the intellect. Perfection is founded on charity toward God, on union with Him and on conformity with Him. Love for God is shown by doing His will—which is manifested by means of the will of the superiors, when this is not evidently and certainly against the divine laws.... I think that the M.I. must be founded on the way of contradictions: It is more fruitful if it is cultivated amid misconceptions and contradictions."

His experience among the intellectuals in the sanatorium made him realize the importance of knowledgeable priests endowed with the qualities necessary to make truth shine over error. For this reason he exhorted his brother Alphonse to deepen his sacred studies:

"By personal experience, I know that it pays to learn not for school but for life, in such a way as to present clear doctrines to others. God forbid that a Knight of the Immaculata should shrug off anti-religious objections with inadequate answers and thus with his ignorance, weaken the faith of his listeners.

"I recommend that you meditate on and profoundly assimilate dogma, especially fundamental dogma."

One of the aims of the M.I. would be to form in its members the love for Franciscan poverty; and Father Maximilian demanded of Friar Alphonse the perfect observance of this virtue.

It was customary for certain parents to send their religious sons and daughters paper and stamps so that they could write more often than was permitted by their rules. Mama Maria must have used the same procedure since Father Maximilian tells his brother:

"All that you write is good and Franciscan, but if Mama would not send you any more stationery and stamps, that would be even more Franciscan."

His concern for the sound spiritual formation of Friar Alphonse, especially as he approached priestly ordination, was only the reflection of his own personal rigorous conformity to the arduous principles of religious life, understood as a means of personal sanctification.

In his notes are found the resolutions he made during a course of spiritual exercises in February, 1920, at Krakow. More than resolutions, they can be defined as a program of life to be read every month. Written in a concise style, they mirror the soul of Father Maximilian who was faithful to them until death.

Here they are in a literal translation from the Polish:

*"Regulation* of life to be read every month.

1. I must be a saint and a great saint.

2. For the glory of God, I must save myself and all souls, present and future, through the Immaculata.
3. Flee *'a priori'* not only from mortal sin but also from deliberate venial sin.
4. Do not permit:

> a) that evil remain without reparation and destruction;
> b) that good be without fruit or increase.

5. Let your rule be obedience—the will of God through the Immaculata—I am nothing but an instrument.
6. Think of what you are doing. Do not be concerned about anything else, whether bad or good.
7. Preserve order, and order will preserve you.
8. Peaceful and benevolent action.
9. Preparation—Action—Conclusion
10. Remember that you belong exclusively, unconditionally, absolutely, irrevocably to the Immaculata.

"All that you are, all that you have or could have—everything: thoughts, words, actions, inclinations, (pleasing, indifferent) are her property absolutely.

"She, and not you, will do what she wants with everything.

"Equally hers are all your intentions: she disposes, does and corrects so that you cannot err.

"You are an instrument in her hands. You must therefore do only what she wants.

"Take everything from her hands. Have recourse to her as a child does with its mother. Confide in her.

"Be concerned about her, for her glory and for things pertaining to her. Entrust yourself and all your things to her care.

"You must recognize that you have received everything from her, nothing from yourself. All the fruit of your work depends on union with her, as she is an instrument of the Divine Mercy....

*"Life* (in every moment), *death* (where, when and how), *eternity,* everything is yours, O Immaculate Virgin. Do with me everything that pleases you.

"Everything is possible in Him who through the Immaculata is my comfort.

"Interior life: first, everything for my own sanctification, and equally for the sanctification of others."

In September of 1920, at the end of a second course of spiritual exercises he made in Zakopane, he added to the previous program:

"1. Indifference to any place, occupation, condition of health.

2. The greatest glory of God: my salvation and sanctification and that of others depends on the will of God.

3. Jesus desires the liberation of souls from purgatory. 'Jesus and Mary,' 300 days indulgence. 'Jesus, Mary and Joseph,' seven years indulgence....

4. Satan: riches, pleasures, esteem, disquietude, desperation, hell.

5. Jesus: poverty, suffering, humility, peace, confidence, paradise."

Armed with these spiritual "weapons," Father Maximilian set out to begin one of the greatest apostolic undertakings of our times for the honor and in the name of the Immaculata.

# The Knight of the Immaculata

On April 28, 1921, Father Maximilian was released from the sanatorium and on May 4, he went to spend a long period of convalescence in the friary of Nieszawa on the Vistula River, far from the polluted air of the city.

His life in the community and its ministry in the Church aroused in him the desire to do something for the M.I., but even there his best activity was to obey the dispositions of absolute rest given by his Provincial. He had to be content with doing the small apostolate of a simple Knight of the Immaculata: good example, edifying conversations wherever he was, friendly, catechetical encounters with the pastor of the Evangelical Church.

Early in November of the same year his health improved enough for him to return to Krakow.

Immediately after his arrival at the friary, he again set to work. From then on, his life would be characterized by even greater activity, as if he foresaw that life would be brief and wanted to make the most of it. The imposing dimensions of his apostolic achievements are astounding. Whatever he undertook had far-reaching effects.

In January, 1922, the young priest began the publication of a Marian magazine, *The Knight of the Immaculata*. In itself this initiative was not especially outstanding. Its foundation, however, completed the work of the M.I.

Confronted with the urgent needs of modern society, Father Kolbe viewed as insufficient the missions preached in villages and cities, which only reached a limited number of souls. Since the forces of evil were spreading immorality through press, radio and other means, he understood the necessity of making use of these same means for the greater glory of God. He began with the most available and widely used of these: the press.

In Father Kolbe's mind, *The Knight* was intended not only for the members of the M.I., but for all the families in Poland and throughout the world. Its purpose was to bring the Immaculata into the homes, so that by coming closer to Mary, families might receive the grace of conversion and sanctity. Once individuals were imbued with the spirit of the M.I., that spirit could permeate private and social life. The development of *The Knight* was therefore intimately linked with the life and growth of the M.I. In fact, it was *The Knight* which often paved the way for future apostolic ventures.

The first issue of *The Knight,* which was published without a cover because of lack of funds, contained this note: "Due to financial difficulties we cannot guarantee that our readers will receive the magazine regularly. The magazine relies on free offerings."

Before beginning the publication of *The Knight,* Father Kolbe had obtained the approval of his superiors. The superiors saw no reason to disapprove the project, rather they praised and encouraged it. However, they were concerned about Father Kolbe's poor health, his editorial inexperience and the inflation of the Polish mark. While the first difficulties could be easily overcome through the help and collaboration of other religious, the financial problem remained. The Minister Provincial, Father Louis A. Karwacki, was more preoccupied with the future than with the present.

Would *The Knight* be able to go ahead and overcome the initial economic uncertainties? If it failed, the responsibility would fall not only on Father Maximilian but on the entire province. The best solution seemed to be to postpone the approval of the initiative to better times.

This decision caused sleepless nights for Father Maximilian, until he decided to try a second time. On his knees, he humbly explained to his superiors that his project was for the good of souls and the glory of the Immaculata.... Would not a denial on his part be a refusal to the cause of the Immaculata and of souls?

The Provincial hesitated until Father Maximilian assured him, "Father Provincial, just give me the permission: I'll find the money."

If Father Karwacki thought Father Kolbe would soon become discouraged, he was mistaken. For the love of his Immaculata, Father Maximilian had recourse to begging.

He later confessed how painful this experience was and how he had to struggle to overcome his natural repugnance to this type of humiliation.

"I entered a stationery shop to ask for an offering for *The Knight,* but, overcome by shame, I instead ended up buying some small object and leaving. I went on, reproving myself for the weakness of not having succeeded in repressing the instinctive sense of personal humiliation for love of the Madonna. I tried again and entered a second store. Again shame conquered me.... Without even saying a word, but completely confused, this time, I found myself outside on the sidewalk without knowing how."

The situation facing Father Maximilian after the publication of the first issue of *The Knight* was extremely difficult. The debts he had contracted were so high that the initiative was in danger of failing at any moment. Fortunately, a good priest, Father Tobiasiewicz, pastor of St. Nicholas' Church in Krakow, was inspired to help. He understood the holiness of the initiative and the financial difficulties of Father Kolbe and gave a generous donation. Following in his footsteps, other priests gave contributions. It was thus possible to collect half the amount needed to defray the expenses of the first issue. But what of the other half, which according to the sources was about 500 marks?

Father Maximilian decided to appeal to his Lady. Kneeling at her altar he invoked her with fervent supplications.

"After he had ended his fervent prayer, a true outburst of the heart of a son who sought shelter in the heart of the Mother full of love, he was starting to leave when his eyes saw a non-liturgical object lying on the altar cloth. He went closer. It was an envelope. In his love for order and harmony and the decorum of the church, he ascended the steps and to his grateful surprise read—written on it, in very small letters—*'For You, Immaculate Mother.'* He opened it, and, marvel of marvels, he found inside the exact amount of the remaining debt for the printing of the first issue of *The Knight of the Immaculata.*

"He understood everything, and in an outburst of tears knelt in grateful adoration.

"Serene and amazed at the unusual coincidence of this event, even his superiors granted to Father Maximilian that amount for his debt, the amount of the miracle."

# Unfavorable Criticism

No one is born an editor or publisher, and Father Maximilian was no exception. In the first years his inexperience met with much dissatisfaction, and the poverty and simplicity of *The Knight* were greeted with criticism.

Rev. John Kozonkiewicz, ecclesiastical censor of Krakow, assumed an attitude of sheer skepticism in examining the first number of *The Knight*. To him the future of the publication seemed very doubtful. Twelve years later he retracted his opinion and expressed his amazement at the development of the publication. At the beginning, however, his views had sown the seed of dissension.

If Father Kolbe had been animated only by a fleeting fervor and enthusiasm for *The Knight,* he would not even have celebrated the first anniversary of its existence. His heart, instead, was on fire with an ardent love for the Immaculata which enabled him to endure any sacrifice, even heroic, with serenity and true Franciscan joy. All the trials of the years 1922 and 1923 were useful and indispensable, serving as the crucible in which the gold of his virtue was purified. And his patience was rewarded. The difficulties that Father Kolbe met in the foundation of *The Knight* were gradually overcome.

In the course of a few years, Father Kolbe had succeeded in winning others to his cause and inspiring them to support his future undertakings.

# A Printing Press

The first issues of *The Knight* were printed by commercial printers. During the first year, *The Knight* had to change printers five times, with disastrous effects. Besides greater expenses, continual strikes prevented the publication from coming out on time. Father Maximilian then turned to the army's printers. Their equipment was magnificent and things went ahead smoothly for some months. However, difficulties arose which were not so much material, as moral, and Father Kolbe was forced to abandon this means.

Suddenly, Father Maximilian had an inspiration: he would open his own print shop in the friary and thus make *The Knight* completely the work of the members of the M.I. It was a most daring project, and its realization gave further proof of the holiness of its founder.

In the mind of Father Maximilian a printing press was associated with two immediate advantages: independence from outside help, and a better blending of the printing operation with the observance of community life. There remained, however, the vexing problem of finding the money. Since he was penniless, how could this be done? It was in this situation that the Blessed Mother again gave an evident sign of her protection, as is proven by the following event, related by Brother Gabriel Siemenski.

"One night during recreation, one of our Fathers decided to entertain Father Lawrence Cyman of the friary of Chicopee in the United States, who later became Minister Provincial of the American Province of St. Anthony. This priest immediately made *The Knight* the target of his sarcasm. He had something to say about the way it was written and cast doubt upon the efficacy of the publication in the work of conquering and converting souls. Meanwhile, Father Maximilian, unperturbed, neither defended himself nor reacted; lowering his eyes, he remained silent. Instead, it was the guest himself who defended *The Knight*. Seriously and frankly he declared, 'If the editing of *The Knight* fares badly, the fault in great part lies with the one who, instead of helping, knows only how to find fault.' And he added that the burden of the writing and layout of the booklet should have been borne not by Father Maximilian alone but also by all other capable religious and friaries of the province, especially in undertaking the expenses.

"Turning then to Father Maximilian, he added: 'To help you, Father, I, for the first, will give my offering'; and in saying this, he gave a check for one hundred dollars."*

It almost seemed that the Immaculate Virgin had called Father Cyman from America just for this purpose. At that time one hundred dollars constituted a small fortune. Father Maximilian's Provincial also loaned him money so that he was able to buy the machine and also some magazines of type. Later his Provincial let him borrow more money and told him to forget repayment of the loan he had given him. This marked the beginning of a printing plant destined to astonish everyone within a few years.

As a seminary for the formation of young vocations, the friary at Krakow was too small for the new apostolate of the press. Moreover, a printing press could become a source of distraction for the students.

Confronted with these difficulties in the autumn of 1922, the Provincial decided to send Father Maximilian to Grodno. The friary of Grodno had just reopened its doors three years before, and the extra space offered a better accommodation for the editorial and typographical stages of *The Knight.*

Year by year, the publication grew in quality and in the number of subscribers. In the course of a few years the whole friary, with the exception of the rooms for the religious, was entirely occupied by the printing equipment, which had multiplied from the first printing press. Later on a new wing of the house was provided to make room for the young men who were asking to become Franciscan religious.

According to documentation dated July, 1927, this printing plant put out two monthly magazines: *The*

---

*Actually, Father Cyman sent the hundred dollar check from America; Father Maximilian received it on January, 1923. Nor was Father Maximilian alone in his editorial work, for the other priest members of the M.I. were contributing articles regularly, as examination of the early issues clearly shows.

*Knight,* with a circulation of 60,000 copies, and *The Seraphic Flame,* the organ of the Third Order of St. Francis, with a circulation of 8,000 copies. There were only seventeen Brothers to carry out this great work.

Father Kolbe did not go to Grodno as superior of the friary. It would have been impossible for him to combine the direction of the M.I. and the activities connected with the obligation of a superior and the sacred ministry. At Grodno he did not even have the immediate direction of the M.I. Father Karwacki had appointed a delegate with limited powers to advise Father Maximilian and especially to give him spiritual direction. Most probably this decision was dictated by the desire to keep harmony in the community, prevent possible misunderstandings between the superior and the local director of the M.I., to calm the still doubting councillors, and to restrain the zeal of Father Kolbe.

The appointment of a provincial delegate brought about a twofold benefit: peace and harmony both in Grodno and in the other communities of the province; and the true development of the M.I., fostered by the spirit of humble submission of the good priest. Once more we find Father Kolbe serene and tranquil, absorbed in his ideal, walking the road most profitable to a religious: that of obedience.

The first spiritual director of the M.I. was Father Melchior Fordon. A wise and prudent man, extraordinarily pious and devoted to the Blessed Mother, he was soon won to the cause of the M.I. Not only did he understand perfectly the spirit and zeal of Father Kolbe, he also became his faithful interpreter during Father Kolbe's second and more prolonged attack of tuberculosis. The leadership of Father Fordon, who died on February 27, 1927, before Father Kolbe's return to Grodno, was truly providential for the M.I. He continued to carry on his office as delegate even during the acute period of sickness which brought him to the tomb.

Father Melchior did not make his mandate weigh upon Father Maximilian. More than a superior, he was a father and an adviser—in the words of Father Kolbe—the voice of the Immaculata, the voice of the will of God in regard both to the M.I. and to *The Knight.*

Fr. Fordon, who was also tubercular, urged Father Maximilian to rest and not to worry about anything. Father Kolbe answered: "According to obedience I will not do anything any longer; the Immaculata will do it by herself."

Father Maximilian held Father Melchior in the highest esteem and constantly urged his collaborators to obey scrupulously not only the orders he gave, but also his advice, and to turn to him in every difficulty. When informed of Father Fordon's imminent death, Father Kolbe wrote to his brother, Father Alphonse: "Tell Father Fordon not to forget from heaven the direction of the M.I., the Brothers, the difficulties, and not to forget me."

Later Father Kolbe wrote:

"Even from heaven, Fr. Melchior will not forget *The Knight,* because he was like its delegate and like a confessor. How many times he exhorted and advised me in the work for the Immaculata! How many times I went to him sorrowful and almost hopeless in spirit! It is right, therefore, that an article in his memory should appear in *The Knight,* and not only there but also in *The Seraphic Flame.*"

As the years went by, the amazing growth of the M.I. and of *The Knight* would not make Father Maximilian forget Grodno and Father Melchior. While traveling toward India in 1932, for the foundation of a third "City of the Immaculata," he would write to Poland:

"You must pray for this third *City of the Immaculata.* Someone tells me that it should be called the fourth, and not without reason. The first city is in heaven, where the superior is the Immaculata, and the workers are Father Fordon, Father Venanzio, Father Alphonse, Father Albert, etc."

In Grodno, Father Maximilian did not let the direction of *The Knight* interfere with his priestly ministry, which he carried out for the spiritual benefit of the people in nearby villages.

Here is the testimony given at the Apostolic Process in Warsaw by Mrs. Sophie Roszkowska, a teacher in the school of Lososna:

"My testimony refers to the catechetical activity carried out by Father Maximilian in the school where I was teaching. Father Kolbe used to come to our school twice a week to teach religion. Each time he came, he shook hands with us, saying: 'May the Immaculata help us.' When taking leave of us he used to repeat the same words. Holiness radiated from him. Both teachers and children were spellbound by his goodness. Young people eagerly looked forward to his coming, children clapped hands when he appeared. At his request a little altar to the Blessed Mother was prepared in each classroom, and the children would adorn it with flowers. In his work as a catechist, he obtained results beyond compare. Each lesson contributed to a better grasp of the Faith and motivated one to become better and closer to God. He established the *Militia Immaculatae* in our school, and both teachers and students belonged to it. He enlisted the teachers in a living rosary and personally presided over the monthly meetings in the friary of the Franciscan Friars in Grodno.

"During these rosary encounters he asked about any problems we or our friends had in living the Faith. Two colleagues of mine were rather indifferent about religion. Father Maximilian asked me to give them two Miraculous Medals, saying: 'The Immaculata will find the way of converting them.' Then he added: 'I am sure about their case.' I gave the medals to these two persons, and they were converted.

"I myself saw crowds of young people go from nearby parishes to the ceremonies celebrated by the Franciscan Fathers in Grodno. I knew some of them personally and I asked the reason for their preferences.

They answered that they liked to attend the Mass of Father Kolbe and hear his sermons. Some of my own friends preferred the church at Grodno to their own for the same reason.

"Father Kolbe used to organize spiritual retreats for children and adolescents, and he diffused among them copies of *The Knight* and *The Little Knight of the Immaculata.* The young people willingly read these publications. Under the influence of his pastoral and catechetical work, many were attracted to the religious life, even from among my own pupils."

## Return to Zakopane

In 1926, Father Maximilian was ill. Tuberculosis had again seized his weak body, and this attack was to be longer and more violent than the previous one.

To prevent irreparable damage to his health, the doctors prescribed that he must be immediately brought to the sanatorium.

Now that the work of the Immaculata was well established, Father Maximilian had to abandon everything to return to Zakopane. In the minds of many it seemed as if the work and sacrifice and prayer had been in vain. Would *The Knight* survive without its director? There was enough reason to be disheartened. Only Father Maximilian, completely abandoned into the hands of the Immaculata and trusting in her protection, gave no sign of alarm. On September 18, 1926, he left Grodno to enter the sanatorium a second time. During these months, contrary to every expectation, the circulation of *The Knight* doubled and the ground for the future development of the M.I. was prepared. It was clear that during this troubled time, Father Maximilian experienced a special protection of the Immaculata and gathered the fruits of his rare prudence and blind obedience.

The characteristic which best describes the whole life of Father Maximilian is obedience. His accomplishments aroused admiration not only for their grandeur but also for having been the fruit of faithful implementation of the decisions of the superiors. This continual self-denial obtained for the M.I. the guarantee of growth and abundant fruits. Moreover, Father Kolbe's obedience convinced and won over his confreres and superiors who had hesitated at first but later became his most firm supporters and collaborators.

We have seen the Provincial, Father Karwacki, assign to the M.I. a location where its activity could be carried out. His successor, Father Peregrine Haczela, on the eve of Father Maximilian's departure for Zakopane, took a wise measure on behalf of *The Knight*. He called Father Alphonse from Lwów and appointed him as successor to his brother in the direction of *The Knight*. This choice proved to be providential. A capable person, a tireless worker, and a good writer, Father Alphonse replaced his brother very well during his illness. In fact, when Father Maximilian returned from Zakopane, the old friary of Grodno was filled to overflowing and its large rooms had become too small to contain the different departments of the growing apostolate. Much of this progress was due to Father Alphonse, who in developing it was not guided by human ties but by the spiritual principles he had inherited from Father Maximilian.

At first Father Alphonse was overwhelmed by the new task. Father Maximilian, however, did not leave him without any kind of guidance. Twenty-nine letters dating from this period show Father Maximilian's concern to strengthen his brother's love for the Immaculata. In his turn Father Alphonse would arouse this love in the vocations who were attracted by the new Marian apostolate and were asking to become part of the Franciscan community in Grodno.

Father Maximilian advised his brother that in order to be victorious in every difficulty he should submit humbly to his superiors.

"Since the Father Provincial wrote that I would have to regulate myself by the counsels of Father Melchior (Fordon), I have always done so because it is the divine will—the will of the Immaculata—the will of the Provincial—the counsels of Father Fordon."

For the spiritual formation of the new vocations he gave this wise directive:

"I have observed that some religious regulate themselves more according to reason than according to faith, more by natural than by supernatural calculations, seeing therefore in the superiors only men more or less learned, rather than the representatives of God. Oh! Be very watchful so that these destructive pests, which take away all merit from holy obedience, do not contaminate the Brothers."

Father Maximilian's state of health was most critical. An X-ray taken in February, 1926, showed that the disease had gradually been eating away at the right lung. A second X-ray showed even more clearly the gravity of the illness, giving a prognosis anything but favorable for a complete recovery.

In the meantime in Grodno, good Father Fordon was close to death from tuberculosis, and many other religious were suffering from the same disease. This explains why the Provincial in January, 1927, forbade Father Kolbe to worry about the way things were going in Grodno. On his part Father Maximilian, completely abandoned in the hands of his heavenly Queen, whose wishes he identified with those of the superiors, could only choose the heroic way of obedience. Because of this, when on January 14, 1927, Father Alphonse in a letter asked for some guidelines connected with the M.I. and the new apostolate, Father Maximilian wrote in reply:

"Father Provincial wrote to me and told me that I must not make any trip and that I should not be concerned about anything. Therefore, I will not give you any counsels, nor make any decisions, since this is the desire of the Immaculata. If I should do anything to the contrary, I would act badly. Regulate yourself according to what the Immaculata inspires you to do."

In the following letter he added:

"Since Father Provincial has written to me that I should not concern myself about anything, it is a sign that the Immaculata desires things this way. If I should do differently, I would only spoil her plans.... May she alone direct your every thought, word and action so that you may be a useful instrument, very useful in her hands. For you, for the magazine, for the brothers, I pray often in the Holy Mass."

Father Alphonse went by train to Zakopane, but there, too, he ran up against the inflexible obedience of Father Maximilian, who repeated: "I am not allowed to busy myself with it. May the Immaculata help you." Father Maximilian was firm in wishing to obey his superiors.

During his second stay in Zakopane, Father Maximilian was thirty-one to thirty-two years old and had already reached a high degree of sanctity. Here is how he is portrayed in the testimony of Sister Felicita Sulatycka, who met him in March, 1927:

"From my first to my last encounter with Father Maximilian, I always viewed him as a saint, not only because of his evident priestly and monastic virtue, but because of his mysterious way of radiating faith, hope and love of God and neighbor. At the first encounter I was impressed by his faith. I had entered the chapel of the 'Pelczarki' Sisters in Zakopane, to whose care Father had been entrusted. The holy Mass had already started and I was rather distracted. Soon, however, the way this unknown priest was saying Mass impressed me and helped me to pray. I thought to myself: 'He must be a holy priest.' On the way out, I asked the Sister door-keeper who he was and came to know that he was the founder of the M.I. One could hardly believe that he was sick, when he began to speak with contagious fervor of the M.I. as the powerful means of spreading the kingdom of God through the Immaculata. Father told me that he was ill and not sure whether he would go back to work. I asked him: 'In that case, what would become of the *Militia?*' Father answered that he was only the instrument through which the Immaculata worked as she wished. He spoke enthusiastically of the miracles performed by the Virgin in souls, and said that no one should hesitate to put himself under her protection. Then he referred to the recent conversion of an unbeliever in the sanatorium as proof that the M.I. was founded to lead souls to God through the Blessed Virgin.

"During this conversation my conviction was strengthened that Father's love for souls, his faith and virtue, were able to overcome any obstacle. I often went to visit him and always found him serene and calm despite his very great suffering. His only concern was for the salvation of souls and the spread of the kingdom of God. Everything else had value only in view of these two basic aspirations of his soul. After holy Mass, I assisted at the thanksgiving of Father Maximilian; it was a recollected and prolonged prayer. In celebrating the Mass, he was deeply absorbed in the mystery of the action, and this had a great influence on me. He often repeated that obedience to the Church was the decisive way of doing the Immaculata's, that is, God's will. Each word, question, action, moment was for him a means for spreading devotion to the Immaculata and leading others to a filial abandonment in her. In this abandonment to the Immaculate Virgin, he saw the summit of man's activities. Father explained to me the necessity of propagating the *Militia,* as a weapon against Satan whose hold over the world was increasing. In the struggle against the devil, no man, even the most gifted, would be able to succeed, except the Mother of God, who had obtained the promise that she would crush the head of the serpent. Father Maximilian tried to instill this confidence in all who approached him. It was an act of love, which shone in his heroic charity, sacrifice, humility, obedience."

In spite of Father Maximilian's illness, the circulation of *The Knight,* in the course of five years, increased to 100,000 copies each month. The first economic difficulties were followed by an availability of funds, thanks to numerous donations. However, now that the economic worries had faded away, and the first difficulties had been happily overcome, another danger arose from expectations of profit. In order to preserve the spirit of the *Militia* and observe strict religious poverty, Father Kolbe reacted by letter immediately and energetically:

"My dearest brother, I myself marvel that, notwithstanding my ignorance, weaknesses and miseries and so much difficulty, *The Knight* still exists and is propagated more than any other religious paper. Many times, standing in front of so many machines I have asked myself: From whence and why all of this? The answer has always been the same: the Immaculata! She shows that she can do things and wants to do them. The greater the incapability, the more numerous the contradictions, so much the more does she show that she does everything. In this sincere recognition lies the whole explanation of our editorial activity...another very important point: the purpose of this publication is to win and conquer the whole world—present and future souls—for the reign of the Immaculata and never for cursed gain.

"It has been said: Now that we have machines we can count a little bit on the income from the machines themselves.

"In such a way, the means becomes the end, and the end the means; while reasoning in this way, no thought is given to future development.

"The souls go to ruin, the diabolical press works feverishly to sow disbelief and immorality, and we reap profit from the machines.

"It is then evident that the curse of St. Francis should fall on this work which would secure a quiet livelihood for the religious. It would then be a blessing from heaven that everything be destroyed....

"I write this so that you may understand what would happen if we were to lose sight of our goal and that you may have reasons to oppose anyone who might think this way."

For this reason, measures were taken so that nothing would be used for a purpose other than the M.I. In fact, Father Kolbe urged his brothers in religion to sacrifice their conveniences and needs for the good of their apostolic works. As an example, during the rigors of the Polish winter, in the ice-cold editorial and print shop rooms, he asked them to sacrifice the habit of smoking, out of love for the Immaculata.

"I urge you not to run out of paper for *The Knight*. I have written to the Brothers that they should not smoke. It is more expedient to praise the fervent so that the lukewarm may imitate them, than to reproach the lazy. With a drop of honey are caught more flies than with a barrel of vinegar. Do not worry about any criticism."

As single stones constitute the foundation of great buildings, these small sacrifices attracted the blessing of the Madonna and laid down not only the foundation of a building but of the "City of the Immaculata."

# Niepokalanow

On April 13, 1927, Father Maximilian having recovered somewhat from his illness, left the sanatorium of Zakopane. Having presented himself at the provincialate at Krakow, he set out again for Grodno. On his return after seven months of absence, he found many things changed. The friary at Grodno had become a crowded typographical complex under the direction of the M.I. which had also undergone growth. Thanks to the wise leadership of Father Fordon, Father Alphonse's efforts had met with much success: the members of the M.I. in Poland alone numbered 126,000; *The Knight* had a monthly circulation of 60,000 copies.

In the friary there was not even an empty corner. One moved with difficulty through the corridors stacked with reams of paper and piles of the bulletin. Even the cells, already inadequate for the growth of the community of Brothers, had been transformed into departments of work, occupied by counters and piles of lead for composition, which at that time was done entirely with movable characters. The machines were arranged in the areas where the kitchen and refectory had first been. In the evening, when the time of rest had come, the brothers had to prepare cots for themselves in the various workrooms.

One evening, impressed by the spectacle of the brothers sleeping in the place of the daily work, Father Maximilian exclaimed in an exuberance of feeling: "This is the beehive of the Immaculata!"

The well-chosen comparison between the labor of the worker bees for their queen and the untiring activity of the Brothers for the Immaculata came spontaneously at the end of a day that would be momentous in the annals of the Knights of the Immaculata.

That day, June 13, 1927, feast of St. Anthony of Padua, Father Ciborowski, known in the area as a passionate bee raiser, had been a guest of the Brothers. During dinner the conversations had centered on only two topics. On his part, Father Ciborowski had praised his bees, the perfection of their breeding, the goodness of their honey and the profit derived from their industry. On their part, Father Maximilian and his confreres had dwelt on their daily apostolate, the stages already reached, and those possible to attain. The comparison between the organized industry of the bees and the work of the religious regulated by obedience came spontaneously. Spontaneously, too, came the logical conclusion: as the bees multiply and swarm, so also the brothers, now many more because of the greater extension of their work, would have to swarm. But where?

Father Ciborowski was soon ready to leave. He had come alone to Grodno and before evening had to reach Poniemun to deal with Mr. Srzednicki about the development of his apiaries. Mr. Srzednicki was the head administrator for Prince John Drucki-Lubecki, a well-known landowner in the area.

On the doorstep of the friary, Father Kolbe asked:

"Does the Prince own other property besides that in the region of Grodno?"

"Yes," replied Father Ciborowski. "He has a vast amount of property at Teresin, near Warsaw."

"Near Warsaw!..." reflected Father Maximilian. Warsaw...at the center of Poland, on the principal railway system. That would be an ideal location for the development of *The Knight.*

Turning to Father Ciborowski, Father Kolbe asked: "Wouldn't you please, in honor of the Immaculate

Virgin, inform Mr. Srzednicki of the needs of *The Knight,* so that he may bring them to the attention of the Prince?"

"Willingly, Father! May the Immaculata help us." With that, Father Ciborowski left.

It is not completely groundless to presume that that evening, as Father Maximilian recited the rosary while passing through the corridors of the "beehive" of the Immaculata, he included among his intentions Father Ciborowski, Mr. Srzednicki and Prince Drucki-Lubecki.

Father Ciborowski kept his word. A few weeks later, Father Maximilian and Father Alphonse, invited by their friend to visit his apiary, were able to meet Mr. Srzednicki. After the introductions, the conversation was marked by the most sincere cordiality.

Mr. Srzednicki later recalled:
"I spent a few hours in confidential conversation with Father Maximilian. Calmly and unpretentiously, Father unfolded the plan for his projects and for the activity he proposed. The enthusiasm with which he presented the results of his experience and reflection for my consideration influenced me. As a typical layman, one of the so-called intellectuals of the nineteenth century, I was indifferent to religion and ignorant of supernatural truths. The concise explanation Father gave of the missionary scope of *The Knight* and of its gradual growth introduced me to the invisible reality which was the foundation of the activity of the good religious. The supernatural tone of the whole discussion won me over. It was the beginning of a change in me, of a tendency to view things from higher standards. Since then my interest in the new field, and my knowledge of the supernatural world has grown deeper."

Having mentioned the crowded and inadequate quarters of Grodno, Father Kolbe invited Mr. Srzednicki to visit the Franciscan friary and printing establishment.

Mr. Srzednicki continued:

"I gave my word that I would go. Meanwhile, continuing our conversation, I promised Father Maximilian to mention to Prince Drucki-Lubecki the possibility of giving the Fathers an allotment of land at Teresin, in the vicinity of the train station. If there would be any difficulty, I was disposed to offer some of my own land at Milosna, near Warsaw."

On the following day, Mr. Srzednicki arrived at the friary of Grodno. The visit convinced him that there was no prospect for further development there. As on the preceding day, the necessity for land at Teresin or at Milosna was reaffirmed. Concerning the decision, Mr. Srzednicki urged Father Maximilian to freely approach the Prince's administrative offices at Grodno.

"When Father Maximilian came to me," continued Mr. Srzednicki, "our conversation focused on Teresin or Milosna. Since Teresin, near the railroad station, appeared more convenient, Milosna, which was a half mile away, was put aside. During a meeting with the Prince, 50,000 square meters in a suitable site were selected in front of the station of Szymanow on the way to Paprotnia and Teresin. In accord with Father Maximilian's express desire, there was at that moment neither an act of donation, nor an act of purchase. Only the use of the land was granted. Upon its consignment which took place immediately in August, 1927, by verbal donation, a statue of the Immaculata was placed on the site by Father Maximilian."

Mary, Queen of the M.I., was to be the cornerstone of the city soon to be erected. She would lead to victory over the difficulties.

As a religious, Father Maximilian could not accept the donation of the land of Prince Drucki-Lubecki without the permission of his superiors. Moreover, the simple authorization of the Minister Provincial was not sufficient, since a new foundation had to be ratified by the deliberative vote of the provincial council, and confirmed by the Minister General of the Order.

The negotiations were begun with the permission of the Provincial; however, the conclusion was to be referred to the decisions of the forthcoming provincial chapter presided over by the Minister General of the Order.

The chapter was held in Krakow from the 19th to the 21st of July, 1927: after Father Maximilian's meeting with Mr. Srzednicki but before his meeting with Prince Drucki-Lubecki, which took place in August.

The case was discussed by the chapter Fathers. The explanation Father Maximilian gave concerning the acceptance of the land and the future constructions did not convince some of those present. The personal intervention of the Minister General became necessary. He took a firm stand on behalf of Father Maximilian's requests and convinced the undecided members to vote favorably.

The voting concerned two questions: the first examined the necessity of a center for the M.I.; the second dealt with the question of complete donation and the possible strings attached.

The first point was agreed upon unconditionally. The second, instead, was conditional, subject to the approval of the Minister Provincial and of his council.

Thus authorized by the superiors, the meeting between Father Maximilian and Prince Drucki-Lubecki took place, as already described. Through his administrator, the Prince verbally handed over the land in August, postponing the details of the definitive negotiations to another date. Meanwhile, on the day of taking possession, Father Maximilian planted the statue of the Immaculata on the land. He had faith that the Immaculata would be the true and only tenant.

Then came the unexpected. The Prince had asked that Masses be celebrated for him in exchange for the donation of the land. Because of the onerous obligation, the superiors decided to renounce the offer.

Being informed by Father Maximilian of his superiors' decisions, the Prince withdrew his gift and requested the removal of the statue of the Immaculata. Father Maximilian insisted that the statue should remain, at least to show that the Madonna had once failed in keeping her promises. This saved the situation.

Father Maximilian's attitude impressed the Prince, who later attested:

"His humility and childlike simplicity attracted me. If there was ever a man who was not proud, it was Father Maximilian."

His abrupt refusal to give the land, which had been triggered by the behavior of Father Maximilian's confreres, gnawed at the Prince's conscience. In his testimony he unhesitatingly affirmed:

"I became irritated. They wanted the land, which I was disposed to give, but not the obligation of the Masses. The conversation ended there, but Father Maximilian said that he would return after three days for a definitive answer. During those three days a state of uneasiness prevented me from performing my work. My uncertain conduct toward the Franciscans gave me no rest until I made up my mind to give him the land he needed. Regarding the donation, I do not think of having any merit for the gift. As time goes by, I become more convinced that such an opportunity was for me the beginning of a friendship which was a real blessing."

To Father Cyril Kita, who learned about each circumstance from Father Maximilian himself, we owe this further information:

"After the first bequest, the Prince did not mind giving one or another extension of land. Whenever Father Kolbe needed more land, the Prince gave him all that he asked for."

This time, too, the Immaculata had intervened in an evident way for the good of Father Maximilian's work. His superiors accepted the free offering, and immediately ordered the transfer of the printing establishment at Grodno to the friary soon to be constructed.

# The Foundation of Niepokalanow

Prince Drucki-Lubecki signed the act of donation on
October 1, 1927. A few days later, Father Maximilian,
already named superior of the religious house about to
be erected, set out for Teresin for the foundation of
Niepokalanow. Father Alphonse and a few religious
expert in carpentry were his first co-workers. The other
Brothers who had remained temporarily at Grodno
were to prepare the editions of *The Knight* for the whole
year before the machines could be dismantled for the
transfer.

A good lady, Mrs. Klimacewska-Jaroszewska, offered
hospitality to Father Kolbe and his confreres, giving
them lodging in the attic of her farm house. They remained there for six weeks. As soon as the chapel and a
house had been built and the area fenced in, the
religious settled themselves, immediately establishing
the conventual cloister.

A providential gift of two cartloads of timber from
Prince Czetwertynski enabled the religious to begin
the construction of the printing offices and attached
buildings.

The testimony of Father Anselm Kubit sheds light on
Father Kolbe's criteria for the construction:

"Father Maximilian shook the entire province with
the introduction of a more strict poverty. The Franciscan friaries were generally modest, but here and there
the tendency toward some convenience had infiltrated.
At Niepokalanow, Father Maximilian constructed the
buildings with *lesz,* that is, with the dross of carbon
coke. The tables were unplaned; rough seats without
supports were used as chairs.... All our dishes were
made out of tin. Father Maximilian was not ashamed of
this poverty, even in front of others; bishops and cardinals alike were welcomed with simplicity. When someone pointed out to him that this was unbecoming for
illustrious personages, he explained that introducing
novelties for the guests could provoke relaxation in the

life of the friars. He shared his own cloak with the Brothers. It displeased him when a durable brick building was constructed. He said that great buildings hold friars back; they cannot be transferred easily. One would not want to leave a comfortable house for one less comfortable, and thus one is held back from moving to other friaries. During social revolutions, the first to fall victim are the ostentatious and comfortable buildings. Then, too, times change, improvements are made, so to what purpose does one build for long years?"

According to these exclusively Franciscan principles, Niepokalanow, from its foundation, was built only through the work of the friars, with the exception of some gratuitous help from a few good elderly men and boys of the area. By the middle of November, a more spacious chapel, a poor, but roomy house for the religious and the quarters for the machinery were ready.

From the beginning of October to the middle of November 1927, Father Maximilian and Father Alphonse remained at Teresin to prepare for the transfer of the publishing house from Grodno to Niepokalanow. However, for a little while they had to divide their time between the two communities. During the first six weeks, Father Maximilian, and more often Father Alphonse, was obliged to go back and forth between Grodno and Niepokalanow. By the middle of November, the last issues of *The Knight* for 1927 had been printed; meanwhile new quarters were ready to welcome the publishing house. Father Maximilian went to Grodno for the last time for the transfer of the machinery and of the religious to Niepokalanow.

Was this activity a feverish work of uncontrolled enthusiasm on the part of Father Maximilian and the others? No; rather, the chronicles recall episodes which surprise us and permit us to measure the degree of spiritual maturity and prudence Father Maximilian had reached in only thirty-five years.

The departure from Grodno was planned for the night of November 20.

On the preceding Sunday, Father Maximilian assembled all his confreres and led them on a pilgrimage to Wilno, first to the sanctuary of Our Lady of Ostrabramska, then to the mountain named Three Crosses. This traditional site of the martyrdom of the first Franciscans of Wilno renewed in Father Maximilian his longing for martyrdom.

Here for the first time, he unfolded his vast missionary plan for Poland and the pagan world to the young confreres of the Order who were attracted by the ideals of the M.I.

The next day he organized a second pilgrimage, this one to the cemetery of Grodno, to pray and pay their last tribute at the tomb of Brother Albert Olszakowski, the first typesetter for *The Knight,* who had died a few years before.

On the evening of November 20, they were given a "farewell" dinner by the new superior of Grodno. The preparations for departure were climaxed by the following exhortation by Father Maximilian:

"Niepokalanow, where we are headed, is a place chosen by the Immaculata, destined particularly for the propagation of her devotion. Everything that is already there and will be there is her possession. We, too, have been chosen by the Immaculata and therefore we, too, must be her possessions. Tomorrow is the feast of the Presentation of Mary in the Temple. As did the Immaculata, who consecrated her whole self to the Lord, we also, on the vigil of this feast, make the offering of ourselves to her, placing ourselves as useless instruments into her hands, without limits, without reserve, forever.

"In the new friary our life must be marked by total sacrifice, by the most perfect observance, especially in the practice of obedience. Great poverty, in accord with the spirit of St. Francis, much work, many sufferings and not a few hardships are awaiting us. The Rule and

Constitutions must be strictly observed, because Nie-pokalanow must set forth an example of regular life for all. If some of you feel weak and have not the strength for such a hard life, say it sincerely, so that Father Provincial may dispose otherwise."

Two of the confreres took a step backward, but all of the others bound themselves more closely to Father Maximilian.

They left Grodno with hardly 200 *zloti,* which was scarcely enough for the train tickets. A few days later, eight railroad cars, overloaded with machinery and printing equipment, left for Teresin. The few papers of the M.I., taken from Krakow to Grodno in 1922, had been contained in only one suitcase. Now, five years later, it took eight railroad cars to transport the publishing house.

The next morning the religious community of Grodno had re-established itself at Niepokalanow. The community was canonically erected on December 7, the vigil of the Feast of the Immaculate Conception.

After the blessing of the machines, all were put into motion, to the surprise and admiration of the invited guests: surprise at the complexity of the editorial plant, and admiration at the extreme poverty of the life of the religious.

The new friary—described in the chronicles as the "factory of the Immaculata"—was made up of twenty friars: two priests and eighteen Brothers.

## The Development and Organization of Niepokalanow

At the foundation of Niepokalanow there was no specific program except the general one of the M.I. It was the subsequent development that enabled its founder to give it the lofty objectives demanded by its rapid growth. But the beginnings of Niepokalanow were humble and modest, as are the origins of all the great works of God, who uses men as His instruments.

Father Maximilian was the superior of Niepokalanow up until the first months of 1930. When he left for the Far East, the superiors chose Father Alphonse to succeed him. However, Father Alphonse died prematurely on December 3, 1930. He was succeeded, until the return of Father Maximilian from Japan, by Father Florian Koziura, one of the first to embrace the ideals of the Marian apostolate of the M.I. Besides the action of the superiors, there was the cooperation of the religious Brothers. Those who had been appointed technicians were called to active and organized collaboration. From the beginning, in fact, Father Maximilian wanted a few "idea boxes" placed near the superior's office, so that each of the Brothers committed to the various duties could freely express in writing his viewpoint or advice regarding the progress of his respective department as well as the common good.

Because of this harmonious activity, in less than ten years Niepokalanow reached the stage of organization and development which we are about to describe.

The following overall view of the organization of Niepokalanow is based on data contained in *Elenchus— 1939,* with explanations and annotations by Father G. Domanski. In charge of everything was the Office of General Management with Father Maximilian as director and Father Bartosik as vice director. They were assisted by three secretariats: for personal assistance to the directors (two Brothers); for civil affairs, handling contacts with the civil authorities (two Brothers); and for general office needs (two Brothers); three Brothers, moreover, were assigned to messenger service. In discharging the most important affairs, the director, who acted also as Guardian (superior), was helped by two vicars and assisted by the council of the conventual chapter consisting of the priests. Moreover, meetings were held for all the directors of the twelve offices for particular affairs, and for all the members of the community.

Niepokalanow was divided into twelve departments managed by the aforementioned offices for particular affairs. The first three of these were immediately connected with the purpose of the M.I., that is, the conquest of the world for the Immaculata (II and III), and with the essential condition for M.I.'s existence, that is, unlimited consecration to her (I); five others (IV-VIII) endeavored to produce the means necessary to achieve the purpose; finally, the last four (IX-XII) served as "auxiliaries" of the other sectors to facilitate their intense and broad activity.

*Department I,* called M.I.n. (that is M.I. for Niepokalanow), provided for the spiritual and material needs of the members of the friary. At its head was the Father Guardian, assisted by his vicar, and a secretariat of five Brothers. The spiritual director (Father Florian Koziura) and other Father confessors were responsible for the "internal forum." Religious education was entrusted to six priests called prefects and to a Brother and a priest for each group of religious: professed of solemn vows, professed of simple vows, postulants, aspirants and Brothers of the night shift. Moreover, there was a master for the cleric novices, and a rector, assisted by two Brothers, for the minor seminary.

As far as material needs were concerned, Department I included six sections: a) receptionists (four Brothers); b) sacristy (two priests and two Brothers); c) food section divided into three subsections: vegetable garden (eight Brothers), animal breeding (four Brothers), kitchen (thirty-six Brothers); d) garment section with four subsections: sewing and weaving room and storehouse (twenty-four Brothers), clothing shop (nine Brothers), laundry (five Brothers) and shoe shop (thirteen Brothers); e) health section with three subsections: infirmary with a small hospital, pharmacy and kitchen for the sick (six Brothers), dental office (one Brother), barber shop and baths (one Brother); f) general storeroom (three Brothers).

*Department II:* administration of the M.I. in Poland (M.I.p.). Its members endeavored with timely action to conquer as many souls as possible for the Immaculata in Poland, and to perform the apostolate of correspondence and of apostolic missions outside the friary. It was headed by Father Maximilian. It included, besides a general secretariat with eight friars, forty-nine other Brothers who acted as secretaries and notaries for the sixteen civil Provinces of Poland, and four for Polish emigrants. Also subject to this department were four "sectional" offices of the newspaper *Maly Dziennik* at Warsaw, Lodz, Poznan and Gdynia (seven Brothers), and some other sectional offices in other cities (e.g., at Krakow and Lwów), directed by others. In 1937, the administration received 750,000 letters from within Poland and 9,000 from the Polish emigrants. In addition, one Brother from this department was assigned to the school of Paprotnia as its prefect.

*Department III:* administration of the M.I. for the world (M.I.w.). Its purpose was to implant the M.I. all over the world. It had just begun to develop its work. Under the direction of Father Maximilian there worked four religious (one priest and three Brothers).

*Department IV:* financial office with one priest as bursar, two secretaries (Brothers), one food supplier (Brother) and one beggar (Brother).

*Department V:* study and initiation of projects to conquer souls. "Study," according to the bylaws of the M.I., is a means of discovering what is to be given to souls, so that the Immaculata may act in them. To this department were assigned, always under the direction of Father Kolbe and his vicar, four Brothers, and three other religious for the library (one priest and two Brothers).

*Department VI:* production. Its purpose was to produce the written copy for newspaper, the periodicals and other media necessary for the apostolate that had been planned and called for by Department V. The principal part of this department was, under the guidance of

Father Kolbe and his vicar, entrusted to the editorial staffs of the various periodicals published by Niepokalanow. On the editorial staff of the monthly publications—*The Knight* and two minor magazines—there were three priests and five Brothers. The editorial staff of the daily *Maly Dziennik* had two sections: one at Niepokalanow (one priest and ten Brothers, among them five secretaries for the eleven editions) and the other at Warsaw (four Brothers, plus two Brothers assigned to the kitchen). Three proofreaders and two artists were also working for the editing stage. The religious were helped by lay editors. In 1938, when a broadcasting station was inaugurated at Niepokalanow (December 8), one Brother was assigned as program director.

*Department VII:* reproduction. The responsibility of this division was to produce the printed matter and other media presentations that had been prepared by Department VI. This division included the printing establishment under one director. Thirty-six Brothers were assigned to typesetting and composing, fourteen Brothers worked in the photoengraving and photography labs, sixteen Brothers in stereotype production, twenty-seven Brothers in the pressroom itself. Moreover, fifteen Brothers worked in the bindery and eight as typists. The radio transmitter was manned by two Brothers.

*Department VIII:* mailing and distribution of the publications and correspondence. There was one Brother director. Assigned to this department were: in the secretariat, ten Brothers; in the mailing of the periodicals, thirty-three Brothers; in the mailing of the daily newspaper, thirty-two Brothers; and in the carrying on of correspondence, five Brothers. Moreover, twenty-eight Brothers took care of the addresses. To Department VIII was entrusted also the library, open to outsiders (one Brother).

*Department IX:* technical assistance. Its purpose was to insure the upkeep of the equipment. There was one director. To this were annexed three sections: mechanics (fourteen Brothers), electricity (five Brothers), telephones (five Brothers). Niepokalanow had its own telephone center.

*Department X:* construction. This division was responsible for the maintenance of the buildings and streets of Niepokalanow. It was divided into six sections: sawmill (seven Brothers), carpentry (nineteen Brothers), masonry (nine Brothers), construction (seven Brothers), cleaning (seven Brothers).

*Department XI:* transportation. Thirteen Brothers were assigned for the maintenance of motor vehicles, carts, wagons, and of the little train which brought provisions of paper, fuel, etc. from the station of Szymanow.

*Department XII:* security. Its aim was to protect the friary and center from the dangers of fire, robbery, etc. This section comprised the night watchmen (nine Brothers) and the firemen; the latter carried out this task only when the need arose, while under normal conditions they worked in other departments. They were divided into three sections with a sum total of thirty-three Brothers.

This organization went into effect on December 8, 1936, and received its final form on December 8, 1938, in the so-called general rule of Niepokalanow elaborated by Father Maximilian.

The total of priests and Brothers working in the twelve departments was more than five hundred.

# Two Houses of Formation
# and Two Novitiates

Niepokalanow grew out of a religious community consisting of two priests and eighteen Brothers, who soon enough had been too few to meet all the needs of the growing apostolate. In fact, one of the first problems the new foundation had been confronted with was that of religious vocations to the Brotherhood and, even more so, to the priesthood. Both of these problems beset the Provincial, Father Cornelius Czupryk, who at the time of his election, in 1927, had permitted the founding of Niepokalanow. In May 1929, the worries of Father Cornelius increased because of the health of Father Maximilian, confined to another rest period, and also because of the criticisms voiced by other religious of the province who feared a colossal bankruptcy. Father Cornelius visited Niepokalanow, and, seeing the seriousness of the problem, was more inclined to foresee the failure of the work than its development. Turning to Father Maximilian and Father Alphonse he said in jest: "Now prepare yourselves also to found a seminary and you will have some priests."

Father Czupryk had just returned to Lwów when Father Alphonse went to him with a construction plan for the seminary. The plan had been drawn up by Father Maximilian in all its details, ready to carry it out. Father Cornelius was simply astounded that his words had been understood so literally. Turning to Father Alphonse, he remarked, "You are taking my joke seriously," and angrily dismissed him.

A month of apparent calm followed. On the one hand, Father Maximilian and Father Alphonse, not at all offended by the bitter remark of Father Cornelius, were in perfect serenity of spirit. On the other, the Provincial at Lwów had lost his peace of mind. He spent many sleepless nights, perplexed and uncertain about the course of action to take. He still loved Niepokalanow. After all, he had given the permission for its establishment! Did he not also have on his kneeler the statue of the Immaculata?... One night, after a prolonged prayer, he went to his desk and jotted down the following note for Father Maximilian:

"In virtue of obedience, for the glory of God, the honor of the Immaculata and the growth of our Order, I order the foundation of a seminary in our poor friary at Niepokalanow, beginning with the scholastic year 1929-1930."

When the letter reached Niepokalanow, the July issue of *The Knight* was about to be printed. Without delay Father Maximilian hastened to insert in it the announcement:

"With the scholastic year 1929-1930 a seminary will be opened at Niepokalanow for vocations who desire to consecrate themselves to the priestly and missionary ministry of the Franciscan Order."

When, a few days later, Father Provincial presented himself at Niepokalanow to revoke the letter previously written, it was too late. *The Knight* had already been printed and shipped out.

Immediately the requests began to pour in, and the necessary steps for the construction of a seminary distinct from the house of formation for the Brothers were taken. And so in 1929, scarcely two years after its foundation, Niepokalanow had two houses of formation, whose rapid development made it necessary, within two years, to establish two distinct novitiates: one for the Brothers and the other for aspirants to the priesthood.

The immediate and marvelous fruits of the great and well-organized work carried on in the City of Mary cannot be explained by human reasoning.

A humble religious from a poor family, himself poor by virtue of his vows, and weakened by tuberculosis, had conceived and brought into existence a work worth millions of dollars, the sort of undertaking which would seem to be possible only for a great corporation. Without money he had founded a city in which life pulsated intensely, in which everything was humming with machines and motors, the buzzing of saws and the clanging of anvils. At the same time this immense factory was a place where an ascetical life was lived, where the silence of men reigned supreme, where mysterious friars in religious habits moved about rapidly, almost like shadows, greeting one another with a simple nod of the head, or even more often with one sweet word pronounced in a low tone of voice: *Mary*.

In this remarkable city, which was at one and the same time factory and monastery, where work was ceaseless and unrewarded, where one did not speak of the consequences of social vindication, but where, rather, material work itself was spiritualized and became prayer in this city young men were attracted to do more than their fellow citizens.

What was the secret of the success obtained by this humble and sickly Franciscan?

It can be answered in two brief phrases: *the Immaculata* and *divine Providence*.

*The Immaculata*: the ravisher of hearts, the Mother of fair love, the delight of pure souls, the Queen of Apostles and saints—from the beginning, she had been Father Maximilian's chief inspiration, the means and immediate purpose of his apostolate, the standard of his "Knights." She was a powerful attraction, the irresistible invitation which enchanted many young people, leading them toward her city so that they might consecrate themselves to her there, live and work for her, and in her name conquer souls for Christ, "the King and center of every heart."

*Divine Providence*: the divine financier of the Apostles, of souls dedicated to evangelical poverty, of the untiring investors of the talents received by God, of all those who receive in order to give, who build not for themselves, but for their brothers, for the Church, for Christ—this was the resource in which Father Maximilian placed all his trust. From it he received abundantly in all his needs.

His collaborators, too, were sustained by the same confidence. Father Florian Koziura confided:

"I myself, when I was permanently transferred to Niepokalanow, for a few days could neither eat nor sleep for fear that this work would collapse. But then, as everyone else does, I got used to the unusual way in which Father Maximilian worked. At times, pressed by difficulties which seemed insurmountable, he would exclaim repeatedly: 'Ah! What am I going to do?' But after an instant he would overcome himself and say with a smile:

"'After all, why am I worried? The Madonna will take care. *I* will work.'

"One had the impression that he must have had some secret assurance which sustained him. In his work he did not rely on temporal means, but counted above all on supernatural help."

Since supernatural help comes from the same inexhaustible source and in the same ways, we might be reminded of another great "city," this one in Turin, Italy, which is numerically even more populated than the city of Father Maximilian. Out of humility, its holy founder, St. Joseph Benedict Cottolengo, chose to call it "the Little House of Divine Providence." It is a great infirmary, whose immense population of patients and dedicated staff rely solely upon the Providence of God.

There is one reality which explains the "miracle" in each of these cities. Mary is the light, the smile, the comfort, because in both she is officially honored as Queen. Likewise in each, there is one center and throne from which, in His real and substantial Presence, the Eucharistic Jesus rules. There He is honored and adored.

St. Joseph Cottolengo wanted to institute perpetual and solemn adoration of the Blessed Sacrament in the central church of the Little House. All the residents of the Little House who are able to do so—the blind, the crippled, the epileptic, the mentally ill—approach the Eucharistic throne with hymns, prayers and weeping.

So it was at Niepokalanow. Father Maximilian wanted the most Holy Eucharist, whether in the tabernacle or solemnly exposed, to be the Center of his city. He wanted the friars to interrupt their work and even their sleep in order to take turns in adoration before Jesus. This perennial praise is the most efficacious means to honor and to receive graces from the Heart of

Jesus. He was not given permission for this adoration at the time, but God heard his desire. As Father and bountiful Ruler, Jesus provides for the children who serve Him and who ask Him for their daily bread. The marvels of Providence cause the man who has a living faith to exclaim: "Clearly here is the hand of God."

The presence of the hand of God in the work of Father Maximilian, not only in the foundation of Niepokalanow, but in also all his missionary work in subsequent years and during the trials of the Second World War, is confirmed by the following testimony of Father Cornelius Czupryk:

"The Servant of God was not guided in his life by human considerations nor by human interests. He used to say: 'We are instruments in the hand of the Immaculata and therefore in the hand of God.' When he was ill, he did not worry about his work, but was accustomed to saying that everything would be as Mary, and therefore God, wanted it to be.

"If something developed only with difficulty, or absolutely did not succeed, he did not lose his serenity of soul. In Poland, the difficulties were minor, but in Japan they were sometimes very serious: difficulties of a financial character, difficulties from the authorities of the place (civil and ecclesiastical), difficulties arising within the religious family. Even though the most suitable men were chosen, the change of climate, surroundings and diet—plus nostalgia for their homeland—disheartened many, and it was not easy to substitute men because of the distance. Yet Father Kolbe never let himself be discouraged, and he strove to raise the spirit of the others. One time, during the nine years I lived with him, he wrote to Father Provincial: 'Sometimes I feel like abandoning everything and dedicating time to work on myself; however, my conscience tells me to also work for the salvation of others.'

"Father Kolbe did not hesitate to spend money when he was faced with a real need. He counted above all on the Providence of God.

"During the German occupation he showed a special trust in divine Providence when, after returning from the first German concentration camp, he reunited the scattered Brothers and again began to welcome candidates into the order. He thus reestablished the novitiate, notwithstanding the fact that troops had thoroughly plundered the friary. Father Kolbe trusted in the Lord, and this confidence did not delude him. He was able to provide for a numerous group of confreres and unstintingly give alms to refugees and to the poor. After the example of St. Joseph Cottolengo, he encouraged the Brothers to hope in the Providence of God."

# The Editorial Production
# of Niepokalanow

In 1927, when the little printing house of Grodno was reassembled at Niepokalanow, the city became the publishing house of *The Knight,* which at that time had a monthly circulation of about 60,000 copies.

Within a few years, the printing facilities of the city developed little by little and the editorial production achieved unexpected and consoling goals.

From her "city," according to figures dated 1939, the Immaculata blessed and nourished the sons of the noble Polish nation with the following publications:

1) *The Knight of the Immaculata* (Rycerz Niepokalanej)—an illustrated monthly with an ordinary circulation of about 705,000 copies and with extraordinary editions of up to 1,000,000.

2) *The Young Knight* (Rycerzyk Niepokalanej)—an illustrated monthly for young people: 157,000 copies.

3) *The Bulletin of the M.I.* (Informator Rycerstwa)— for the Marian Groups: 900 copies.

4) *The Little Knight* (Maly Rycerzyk Niepokalanej) —an illustrated monthly for little ones: 36,000 copies.

5) *The Little Journal* (Maly Dziennik)—a daily Catholic paper of current events: 150,000 copies daily, 250,000 copies on feast days.

6) *Miles Immaculatae*—a quarterly in Latin for priests of other nations: 15,000 copies.

7) *Missionary Bulletin* (Biuletyn Misyjny Niepokalanowa Japonskiego)—a monthly with 4,000 copies.

8) *The Echo of Niepokalanow* (Echo Niepokalanowa) —a bulletin of information for the friars of Niepokalanow.

To these periodicals we must add the numerous and continual editions of booklets, pamphlets and volumes of pastoral, educative, ascetical works and lives of the saints, all in keeping with the end: the glorification of the Immaculata.

From the above-mentioned list, the reader will be able to understand how vital and fruitful the little seed of *The Knight* was and how around it there sprouted forth and developed a magnificent blossoming of magazines, newspapers and other printed matter.

Father Kolbe enlarged the sphere of action of the M.I. always more. Whenever the opportunity presented itself, he never hesitated to undertake initiatives, even the most daring, to diffuse his ideal and widen the scope of beneficial action.

Among all the publications, *The Little Journal,* a Catholic daily, merits particular attention, because it was to present the news according to Catholic principles in the face of much anti-Catholic sentiment.

Everything was wisely and prudently organized, in the administrative as well as in the editorial field. Around the editorial center at Niepokalanow, seven editorial offices arose at Warsaw, Poznan, Gdynia, Lodz, Krakow, Wilno and Grodno.

The importance of *The Little Journal* and the hearty welcome it received from its readers are demonstrated by the number of copies distributed: 150,000 everyday, as we have said, and 250,000 on feasts.

His Eminence, Cardinal Kakowski, Primate of Poland, defined the newspaper's lofty mission in these terms:

"To instruct and educate people in Catholic doctrine, informing them about the commandments and the precepts of the Church. To defend the Church from the attacks of freemasonry, non-believers, and radicals, who, with their spirit of laicism, would want to eliminate the Church and replace it with their own principles."

Mons. Gawlina testified:

"The Apostolic Nuncio, the Polish Episcopate, the clergy and faithful welcomed the publication with joy because it was very Catholic and forceful, and of lower price than the other newspapers."

# On the Battlefield

With the aim of emphasizing the wise conduct of Father Maximilian in the different foundations and in the apostolate of the M.I., we have had to repeatedly mention the difficulties that he encountered. Because he was a religious, his every action was carried out in obedience to the approval of his superiors, who in their turn —obliged by their religious statutes—had to consult their senior confreres. Difficulties cannot be attributed to bad intentions; rather, they were an understandable result of life in common, where not all have the same viewpoint, the same degree of virtue, and where, especially regarding finances, the calculation of human prudence prevails.

Of a very different nature were the difficulties that broke loose after the foundation of Niepokalanow. Not only Father Maximilian, but also "the City of the Immaculata" and his apostolate of the press, became the object of misunderstandings and obstacles.

Niepokalanow had external enemies of every kind. It had to face opposition, envy, boycotts and assaults. It finally achieved victory, thanks to the protection of the Immaculata, the prudence of its founder and the spirit of sacrifice of its members.

The external enemies were the sectarians, the Masons, the anti-Catholics and the anti-clerics. But Niepokalanow had been bolstered to thwart their plots. It was especially when Niepokalanow came out with the newspaper *The Little Journal,* that attacks became strongest.

Because of its decisively Catholic content, it was natural that *The Little Journal* would excite the anger of the adversaries, who had recourse to every form of boycott to stop its success and to bring about its downfall.

Since the *Little Journal* met popular favor, even because of its low price of five "groszy" as compared with twenty-five and thirty for the other newspapers, it was immediately accused of injustice by the directors of the other dailies. The immediate effect of the struggle, which sprang from self-interest, was that *The Little Journal* was not accepted by the newsstands. The measures taken by the papermills were even more grave. Influenced by the M.I.'s opposition, the mill owners suspended the supply of paper on credit and demanded cash payment. But Niepokalanow did not give up.

Because of its internal organization, by which all the workers were friars, *The Little Journal* was able to offer the money for the acquisition of the paper. To diffuse the journal, Niepokalanow appealed to the spirit of sacrifice of its members, who erected newsstands all over Poland to offset the boycott of the opposition. Thus made independent by its self-sufficiency, and free from the threat of strikes on the part of its workers, because these were religious, Niepokalanow peacefully won its battle. The adversaries, seeing that their attacks were fruitless, ended by giving *The Little Journal* all the rights of the other daily papers.

This victory of *The Little Journal* was not enough to bring tranquillity to Niepokalanow. Soon, because of ever-growing popular approval, it had to face jealousy and snares, and even more dangerous situations. The following episode is given in the testimony of His Excellency, Mons. Joseph Gawlina, who was then a member of the Episcopal Commission for the press:

"Father Maximilian was very devoted to the Holy Apostolic See. He had continual contacts with the Apostolic Nuncio and followed his directives, especially those which referred to the publication of his journals. He enjoyed the full trust of the Polish episcopate and manifested great submission to all the bishops. I refer to an episode in which he showed prudence and respect toward a priest and a bishop. At a certain moment the priest, who was responsible for the press, tried through a bishop to influence the work of Father Maximilian. Both went to Niepokalanow to Father Maximilian and claimed the direction of his daily "Maly Dziennik" *(The Little Journal)*, as though this were a decision of the Episcopal Commission for the Press. Father Kolbe received the news with great respect but asked that the carrying out of the order be postponed. In the meantime he came to me and asked if this were true and if the Episcopal Commission had established it, in which case he was ready to carry out the order. I assured him that it was not true but that it was only the action of the priest. Then I advised him to refer everything to the Apostolic Nuncio, who supported the rights of the Franciscans. So Father Kolbe continued in his work. In this sorrowful episode Father Maximilian did not show any resentment or aversion toward the persons who had attempted to take over the newspaper for their political aims."

Other difficulties, no less grave, arose when Father Maximilian planned to start a little radio station at Niepokalanow. This time, however, because of the outbreak of war, the victory was not complete.

Father Slominiski related that Father Maximilian started to think of other modern means, such as the radio, to be able to draw more and more souls to the Immaculata. Could not the radio, which can do much evil, also be used at Niepokalanow for the glory of

Mary? Without giving thought to eventual difficulties, Father Maximilian had the building for the radio station constructed.

On the vigil of the feast of the Immaculata in December, 1938, with a shortwave transmitter borrowed from the army, they were able to broadcast, for the first time, the Hymn of the M.I., played by the orchestra composed of Brothers. But after a few broadcasts, difficulties arose. The opponents of the M.I., mostly representatives of the government, refused to grant legal authorization to broadcast. They feared that the radio broadcasts from Niepokalanow would stir up still more enthusiastic uproar than *The Little Journal* had done.

However, to satisfy the requests of Father Maximilian, the government granted an hour a week—only—for the broadcast of news regarding Niepokalanow, from the government station.

Father Maximilian remained firm and kept making his request. In the end, because of the war, everything was suspended.

## Saint Francis, the Printer!

While visiting the printing plant of Niepokalanow one day, a certain Polish Canon stopped before the imposing rotary press, an expensive piece of equipment, and ironically asked Father Maximilian:

"If St. Francis were still living, what would he say, seeing these expensive machines?"

Father Maximilian tranquilly responded:

"He would roll up his sleeves and, speeding up the machines as much as possible, he would work like these good Brothers to diffuse the glory of God and the Immaculata with the most modern means."

It is really so. If the herald of the great King lived in our day, he would use the modern inventions of science and technology to radiate his message of "Peace and Good" in the name of and for the glory of Christ and of Mary.

The Poverello, the enemy of idleness, would today have exhorted his sons, as he did in the middle ages, to carry on work more suited to the times, while observing the condition expressed in his Rule: "that the friars not extinguish the spirit of prayer, which must prevail over all temporal things."

Father Maximilian interpreted and practiced to the letter the commandment of the Seraphic Father.

Niepokalanow, "the city of the Immaculata" with its religious inhabitants, had in fact one law: the Rule of St. Francis. This was observed most faithfully. One would think that in the midst of such feverish activity the religious spirit would languish. Instead, Niepokalanow was an oasis which offered the contrast between quiet and work, silence and the noise of machines. On the occasion of a visit, Father Provincial remarked that life at Niepokalanow was a little more rigorous than elsewhere. Father Maximilian replied:

"If Niepokalanow, instead of serving to radiate the glory of the Immaculata, gave in to laxity, or worse yet gave scandal, it would be better for God to immediately send fire from heaven to reduce everything to ashes."

The impression of the Provincial was shared by the Father General of the Order, who visited Niepokalanow in 1936:

"I was able to verify with my own eyes how true it was that from Niepokalanow shone forth the truly Franciscan spirit, a fervent devotion to the Immaculata, much zeal, the greatest poverty and the utmost simplicity. Among the Brothers there was an intense spirit of charity. Great harmony reigned, and on their faces one noticed a serene, Franciscan joy."

In Niepokalanow the visitor was habitually welcomed with the greeting: Mary!... In the name of Mary one prayed, worked, rested. Silence was kept in the religious house and in the working quarters as well.

Once, no one knows why, the machines stopped because of a power failure. Unsurprised, Father Maximilian said in all simplicity: "The devil has put his tail into it." A fervent prayer to the Virgin sufficed to put all the machines back in motion.

# The Ideal of Niepokalanow

As has been indicated, the very name Niepokalanow stated the foundation's purpose and, with greater precision, its ideal. It must be noted that Father Maximilian was an enemy of "programs." One time when a brother collaborator asked him for a program, that is to say, a rule of action, the good Father answered:

"It is impossible to determine programs, because we are totally consecrated to the Immaculata. Therefore we cannot hold to a program which would limit our activity. We must do more than we can for the Immaculata."

Niepokalanow, begun without a determined program, would have to remain this way. Better results thus ensued, and it was ruled by the Immaculata.

Father Kolbe wrote thus:

"In Niepokalanow we live by a voluntary, beloved and fixed goal which we call the Immaculata! For her we live, work and suffer, and for her we want to die. We desire with all our soul that through all means and inventions this fixed goal may be welcomed by all hearts."

And nothing more!...

"The ideal of Niepokalanow is unconditional consecration to the Immaculata according to the *Bylaws* and *Act of Consecration* of the *Militia Immaculatae:* thereby conformity to the will of the Immaculata in everything. Do the will of the Immaculata. Be perfect instruments in her hands. Let us allow ourselves to be totally guided by her—have, that is, *perfect obedience,* through which she reveals her will and disposes of us as her instruments.

"I repeat: the will of the Immaculata, because we have consecrated ourselves to her unconditionally and therefore it is she who must lead us.

"If it is licit to express ourselves in this way—since the universal will of God is not the same as that of the Immaculata, insofar as the divine will is also of justice while that of the Immaculata is of mercy alone, of which she is the personification—we as her instruments do not serve to punish according to justice but to convert and sanctify.

"Therefore, as she is the perfect instrument in the hands of the divine mercy of the most Sacred Heart of Jesus, thus must we be instruments in her hands and through her we become instruments of the most Sacred Heart of Jesus, that is of the divine mercy.

*"Through the Immaculata to the Heart of Jesus,* behold our motto.

"As a consequence, the spirit of each member of Niepokalanow must be *perfect and supernatural obedience* to the Immaculata, as expressed by the superiors.

"One who does not have this spirit is not made for Niepokalanow; and because the consecration of Niepokalanow is unconditional, Niepokalanow does not exclude the *missionary ideal,* although in this the Rule leaves us liberty.

"We therefore do not desire to consecrate only ourselves to the Immaculata, but we also want all the present and future souls in the world to consecrate themselves to her.

"Our mission is to convert and sanctify all souls through Mary.

"One who is totally consecrated to the Immaculata has already reached sanctity, and one who more perfectly lets himself be led by her in his interior and exterior life has a greater share in her spirit.

"For this reason, every member of Niepokalanow—to imitate the Immaculata, imitator of Jesus; to imitate St. Francis, imitator of Jesus—must limit personal needs to the bare necessities, seeking no comforts and pleasures; he must be satisfied with only what is necessary for extending more quickly the *Reign of the Immaculata.*

"This renunciation and spirit of sacrifice in poverty renders it possible to multiply the printing of *The Knight* which must be diffused throughout the whole world: poverty in customs, in dress, in food—that is, *Franciscan poverty in the light of the Immaculata.*

"One who does not love the Immaculata in this way so as to sacrifice everything for her (poverty), sacrifice himself totally (obedience), that is, who does not intend to consecrate himself unconditionally to the Immaculata to be her instrument—let him leave Niepokalanow.

"Therefore: supernatural obedience, so that in all things our will may be the will of the Immaculata; the most rigorous poverty, so that the reign of the Immaculata may be spread all the sooner; conformity to the Immaculata—behold the characteristic of Niepokalanow."

# Niepokalanow, the "Greenhouse" of Missionaries

Speaking of the Catholic renewal of his nation, the Polish author Majdanski, in his book *Giants,* points to Niepokalanow as an example of a new direction and of a new religious-social action bearing the stamp of heroism. He concludes:

"From Niepokalanow, where every commodity is sacrificed, will come the spiritual reform of seminaries, from which will be sent away all those who do not have true paternal sentiments toward souls. The development and work of Niepokalanow, founded not on human calculations but upon faith in Providence, shows what heights priestly heroism can reach."

During Father Kolbe's beatification process, a member of the Polish Parliament pointed out the beneficial social influence derived from Niepokalanow and expressed his wishes for its extension, declaring:

"The spirit that reigns at Niepokalanow should be in everyone; the spirit that makes one sleep on a bare board and eat bran."

When Father Maximilian had returned to Poland as a newly-ordained priest, the Franciscan Province in that nation consisted of a little more than one hundred priests and brothers.

Within the span of a few years, Niepokalanow became the largest Franciscan friary in the world: "In 1939 it consisted of 13 priests, 18 professed seminarians, 527 religious Brothers, 122 aspirants to the priestly state, 82 candidates to the Brotherhood—in all, 762 Franciscans."

Confronted with these amazing figures, one may be tempted to think that in order to succeed in his aim of establishing a "media city" in keeping with the purpose of the M.I., Father Maximilian may have been indulgent and lenient in the acceptance of young vocations. This was the fear of the ecclesiastical superiors.

But the humble Franciscan did not gather around himself only young workers or poor illiterates. He attracted religious vocations by the hundreds, recruiting them even from the higher classes.

At Niepokalanow it is not difficult to meet journalists, public relations men, engineers, and technicians of every kind. Attracted by the smile of the Immaculata, some had renounced with Franciscan humility not only brilliant careers, but also the possibility of becoming priests, preferring to serve the Lord by living as simple religious Brothers and cooperating intellectually and materially with the publication of *The Knight.*

These Brothers were and are the pillars of Niepokalanow, "the media city." In its subsequent development,
the remarkable city housed a seminary or college for
the priestly formation of future missionaries for Poland
and other countries.

Enthused by the rapid multiplication of buildings
and establishments, Father Maximilian did not for an
instant cease thanking the Immaculata with his heart
and with his lips. He had an equally lively and constant
care that Niepokalanow flee from notoriety.

Today the fortunate inhabitants of the "Marian
City" still recall these exhortations of their good Father:

"It is necessary that the spirit which reigns in Niepokalanow be in everything, present in the bare table and
in the bran we eat.

"We must say that our work is beautiful and important: but this is external. Before all else we must take
care of our interior life, the life of grace from which
every external activity must proceed.

"Does the development of Niepokalanow consist in
expanding and in enlarging its walls?

"No!

"Not even new houses are an index of progress.

"Even when in the future there will be the latest and
more perfect machines, not even that will be progress in
the strict sense.

"Even if *The Knight* were to multiply twofold or
threefold the number of copies printed, not even in
that would the development of Niepokalanow consist,
because often all exterior things fail.

"In what then, does the development of Niepokalanow consist? Upon what does it depend?

"Niepokalanow is not only external work, inside or
outside the cloister; first of all it is work in our souls.

"Everything else, even science, is exteriority.

"The true progress of Niepokalanow lies in the sanctification of our souls. Every time our souls register a greater conformity to the will of the Immaculata, we will be making a step ahead in the development of Niepokalanow. Therefore, even if it should happen that every activity should cease, if all the members of the M.I. were to disappear, if we at Niepokalanow were dispersed like leaves in autumn, and yet the ideal of the M.I. remained more deeply rooted in our souls, we could then say boldly that this would be the moment of the greatest development of Niepokalanow."

In the mind of Father Maximilian, Niepokalanow was and will always be "a heavenly oasis on earth" where the Brothers, imbued by ideals of sanctity and apostolate, are educated and inspired with fervor and where they prepare themselves to conquer the world. This thought is expressed in a letter he wrote from Nagasaki to Father Florian Koziura:

"The printed word, the word transmitted through the radio, through still projections, through television, the film and other means, is already much, but it is not everything.

"In order to make the Immaculata known to souls and to make her loved, by arousing in them that love which is true, not sentimental, and which proceeds from the will, united in perfect conformity to her will, it is necessary that the worker 'Knights'—writers, announcers, directors and others—leave Niepokalanow, that they travel, approach souls personally in courses of spiritual exercises, in missions, in conversations, in confession, and in visits to the offices of the M.I., so that when returning, they may better know how much and what must be written for this or for that nation.

"But one who wishes to convert others to the cause of the Immaculata must have his own will united to that of the Immaculata, that is, united to the will of the Divine Mercy, conformed that is, to the desires of the most Sacred Heart of Jesus.

"After these travels outside the sacred walls of Niepokalanow, they will want to return to it, as iron is attracted by a magnet, to hide themselves there for the purpose of purifying themselves from the stains of the world, to heal the wounds received among the thorns of the world and—renewed in spirit—to assimilate new energies for other trips.

"Even the Brothers, with the press and the medal, according to the needs of different countries, will penetrate everywhere, but always with their thoughts at Niepokalanow, where, in humble obedience and with joy, they too will purify themselves from the little stains contracted in their travels.

"In this way, the Immaculata will dominate as Lady in every soul consecrated to her in Niepokalanow and through that soul she will penetrate others to purify them, render them more beautiful, and lead them to Jesus.

"Through the Immaculata to the Most Sacred Heart of Jesus."

In Father Maximilian's vision Niepokalanow was to be a heavenly oasis of spiritual strengthening for the missionaries of Mary and at the same time a magnet for heavenly blessings. His desire to institute perpetual adoration of the Blessed Sacrament was aimed at achieving this objective. (He was unable to achieve this latter ideal until after the outbreak of the war—and then only for the daytime hours, and without exposition of the Blessed Sacrament.)

One who visits Niepokalanow is greeted at the entrance by a statue of the Immaculata, the Lady of the City. Continuing on, the visitor finds feverish activity, interspersed with invocations, ejaculations and aspirations to the Queen and inspiration of all. However, the heart of the City is the throne where Jesus, present in the Blessed Sacrament, is reverently and perennially adored. Everything is centered and sanctified in Him through Mary, as is expressed in Niepokalanow's motto:

"Through the Immaculata to the most Sacred Heart of Jesus."

# In the Cemetery of Niepokalanow

Asked about the space needed for the cemetery of Niepokalanow, Father Maximilian replied, "It should not be too big because I foresee that the bones of our friars will be dispersed throughout the world."

Niepokalanow, however, could not do without a small cemetery. Already a grove of trees jealously guarded the tomb of a great "Knight" who had died prematurely: Father Alphonse M. Kolbe.

We have referred to Father Alphonse many times. However, it will not be inappropriate to dwell for a moment on some aspects of his life before we leave Niepokalanow.

After the founder, Father Alphonse was the first superior and father of the City of Mary. He was given that office when in 1930 Father Maximilian left Niepokalanow for the Far East. Unfortunately, his term as superior did not last long. Less than a year later, struck by bronchial pneumonia, he peacefully passed from the earthly Niepokalanow to the heavenly city of Mary. This passage took place on December 3, 1930, during the novena in preparation for the feast of the Immaculata!

It is said that as Father Maximilian left, he had a presentiment about his brother's death. When he entered Father Alphonse's cell to say goodbye, he found him resting. Not wanting to disturb him, Father Maximilian kissed him lightly on the brow. As he left, he exclaimed with emotion: "Sleep, my brother. There was never a more merited rest in the service of the Immaculata! Farewell...who knows if we will see each other on earth again!"

A eulogy delivered extemporaneously at Father Alphonse's funeral by a journalist who represented the Polish press beautifully portrayed Father Alphonse thus:

"Reverend Father Editor, you live no more! You sleep in eternal rest; your body sleeps but your spirit lives and is among us.

"Why have thousands of persons come together here to gather around the mortal remains of this friar? Certainly something mysterious, something incomprehensible, is hidden here and elevated above this coffin.

"Do you dislike this sobbing, these laments, this weeping? Reverend Father Editor! These are tears of sorrow but also tears of gratitude!

"Here is the poor friar, Rev. Father Alphonse, who with the help of his confreres, and almost without material means, began a burdensome and very difficult work, printing *The Knight of the Immaculata*. Painful and sorrowful was the initial stage of the printing and editing, when it was necessary to beg for even a penny for the print shop.

"But now you can rest, because your strong faith in the help of the Queen of heaven has abundantly taken care of the finances of *The Knight*. The circulation of the magazine has grown always more, increased always more, consolidated itself always more. This is the miracle: an event unheard of in the history of journalism in our nation. The circulation of *The Knight* is 350,000 copies (December, 1930). This is the greatest of the magazines among us, in which no other publishing house can glory. What is it? *The Knight of the Immaculata*? Yes, it is! This little magazine with a blue cover marches in the front lines of our nation's press. And who was its leader?

"Here he is. A poor friar whose editing office was a poor and simple cell. Clothed in a Franciscan habit, faded and patched, he persevered in work and prayer directed to the great Mother of God.... He taught crowds of young people about God.

"The Immaculata accomplished this miracle with the strength and power of her grace, diffusing hundreds of thousands of magazines throughout the world....

"You are the one, Reverend Editor, who, forgetful of yourself and confident only in the help of the Immaculata, accomplished this work. I salute you as a legionary, and as an editor. I salute you, O Knight of Mary, I salute you for the work begun by you. I salute you, O Knight of the Immaculata!"

The death of Father Alphonse left an immeasurable void at Niepokalanow.

One could really call him the father of the mystical City. It was he, the faithful interpreter and executor of the will of the founder, his brother, who maintained in the Franciscan "City" that austerity of life which was its most luminous and edifying mark.

His spiritual testament reflects this diligent care for exact religious observance in the "City" of Mary:

"Always conserve the Franciscan spirit of poverty at Niepokalanow."

The sorrowful event of Father Alphonse's death serves to better highlight the faith of Father Maximilian, a faith shown in the letters he wrote to his mother after the news of his brother's death. The following was written from Japan where he was given the news on December 7, the vigil of the feast of the Immaculate Conception:

"I used white vestments in celebrating Mass in suffrage for Father Alphonse, because it was the feast of the Immaculate Conception. Certainly he was already in heaven. The Immaculata took him to herself during her novena. One can only envy him. For the Immaculata he lived, suffered, worked and immolated himself. She called him to herself during her novena. We, too, will follow him, because we live only in order to go to heaven.

"Now Father Alphonse will not be inactive: he will work even more and even better, so that he can do more. He will have more solicitude to spread the glory of the Immaculata than he had on earth. He will also be able to help Francis* more effectively."

---

*Francis Kolbe, the oldest of the three brothers, had been a Franciscan but had later left the Order to join the Polish army.

# Mugenzai No Sono

It is related that one day Father Maximilian was seen attentively studying a map of the world, calculating the distances from place to place. Then after voicing a few reflections on the customs and religions of those who populated the various continents, in an inspired manner he exclaimed: "The Knights of the Immaculata must have missions! In spite of all the difficulties, we must have faith in the Immaculata. For this purpose, she will send us many vocations."

Father Kolbe's missionary efforts, which had as their objective the entire world, were first to be directed toward the Far East where there would rise the second "City of the Immaculata." This ideal of an apostolate among the infidels had roused his enthusiasm from the time of his Roman residence at the Seraphic College on Via San Teodoro. In his burning desire for the spiritual conquest of the Far East, he had often made the missionary Institutes of Rome the goals of his walks to obtain from the seminarians there information about the customs, religion and civilization of those populations.

In the years 1924-1930, under the Pontificate of Pius XI, called the "Pope of the Missions," the Friars Minor Conventual gave new impulse to their missionary apostolate. The Minister General appealed with vigor, especially to the young priests, inviting them to voluntarily set out on missions according to the spirit of the Franciscan Rule.

Father Maximilian responded with the enthusiasm of a newly-ordained priest. He promptly put himself at the disposal of the superiors, ready to go wherever they would send him. It is moving to read in this regard the testimony of the Minister General of that time, Father Alphonse Orlini: "He accepted the mission program of the Order, engrafting into it his Marian ideals."

Although the towering project of Niepokalanow was still in the phase of development and claimed his full attention and effort, Father Maximilian was one of the first to answer the appeal for the missions. In so doing, he gave a rare example of detachment from an enterprise which had cost him untold sacrifice and humiliations. In his poor esteem of self, he did not deem himself necessary for the fulfillment of the work he had begun. On the contrary, happy that others could gather the fruits of his labors, he asked his Superior General permission to come to Rome in order to submit the project of a new Niepokalanow among the nonbelievers.

The request was welcomed by the same Father General who, in 1927, had recommended the foundation of the "City of the Immaculata" in Poland, and the permission was easily granted.

On January 17, 1930, after the eventual juridical status of the new foundation was agreed upon by the Minister Provincial, Father Maximilian went to Rome. On January 18, he was in Orvieto, and he celebrated Mass in the monastery of St. Bernardine of the Poor Clares, to whose prayers he most probably must have entrusted the new foundation. In the evening of the same day, he was already in Rome, where he would remain for four days—days which proved not to be useless.

First of all, just as the foundation of the M.I. and Father Maximilian's very priesthood had begun at the altar of the miracle in the Basilica of S. Andrea delle Fratte, so did the new apostolate begin there. According to sources, on January 20, anniversary of the miracle and of the conversion of Ratisbonne, Father Maximilian offered Mass at the same altar at which he had celebrated his first Mass. He was also able to make several contacts, for example, with the Vicar of his Order, who at that time was Father Francis D'Ambrosio; with some seminarians of *De Propaganda Fide College;* with the Secretariat of the Missions, near the generalate of the Jesuit Fathers, and, finally, with the Sacred Congregation for the Propagation of the Faith. His program of Marian apostolate among the nonbelievers was not only approved by the Vicar of the Order but was approved by the leaders of the Congregation for the Propagation of the Faith.

Because of the social character of the apostolate of the press, Father Maximilian's foundation was not to be established in an out-of-reach pagan region. Only a center of communication with a good percentage of Catholics and subject to the jurisdiction of a local bishop could be ground favorable for its realization. As a consequence, Father Maximilian set out on his missions without the apostolic credentials usually granted to the other new missionaries. The Roman superiors of the Order, in agreement with the Congregation for the Propagation of the Faith, had approved a plan according to which Father Maximilian would first go in search of a place favorable to his project. Once he had been authorized by the local bishop, he would be granted the ecclesiastical documents necessary for the new foundation.

On January 23, Father Maximilian set out for Padua to meet with the Minister General. He arrived there only to learn that the latter had just left for Rome. After a stopover of two days, on January 25, he took the train for Rome and met with the Minister General who, while being pleased with his programs, nevertheless postponed a decision, following a more careful deliberation. Their next meeting focused on the financial aspect of the work, and the Minister General candidly confessed that he could not give Father Kolbe any money. The opening of a new mission in Africa and other expenses of the Order would not allow this new initiative of Father Kolbe's to be backed up financially.

But Father Maximilian had not come to Rome to look for money. All that he asked of his Minister General, successor of St. Francis, was the command to leave for the missions "in virtue of holy obedience." Everything else had been thought of and provided for in true Franciscan style.

What had been "provided for" was very little, materially speaking: a ticket for the trip and a suitcase with a few personal articles. Spiritually, instead, Father Maximilian and his companions were clothed with a vivid spirit of faith and an unfailing trust in the assistance of the Immaculata.

"The Immaculata will provide!" This exclamation was already familiar to Father General: it had been on the lips of Father Kolbe during the Provincial Chapter of 1927, when the expenses of the construction of the first "City of the Immaculata" were dealt with. After three years, he had personally experienced the impact of that expression. With tears in his eyes, the Father General repeated: "The Immaculata will provide!"

"Well," he continued, "come back in a few more days and you will be given the *obedience* with a letter or recommendation for the bishop who will be willing to have the new Niepokalanow built in his territory."

# Two Pilgrimages

We ought not to picture Father Maximilian merely as a man of action, ready to sacrifice everything to activity. Had he been such a person, he would have been just one among the thousands of men who are hardworking but lacking in supernatural outlook and sanctity. In him, action was an overflow of his Marian love and piety. All his initiatives were born from the Immaculata. His exquisite sensitiveness for any bond of solidarity and fraternal love was inspired by supernatural principles. Having deep faith in the "communion of saints," he put unlimited trust in the cooperation and solidarity of his living Brother "Knights," but especially the deceased Knights. The following episode highlights this:

At Camposanpietro, near Padua, was the grave of Father Jerome Biasi, one of the first seven; in Rome, in the cemetery of Verano, the grave of Father Anthony Mansi, and, in Assisi, the grave of Father Anthony Glowinski. Before leaving for distant lands, Father Maximilian went to take leave of these Brother "Knights" already in the heavenly "Niepokalanow." Praying at their tombs, it seemed as if he wished to entrust his future work to their intercession near the throne of the "Heavenly Lady." This is the reason why, on his forthcoming departure for the Far East, he went on a pilgrimage to the cemeteries of Verano, Camposanpietro and Assisi. A meager note in his diary confirms it: "Camposanpietro—by the tomb—I await an answer." Which answer? Undoubtedly, through the intercession of his deceased confrere, a particular blessing of the Immaculata on the new foundation. Spiritually united to them, he directed his pilgrimage to the Marian sanctuaries which inspired the activity of the M.I.: Lourdes, famous for the apparitions of the Immaculata to Bernadette, and Paris, in rue du Bac, where St. Catherine Labouré received the Miraculous Medal from the hands of the Immaculata. From there he visited the shrine and convent of the Little Flower at Lisieux, and then made his way to Turin to the shrines of St. Joseph Cottolengo and St. John Bosco.

The trip was most uncomfortable, undertaken in six days, traveling at night to arrive at the individual sanctuaries in time for the celebration of morning Mass. His longer stops in Lourdes and Lisieux were referred to in his diary with much detail and vividness of description. Especially significant—although written in fragments—is the page regarding Lourdes. It portrays the whole spirituality of Father Maximilian: devout and tender, yet strong and prudent, even more so in this period when his soul was experiencing aridity and coldness. It seemed as if the Madonna wanted to test his fidelity and zeal on the eve of his departure for the missions as a foretaste—as he confesses—of the hardships that would await him abroad. Here is his account:

"Lourdes. To the grotto with tram number thirteen. Holy Mass at a side altar of the crypt. Signature in the registers, then to the grotto, where a gentle rain falls steadily.... Crutches bear witness to the graces received; candles signify prayers; part of the rosary. Afterwards *sadness*. Again under the rain. There is no place to rest for a moment. I go by tram to the station to ask information about the "rapid" [an express train] for Paris. I go back to bid farewell to the Virgin. Even in this mission what nostalgia! It is necessary however. Why am I looking for happiness? Father Jerome [Biasi] was also sad when he left Lourdes. To return instead was consoling: I drank the miraculous water; I dipped my finger into the water; I said goodbye to the Immaculata.... I remembered everybody and everything to her! I kissed the sacred rock. Goodbye, Madonna!

"As soon as the train moves, I start to write, and the train brings me back to the grotto on the other side of the Gave for the whole length of the grotto and the basilica. I speak with my heavenly Mother. I tell her that I am all hers in body and soul. How thoughtful is the Immaculata! Had I not taken the train for Bordeaux, I would not have these consolations! I start to write again.... The mountains which seem to be holding in their lap these blessed places bid me their last farewell! One more time...the Gave runs along the train tracks to disappear little by little. In the meantime, the sun shines, spreading its sweet warmth. Glory to the Immaculata! When I left the grotto, wet and worn out by fatigue, I did not expect such a farewell. Everything always as it is pleasing to the Immaculata. On the way to the station, I reflected on my sadness: what are you looking for? Although so cold in soul, you celebrated holy Mass in the basilica, went to the grotto and now to

Bordeaux, and on to Paris in rue du Bac where the Immaculata showed the Miraculous Medal!"

Father Maximilian's pilgrimage to the sanctuaries of the Miraculous Medal is briefly and hurriedly described in his *Notes.* A more detailed account is found in the testimony of Father Ferdinand Machay, a priest from Krakow who was studying in Paris at that time. He was also chaplain at St. Casimir Hospice.

Upon his arrival in Paris, Father Maximilian had gone by taxi to rue du Bac. While paying the taxi driver, he had been saddened by a painful incident. Unaware of French customs, he had failed to add a tip to the amount determined by the taximeter. Instead, he had handed the driver a Miraculous Medal. Moved by anger, the driver had thrown it on the ground and had stepped on it.

Father Kolbe had not understood the reason for this and had attributed it to an anti-clerical spirit. After the celebration of Mass at the altar of the Miraculous Medal—only God knows with what spirit of reparation—he met Father Machay, and together they went by taxi to St. Casimir.

At the convent of the Sisters of Charity Father Machay gave the driver some extra marks besides the due amount. Noticing this, Father Maximilian asked whether it was customary to give a tip to the taxi driver. At the answer that it was his main source of profit and customary indeed, Father Kolbe was deeply sorry and tears slid down his cheeks. "I did wrong to the taxi driver," he exclaimed, "when I refused him a tip. I thought that he was expecting more of me as a foreigner."

His grief made a great impression on Father Machay who from that moment held him in high esteem.

A description of the pilgrimage to Lisieux, given by Father Severin Dagis, betrayed Father Kolbe's attraction to the Saint who had promised to spend her heaven doing good on earth:

"At Lisieux, he was delighted by everything related to the life of St. Therese of the Child Jesus: the cottage at

Buissonets still reechoing the years of her childhood, the many toys, and even the chess game. He reflected: 'As it is peculiar to her sanctity, there is nothing miraculous in her life; only the routine of everyday existence elevated by pure intention to a supernatural degree.' It seemed as if our missionary could not leave that place without regret. He asked to speak also with St. Therese's sister, to assure to his missionary labors the protection of the Saint through the prayers of her sister. After all, Saint Therese is the patroness of all the missions.''

We possess the following few details from Father Maximilian himself:

"After the conversation with her sister, a further visit to the tomb of the Saint and then on with the journey. Gentle rain as on the arrival at the station and again sunshine as at Lourdes. It is a sign that we will have many difficulties but then a clear sky."

Father Maximilian went back from Lisieux to Niepokalanow on February 6, via Paris, Strasbourg, Nuremberg and Berlin.

# From Niepokalanow to Shanghai

On February 26, 1930, Father Maximilian Kolbe, together with four brothers chosen for the foundation of the new "City of the Immaculata" among nonbelievers, set out for the Far East. They embarked at Marseilles, France, on board the liner Angers, on the evening of March 7. The cabin assigned to them was immediately named the Niepokalanow of the ship. A little statue of the Immaculata, placed on a portable altar, created an atmosphere of trust in the good outcome of the voyage and nourished their hopes in the success of their apostolic endeavors on behalf of immense Asia. Then life on board began its regular daily course as if they were in community. Their daily schedule included the study of foreign languages, conversations of an apologetic character, and the programming of their future missionary work. It goes without saying that everything was preceded by the Holy Sacrifice of the Mass and alternated with the recitation of the prescribed prayers.

In his spare time, Father Maximilian liked to walk on deck, always with a view to reaching souls. He mingled with people from all classes of society and walks of life, and with his rich and warm personality won many friends. One day he carried on an animated discussion with a Russian who defended Darwin's theory. Another time he spoke with a Syrian about the religious practices of his country. Still another time he spoke with an Abyssinian, set in his ways, with whom Father Kolbe endeavored to come to an understanding.

Having received full authorization to found a mission in China and Japan, Father Maximilian did not forget the rest of the world. At every port where the ship docked, through his contact with the hierarchy or local missionaries, he scrutinized the "pros" and "cons" concerning an eventual insertion of his apostolate among those people.

A stop of a few hours at Port Said strengthened him in his project to win to the Immaculata the nations on the Eastern side of the Mediterranean Sea. He had noticed that a publication which had begun in Egypt had gradually extended its plan of action to embrace Arabia, Palestine, Syria, Iraq and Iran. A Syrian businessman, who discussed with him the living conditions of the Near East, was impressed by Father Kolbe's plans, and invited him to his house in Syria.

The hardships of this voyage were extensive; often the friars were tossed and tormented. Along the coast of the Arabian desert, the ride was particularly difficult. During that time, the missionaries suffered terribly from the heat and the desert's sand. The thin dust from the desert, rising over the surface of the Red Sea, rested on the decks and penetrated the cabins. It was hard to remain inside; but on the deck, one's nose, ears, lips and eyes were covered with it. For Father Maximilian, with poor lungs, this excruciating torment caused him to cough terribly. At times his whole body twisted with pain. But never the slightest lament was heard from his lips. When his sufferings, as one could suppose, had reached the highest degree, it was then that he asked his Brothers how they felt. Unable to move from his location, still he took an interest in the others' pains, and apologized for having caused them any inconvenience.

After landing at Diibouti on the boundaries of the French Somali, Father Maximilian began to channel his thoughts toward India, since Ceylon was the next stop. He spent his time on deck with his confreres or in having discussions with some of the passengers, especially a young Chinese architect who had recently graduated in France. Father tried to "win him over" with a view to having him translate an introductory article for the first Chinese issue of *The Knight.* He partly succeeded in his intent.

At Colombo, they received a heartfelt welcome from the Archbishop, a Frenchman of the Congregation of the Oblates of Mary, who explained to them the administrative division of his diocese, its boundaries and the many languages of the population of Ceylon. Here, for the first time, Father Maximilian became acquainted, first hand, with the power of the press in mission lands. He witnessed the capacity of the press to reach those who could not otherwise be reached. He took great interest in the varied aspects of the daily life of the Hindu and looked with nostalgia at the distant coast of Malabar, which little by little was manifesting itself through the ocean's haze. How willing he was to do something for those 350 million people! But the time was not yet ripe.

On voyage from Colombo to Singapore, India was the theme of Father Maximilian's thoughts. When Ceylon finally disappeared from the horizon, Father Maximilian called his confreres into his cabin and all together they prayed for the conversion of India.

After another few days of journey, there appeared the coasts of the peninsula of Malacca, and not too far distant, covered with fog, was Sumatra. This was the same course that centuries before had been taken by

St. Francis Xavier. The four missionaries dwelt on the
spirit which had animated the great apostle of India and
Japan. In spite of the perils and hardships of a sixteenth-
century voyage by sea, Francis Xavier had not hesitated
to cover immense distances to the last limits of human
endurance, spending himself mercilessly in order to root
the Faith in those people, so that it would never
diminish. Father Maximilian sang the praises of the
great apostle of India, as if he never would be able to
compete with him in heroism. But was not more heroism
demanded of him who covered the same immense distances and was so ill that he had to lean on a stick or
the arms of his confreres?

At Saigon, Father Maximilian was wholeheartedly
welcomed by the clergy of the Annamite rite who showed
themselves most favorable to his missionary project. He
saw, however, in the opposition of the local bishop, the
sign that the Immaculata did not want him there.

Hong Kong, the gateway to China, offered him clues
for his eventual work among the Chinese people. He
met missionaries with many years of experience. As in
Colombo, here too he visited those who could be of some
service in his missionary work.

On April 4, against the backdrop of a rainy morning,
there appeared the golden waters of Yangtze Kiang. It
was necessary to sail for a stretch of a few more miles on
the Hwang Pu River to arrive at Shanghai. The fourth
largest city in the world, Shanghai held many surprises
for him—some pleasant and some unpleasant. On their
arrival the friars went to the mission office there and
were informed that other missionaries had tried to
begin the publication of a magazine but without positive
results. While they were considering what to do and
where to begin, a car stopped in front of the building.
A tall, distinguished Chinese gentleman emerged, who
addressed a witty greeting to the superior of the Institute. Immediately after, he was introduced to Father
Maximilian. He was the well-known, well-deserving
Chinese gentleman named Joseph Lo-Pa-Hong, whose

ancestors three hundred years before had received Baptism from the Franciscan missionaries. From that time on, his family had been the pride of the Catholic Church in China. Lo-Pa-Hong, one of the richest men in China, immediately recognized the kind of man Father Kolbe was and invited him to his house to discuss together the kind of help he could give him.

With his large fortune, Lo-Pa-Hong had built hospitals in Nanking, Peking and Shanghai. He had founded schools and trade schools for neglected youth. One of these, recently erected and magnificently equipped, still had its doors closed because Lo-Pa-Hong wanted Catholic missionaries to conduct it as a guarantee that a Catholic education would be imparted to Chinese youth. If Father Maximilian would accept Hong's proposal, Hong would put himself at Kolbe's service, offering him the money to begin the Chinese publication of *The Knight*.

On the following day, Father Maximilian had a private audience with the Bishop of Shanghai, during which he was informed that he could act only in the Franciscan zone, a proposal which Father Maximilian could not accept. In another meeting, the bishop, attracted by the simplicity and sincerity of Father Maximilian, gave him full authorization to found the apostolate of the press and to diffuse his magazine in Shanghai, but advised him that, to avoid serious problems, he should refuse the direction of the school of Lo-Pa-Hong. Moreover, attached to his permission was the condition that at the beginning of the new foundation, there would be at least two priests and two Brothers.

In a letter to the Provincial in Poland, Father Maximilian informed him of his difficulties and hopes about a Chinese publication of *The Knight*. None would read it without feeling his heart filled with deep emotion:

"Most Reverend Father Provincial,

"Concerning the mission of Shanghai, the Apostolic Vicar placed the condition that only one priest could remain in Shanghai.... It is a pity to abandon Shanghai because it is such a central location. The Bishop has given permission for an administrative office for *The Knight,* but he did not give permission to set up a typography because all of China has a distinct division for the places of the different orders and congregations, and each one must work exclusively in its own territory. To us would remain only Shensi, but it is impossible to work there because it is an inaccessible mission, without rail and water transportation.

"We have many difficulties, not on the part of the citizens, but from the European missionaries. Yet, also in this, there is the will of the Immaculata. There are some of the Chinese ready to translate into the Chinese language and to maintain expenses. Mr. Lo-Pa-Hong has put at our disposition his whole house, but the difficulties mentioned persist for *The Knight.*

"Today I leave for Japan and I hope to be able to do something there even in the Chinese language. Blessings.                                    *Father Maximilian*

"P.S. At Shanghai we were given hospitality by the Friars Minor Observant, who welcomed us very fraternally, cordially and gratuitously."

In the meantime, he left two of the Brothers at Shanghai with the hope of starting the M.I. there and proceeded with the other two to the last of his possible goals, to Japan. This was the place where the Immaculata wanted him; here the Immaculata awaited him.

# Nagasaki

The three weary missionaries landed at Nagasaki on April 24. As they arrived at the cathedral, to their surprise and delight, as a sign to them of successful apostolic labors in the land of the blossoming cherry trees, they found the statue of the Immaculata surrounded by beautiful exotic flowers, enthroned in the cathedral's square. With outstretched arms and a smile, the statue seemed to welcome them. Deeply moved by this unexpected sight, Father Maximilian uttered the prophetic words: "If we have found her, it is a sign that all will go well."

The missionaries were cordially received by His Excellency, Bishop Hayasaka of Nagasaki, one of the first native bishops to be ordained by Pope Pius XI. Bishop Hayasaka needed a professor of philosophy in his diocesan seminary, and learning that Father Maximilian was a doctor of philosophy, asked him to give lectures. Father Maximilian gladly accepted but on condition that he could have permission to publish his magazine.

Soon enough, Father Maximilian found near the Cathedral of Nagasaki a dilapidated wooden house which he rented for nine months for 405 yen, and in which the religious arranged their few belongings, happy at least to have a roof over their heads. Their life on Japanese soil began its new course characterized by an extreme and perfect, yet joyfully Franciscan, poverty.

Father Maximilian's teaching duties did not "estrange" him from the work he had so much at heart. Rather, he was more active than ever in the attempt to put immediately into execution his program of publishing the first issue of *The Knight* in Japanese before the month of May, Mary's month, had gone by.

By earthly standards, it would have seemed ridiculous to think of beginning a publication in Japanese only a few days after their arrival. The friars were ignorant of the language, lacking any means, and completely unknowledgeable about composition in Japanese signs. Father Maximilian, however, did not reason in terms of imperfect human logic. Leaving nothing untried on his part, he put an ever greater trust in the Immaculata. The extraordinary way in which he spoke of Mary made a great impression on his Japanese listeners.

The vexing problem of producing articles in Japanese was the first problem to be met. Father Maximilian solved it by writing the articles in Latin. These were then translated into good Japanese by his student colleagues at the seminary. Then he took them to a local printer and arranged to have his magazine printed. While this was going on, he went out and bought an old printing press and 145,000 characters of Japanese type for the future print shop.

Thus within four weeks of his arrival in Japan, sheet after sheet of *Seibo No Kishi,* the Japanese *Knight of the Immaculata,* was rolling off the press. On May 24, a telegram was sent to Niepokalanow with the message: "Today we are mailing out *The Knight* in Japanese. We have a printing shop. Praise be to the Immaculata! Maximilian."

His own print shop was not yet set up and operating, but he had the equipment, and the Japanese mission was definitely on its way!

On June 12, 1930, Father Maximilian left Nagasaki to go back to Poland by way of Siberia to attend the Provincial Chapter. This he had agreed to do before leaving Europe. Vital issues were at stake in this Chapter. He would have to speak on behalf of his dear Japanese mission, and ask the Chapter to establish it as a Province-sponsored mission. Moreover, the first issue of *Seibo No Kishi,* was followed by a rather difficult situation which exacted much diplomacy on the part of Father Maximilian.

The authorization granted to Father Maximilian by the local bishop to found a mission in his diocese had two conditions attached: first, he must obtain the permission of the Holy See; secondly, he should exclude from his aims any form of direct apostolate reserved to the diocesan clergy, and limit himself to the apostolate of the press. By going back to Europe, Father Kolbe intended to inform his new Minister General of the work done and to be done in Japan, and to obtain from the Polish Franciscan Province financial aid and more religious.

The Immaculata this time obtained the favorable vote of a majority of the Chapter fathers so that the second "City of the Immaculata" did not encounter the obstacles of the first. The Father General, on his part, approved what had been unanimously established by the Provincial Chapter, that is: "The Polish Province seeks to build up a mission in Japan for the purpose of spreading devotion to the Immaculata, dependent upon the consent of the Holy See and the competent superiors."

A telegram announced this decision to Bishop Hayasaka, who was pleased to definitively receive Father Maximilian in his diocese. He immediately sent his consent to Rome, so that further steps could be taken.

On August 13, 1930, Father Maximilian was on his way back to Japan via Siberia. Contrary to his plans, he could not go to Krakow to see his mother. But from Nagasaki he wrote her a short letter to justify his conduct:

"I beg your pardon, mother, if before my trip I did not pay a visit to you; I could not delay departure, since the missions are of primary importance."

Alarming news from Nagasaki had prompted his immediate return. The mission was on the verge of going out of existence. For one month, the publication of *The Knight* had been suspended. Interpreting the sudden departure of Father Maximilian for Europe as a sign that he had given up, the Japanese priests who had offered their collaboration had now withdrawn.

The long and weary journey across the continent gave him the long-awaited opportunity of seeing other regions for which he had also conceived apostolic plans that merely awaited more favorable times for their implementation. Korea, especially, aroused his interest and inspired him with a vocational program which was put into effect shortly after with consoling results. In a few years time, the Japanese Franciscan seminary would have a good number of Korean aspirants, as he wrote in a letter to his brother:

"Dear Brother,

"I have hardly had time to look around a bit and to get things in order. Since this is Sunday, I take advantage of the opportunity to write you a few lines. I am bothered, however, by mosquitoes and I still feel in my left hand the pain of a mosquito bite. But even this for the Immaculata. At night, to avoid being bitten, we have to cover our faces, but in this condition it is impossible to sleep because of the heat and perspiration. Everything for the Immaculata and so that we can win to her heart the greatest number of souls.

"The Immaculate Madonna has happily brought us to Nagasaki. At 7:30 we left Warsaw, and precisely at the same hour, after a twelve-day journey, through Siberia, Manchuria and Korea, the train stopped. Then we traveled eight hours by ship from Pusan to Shimonoseki. We also made a short trip by ship to Moji, and finally, by train, to Nagasaki.

"Korea was for me a country completely unknown.... The journey through it was so stupendous that one could never tire of contemplating it. At Pusan, the last stop in Korea, we had a surprise. We wanted to take advantage of the four hours of free time between the train and the ship to celebrate Mass. But no one was able to tell us where there was a Catholic church. Only much later did we learn from a policeman that there were six Protestant churches in the city, and that in all of Korea there were scarcely three Catholic churches!

"When will the Immaculata establish in this very beautiful country the kingdom of her Son?..."

*Father Maximilian Kolbe*

Back in Nagasaki on August 25, 1930, Father Maximilian set himself to the task of re-establishing order and efficiency in his apostolate. Now the Franciscan community had two new members: the two clerics who had come with Father Maximilian from Poland to complete their priestly studies while learning Japanese. One of them mastered the language so well that he became the personal interpreter of Father Maximilian when more complex conversations demanded it.

The last months of 1930 were stormy, harassed by difficulties which weighed heavily on Father Kolbe. We are able to get some insights into the nature and extent of these troubles from some accounts which highlight them. A short account from the Provincial, Father Czupryk, explicitly states:

"Being unfamiliar with the language, he met many difficulties. He suffered from his confreres; he was forsaken by two of the four clerics [another two students had come later] who had come with him from Poland. He was suspected by the police of being a spy. In this state of affairs, he reached the point, as he wrote to me, of desiring the peace and tranquillity of one of our small friaries. He overcame the temptation, saying that life was short and he had given himself totally to the Immaculata."

More details are given by Brother Severin Dagis:

"The Japanese typesetters used all their cleverness to increase the technical difficulties for the missionaries. Day by day they became more exacting in their demands for pay until they completely stopped coming. Nagasaki was determined to boycott the new publication. As later evidence seemed to confirm, the Japanese typesetters as well as the bonzes had a preestablished end. Further attempts of the Brothers to come to an agreement with the workers were doomed to fail. There was no way out. Trusting in the Immaculata, the poor Brothers began setting up type for the articles of the magazine, but often were lost in the maze of the four thousand signs of the Japanese alphabet.... When finally the November issue came off the press, Father Maximilian displayed a childlike delight. It was the first composition in the typographical history of Japan completely done by representatives of the white race.

"Father Maximilian rejoiced in telling every guest how the Immaculata took care of everything even when the problem of the language seemed hopeless. Afterwards, measures were taken to bring the publication from sixteen to twenty-four pages. The most urgent need was to find a translator.

"One day, Father Maximilian was introduced to a Japanese high school teacher, a fiery Methodist who had heard much about Father Maximilian and wanted to discuss his religious doubts with him. This man was Mr. Tagita Koya, professor of Japanese literature and history. From the start, Mr. Tagita made it clear that he would never adopt the Catholic point of view. But Father Kolbe made such an impression on him that he brought some of his friends to see what a true imitator of Saint Francis looked like. One of them, Mr. Yamaka, high school teacher and minister of the Methodist Congregation of Urakami, had once translated into Japanese the *Little Flowers of St. Francis*. His first encounter with Father Maximilian was characterized by a certain skepticism. The missionary had, however, the gift of winning over even the persons most prejudiced against him. And so it happened that Mr. Yamaka was so impressed by that visit that he offered his contribution, entirely unsolicited, for the editing stage. Father Maximilian wrote the articles in Italian and Mr. Yamaka, who knew that language, translated them into Japanese.

"Even more, Mr. Yamaka was so captivated by this true follower of St. Francis that he became the most strenuous non-Catholic defender of Catholicism. This was particularly shown at a Methodist convention when, as a consequence of the unsympathetic attitude of some members toward Catholicism, Mr. Yamaka bitterly reproached them. Another time, at a meeting of Methodist professors, his outspokenness caused him to be threatened with transferral if he did not change his viewpoint. Mr. Yamaka replied that the Protestant view was completely wrong and that his opinion was unchangeable. He was transferred to Tokyo.

"Was he converted? It is difficult to know because after a year he stopped correspondence. Instead, Mr. Tagita, in the course of a few years, was baptized, together with all his family, and became a most zealous Catholic. Mr. Tagita, too, helped translate into Japanese the articles for *The Knight*."

Another cause of suffering for Father Kolbe was the change of attitude of Bishop Hayasaka toward the Polish missionaries. The delay of the official documents for the foundation of the new apostolate caused him to become more and more suspicious, until he finally withdrew from them the permission to celebrate Mass in the private chapel for the religious. When, in November, the documents arrived, the bishop became convinced of the right intention of the Polish priest and, from that time on, held him in the highest esteem.

There followed a period of relative calm and serenity. Everything seemed to turn out well, until the news of the death of Father Alphonse arrived from Niepokalanow. A thick cloud of uncertainty appeared again on the horizon. Being unable to find a capable substitute for the deceased priest, at first the Minister Provincial thought of calling Father Maximilian back and closing the Japanese mission. A sense of bewilderment shook all in Niepokalanow as well as in Nagasaki. Only Father Maximilian, totally conformed to the will of God, did not lose his calm, as is marvelously reflected in this letter to his confreres of Niepokalanow:

"I am resigned to the will of God which I intend to do especially in the most difficult and critical moments. The cross is the school of charity. Crosses purify the intentions because suffering permits us to work only out of love."

The unofficial news that Father Koziura would be appointed as successor of Father Alphonse brought him to write:

"Let us pray together that the Immaculata provide for the future of her Niepokalanow."

## Mugenzai No Sono

The small house, near the cathedral that first sheltered the Polish religious and their printing operations, was called by Father Maximilian "The Japanese Grodno." It was to have only a temporary function until the foundation of the Japanese "City of the Immaculata." In the meantime, Father Kolbe bought a piece of land in the suburb of Hongochi on the slope of the mount Hikosan. It was an enchanting place from which one could enjoy a gorgeous view of the whole city and toward the east the immense stretch of the ocean. In spite of many difficulties, the new house was soon completed on May 16, 1931. Only one year after the arrival of the missionaries at Nagasaki, it was inaugurated. *Mugenzai No Sono*—City of the Immaculata—gave concrete expression to the missionary dream of Father Kolbe. It would always be the "Benjamin" of his heart, and would enjoy his special protection from heaven. This became clear during the fateful explosion of the atomic bomb over the city. While the greater part of Nagasaki was destroyed, Mugenzai No Sono was totally spared, perhaps because it was protected by the mount, but more certainly because of a special assistance from heaven.

The Mugenzai No Sono marked the beginning of a new missionary era for Japan. Its apostolate was greatly beneficial to the entire missionary action, since the spreading influence of the Marian press removed many of the obstacles which were placed in the way, undermining the efforts of Christ's heralds in that land.

In 1933, only three years after the apostolate of the M.I. was begun, the *Seibo No Kishi,* that is, *The Knight* in the Japanese language reached a monthly circulation of over 50,000 copies, taking precedence over all the other Catholic periodicals among the non-believers.

The secret of the success achieved by the apostolate of the M.I. in a non-Christian country is found in these notes: first, the attraction exercised by the Immaculata on the non-believers; second, the example of perfect and joyful poverty given by the Franciscan religious. Inexhaustible enthusiasm for their mission, confidence, truthfulness beamed from their faces when, in spite of unfavorable criticism, they brought their greeting: "Mary," and their message of faith in Jesus Christ.

One day, the superior of a Buddhist monastery of Kyoto knocked at the door of the Mugenzai No Sono. Deeply moved by that spectacle of poverty, he took interest in the work of the religious and in their style of life. On taking leave of Father Maximilian, he invited him to his monastery in Kyoto. Father Maximilian availed himself of this kind invitation to make the light of truth penetrate among the bonzes. Most of the conversation was on the Madonna. What Father said was plain and forceful, filled with the fire of a man in love, and made a great impression on the Buddhist priest who said: "From now on, before accepting candidates I will ask them whether they know or are willing to know and love Mary, the Mother of God."

Father Maximilian has explained the reasons for the enthusiasm of nonbelievers for Mary in these terms:

"The purity of Mary attracts the Japanese as the purity of the Catholic missionaries arouses their admiration and their willingness to listen to them."

With regard to the poverty of Mugenzai No Sono, simple but eloquent examples testify to the friars' fervor in this regard. The most firm friends of the "Knights" were Catholic priests, among whom there was one who was eighty years old. One day he said to Father Maximilian: "You are true Franciscans because you are so poor and before you I never saw such missionaries."

We owe to Brother Severin Dagis this touching episode:

"The first Japanese person to show much help to the missionaries was the merchant Uraoka. One day, the old Uraoka, returning from a Sunday function in the Cathedral of Oura, noticed that the house which had been empty for a long time showed some sign of activity. With interest he looked inside and saw many smiling faces of religious. They tried very hard to ask what he wanted, however, they could not in any way make themselves understood. Later, as he narrated, the great poverty of the religious impressed him very much. They had no beds. Usually, they slept on the ground, and the chairs and tables would have served better as material for fire in the stove than for furniture. The old man was deeply moved. However, since he had no teeth, he could not express himself very well. One phrase the missionaries understood was: 'Watakshi no kodomo kimashi,' that is, 'my son will come here.'

"The following day he really brought his son, forty years old. The young Uraoka shared his father's opinion and from that time on they continuously helped the missionaries with food."

Another time, one of the missionary Brothers went to the shoemaker to reclaim a pair of shoes, and had the joy of receiving back the money for the payment, with these words:

"'You are poor. You live on offerings. Your friary does not have servants and this faith of yours must be the true faith.'

"Even the local pharmacist, although a nonbeliever offered to give medicines gratuitously in exchange for the publication: Seibo No Kishi."

The poverty of these missionaries is highlighted also by the following statement related in the chronicle in 1931: "The Sisters of Urakani, coming to know of our poverty, sent us a bit of food...."

Notwithstanding such poverty, The Knight prospered because all the offerings of the non-Christians and the assistance which came from Poland served exclusively to acquire machines, paper and to cover mailing expenses for the Marian magazine, while for Father Maximilian the last thought was for personal necessities. The ideal of Father Maximilian was to increase the diffusion of The Knight, as has already been seen elsewhere.

The most difficult work consisted in the search for subscribers and for addresses. In the West we have recourse to agencies and directories, but this was not possible in Japan where extreme gentility and the courtesy of social living did not admit of intrusion, not even for the mail. Behold then, these missionaries going out on all the central streets, going on buses, penetrating the hospitals, going to schools and giving away copies of *The Knight* gratuitously and asking in return a calling card for a visit, which almost all the Japanese have. And thus, after a personal acquaintance, new addresses were obtained. Then during their reading, the Immaculata would inspire the readers and touch their hearts so that they would send a small offering.

"Are you not afraid that the police will arrest you as disturbers of the public order because of your daring?" the people would ask jokingly. In the beginning, there truly was a fear of arrest, because being Polish, they were suspected as being spies for the Russians. But later the police knew them so well for their goodness that Father Maximilian could answer: "The policemen are our friends and many of them work with us."

It was due to the protection of civic guards that the mission was never visited by thieves, nor damaged by fanatics, as happened in the first days when Mugenzai No Sono was not yet surrounded by walls and barbed-wire fences.

# Favorable Consensus

The unique Marian magazine little by little made its way among nonbelievers who received much good and inspiration from its contents, as numerous letters to Mugenzai No Sono from every part of Japan give evidence. It is refreshing to go through such letters, but for reasons of space we have to limit ourselves to select for the readers only the few examples that follow:

"I have already read seven issues of *Seibo No Kishi* and I am convinced about the existence of God. In the future, I will try to deepen this knowledge. I am not a Catholic but I suffer because I do not know God.

"Please send me other issues of *Seibo No Kishi*.

"I wish you a prosperous development." *Okada Kisei*

Tokyo, May, 1933

"Sometime in May, when I went with a friend of mine to the Ministry of Finance for an errand, I met a stranger on the street who gave me a medal of Mary and a copy of *The Knight.* From that time on, I have been receiving the bulletin every month and I read it with joy. I am sending a yen as an offering; it is truly little, but I beg you to use it for *The Knight.*"       *Hasagawa Junzo,*
                                                    *university student*


Chosen, August 7, 1934

"Are you all well at Mugenzai No Sono? We receive *The Knight* every month. I thank you wholeheartedly. I did not have faith; I did not know the truth. After having read *The Knight,* a miraculous force took hold of me. Every day I drew nearer to the faith and finally I know it. Now I go to church and I pray and I feel that I love Jesus and Mary.

"I received the magazine in this way: my father was given it on the train by an unknown friar, who passed it out to everyone. From that time on, we have been receiving *The Knight.* Thinking back over this, I realize that the Madonna has granted me many graces and I am grateful to her. Now every day, I hope to gain heaven. I try to live well. I pray for the progress of *The Knight,* and pray to work much for those who do not know the faith. I thank you for everything."       *Hashimoto Fumika*


Kanagawa, January 7, 1936

"Joyous greetings to all those who live at Mugenzai No Sono. As I had written previously, I am a student in the school Meijigakauin and am Protestant. I read the December issue of *The Knight* about the M.I. and about the medal that brings graces to those who wear it around their neck. I do not have much education, but even without this, I believe in God. Each time that I read *The Knight* I feel within me an urge to love the Mother of Jesus Christ who redeemed us from sin.

"I recognize the usefulness of the *Militia*. If anyone can belong to it, I also wish to be a member. I desire to be baptized in the Catholic religion.

"I wish prosperity and success to all at Mugenzai No Sono...."                              *Fujisawa Fujisaburo*

These written testimonials, of which there were hundreds, infused an ever greater fervor in Father Maximilian, who, with his heart full of intimate joy, only one year after the first issue of *Seibo No Kishi* had come off the press, wrote to his Minister Provincial:

"At present over twenty bonzes have subscribed to *Seibo No Kishi* and a great number of nonbelievers. Glory to the Immaculata! Today the little statues of the Immaculata arrived. While opening the package, the nonbelievers at the customs house exclaimed: 'Kinejdes,' that is, 'How beautiful! How beautiful!' and they wished to know more about her."

But even more! Having overcome the first perplexities, and backed by the evidence of the facts, *Seibo No Kishi* soon won its "civil rights" among the pre-existing Japanese Catholic press. The following information is based on an account given by Father Maximilian himself to his superiors:

"Mr. Shibalrara, the well-known publicity agent of the Catholic press of Osaka, has contacted us and offered his cooperation for advertising *Seibo No Kishi* also. Even the religious of Sapporo, who have a publication, and at first were rather cold in our regards, have acknowledged us. Glory to the Immaculata! Moreover, Father Krzyszkowski, director of the *Catholic Missions* of Krakow, sent again twenty-two dollars, asking us for an article to be published in his magazine."

Later, articles on Mugenzai No Sono appeared in the secular newspaper *Nagasaki Shimbum,* which led to favorable public opinion for the Mugenzai No Sono and the Immaculata.

# The *Seibo No Kishi*

If the editorial department of *Seibo no Kishi* did not have the exact organization as that of the Polish Niepokalanow at first, it was nonetheless admirable because it demanded greater work. The head editor was Father Maximilian, since, of the four brothers who had come with him, two were assigned to the print shop, and two to the diffusion of *Seibo No Kishi*. But who was collaborating with Father Maximilian in the difficult work of writing and editing? Already mentioned was the Methodist minister, Dr. Yamaki.

Father Maximilian wrote in his letter to the provincialate:

"Helping us in the translation of articles into Japanese is Mr. Yamaki, a Japanese Methodist minister. Today I received from him a card which read: 'I am not yet converted to Catholicism, but I feel that I am a member of the family of St. Francis. Another Protestant, a Mr. Takit Kyoya, also helps us. He lives next door to us.

"A professor of medicine at the local university comes often to talk to me in German and he has already offered to translate the articles from German, although he admitted that he did not know anything about Catholicism. However, he will try to study it."

In the print shop, with Brother Severin Dagis at the head, the compositors were non-Christians who were, however, studying to be baptized. A letter to the Polish provincialate from Nagasaki contained this information:

"The *Seibo No Kishi* thus begins its apostolate within the editorial office and the print shop. In a short time, the Protestants and nonbelievers will be baptized and will work in the spirit of the M.I."

It is necessary to recognize that in the beginning, the *Seibo No Kishi* was simple, humble and at times little suited to the mentality of the Japanese people.

As Bishop Hayasaka himself gave evidence:

"The first issues of *Seibo No Kishi* contained articles which were written more with sentiment than with reasoning. Fearing that the nonbeliever and above all the educated readers would be scandalized, I was obliged to call the fact to the attention of Father Maximilian. Later on, however, the editorial office adapted itself to the mentality, taste and way of reasoning of the Japanese and little by little succeeded in arousing in their hearts first admiration then love for the Immaculata, leading them, through the Immaculata, to the true Faith.

Brother Severin Dagis recalls the debt of gratitude owed to the clergy of Nagasaki:

"The collaborators who wrote willingly for *The Knight* were the priests: Urakawa, Matsukawa, Yamaguchi and Umechi.

"Father Urakawa, then Vicar General of the diocese of Nagasaki and noted Catholic writer in Japan, worked much to put the *Seibo No Kishi* on its feet. Meanwhile, he also had the care of the Catholic weekly. He wrote apologetic works, as well as scholarly books on the history of Christianity in Japan. He was at times urged not to collaborate with Father Maximilian because some thought that *The Knight,* sooner or later, would fail, and Father Urakawa's name, so esteemed among historians, would be exposed to criticism. However, the priest highly regarded Father Kolbe. At times, urged on insistently by unfavorable people, Father Urakawa criticized the magazine intensely in regard to the content, yet he never refused his collaboration. He was one of the most valuable writer-collaborators on whom Father Maximilian could rely.

"Father Paul Matsukawa, an elderly priest, had a beard that reached to his belt. He held the position of spiritual director of the seminary. He also wrote willingly, and he loved Father Maximilian very much. It seemed that these two souls understood each other very well. They resolved many difficulties together. Father

Matsukawa was also the spiritual director of our missionary [Father Maximilian] during the whole time that he lived in Japan.

"The priest, Yamaguchi, a student of the college of Propaganda Fide in Rome, and later Bishop of Nagasaki, was then professor in the diocesan seminary. From time to time, he also wrote for *The Knight*. Often he and Father Maximilian discussed the difficulties that the publication would have to face in its development. He was always smiling, full of energy and youthful ardor. Therefore, it was not unusual that he, too, understood and valued the work of *Seibo No Kishi*.

"The priest, Umechi, secretary of Bishop Hayasaka, a young and energetic priest, rarely wrote articles for the magazine, but he was invaluable in the administrative matters of the new publication. He helped us to buy the land for the Mugenzai No Sono, and even personally operated the press manually, when, because of lack of money, there was not yet the electric motor.

"Thus, the clergy of the country seemed to understand totally the intention of Father Maximilian and collaborated with him."

# A Franciscan Seminary

Father Maximilian, who already in the Polish Niepokalanow wanted a separate seminary for the education of the apostles of the M.I., planned that the Mugenzai No Sono would have its own novitiate and school for Japanese vocations. Japan gives few fruits in conversions as well as vocations. This is the discomforting realization of all missionaries stationed there. But the apostolate of the humble Franciscan was visibly blessed by God. Even the Bishop of Nagasaki could not hide his amazement. Astounded, he exclaimed: "On first sight, his trust in the divine Providence seemed an exaggeration, but judging from the effects, I must admit how right and supernatural was his trust in God."

In less than two years, not only baptisms followed, but among the youths baptized there were many who, attracted by the Immaculata, desired to wear the Franciscan habit and to become priests. In August, 1931, the Franciscan novitiate was built for the native vocations. The following year, the small seminary for philosophy and theology was begun. This seminary was for local vocations, as well as the Polish seminarians whom Father Kolbe had asked for. The Minister Provincial would send them for their training in Japan so that by the time of ordination, they would already have a thorough command of the Japanese language.

In this way, Mugenzai No Sono was now like the Polish Niepokalanow. It not only had the same editorial and technical organization for printing *The Knight,* but with its native seminary, direction was taken for progressive development in future years, when to the apostolate of the press there would be added the pastoral apostolate, and it would provide for the foundation of other religious houses at Tokyo, Osaka and Nagasaki itself.

## Mugenzai No Sono—Beacon of Light

When Father Maximilian founded Niepokalanow, he wanted the first stone of the singular "city" to be the beautiful statue of the Immaculata, which even today, although replaced after the destruction of the war, towers in the same place where the founder had it placed, at the main entrance. In Japan, he did the same for the Mugenzai No Sono. One day, while contemplating the newly erected "city" from Nagasaki plain, Father Maximilian had an idea which was put into execution immediately.

Many times in the morning, on his way to Nagasaki, Father Kolbe met groups of Japanese, who before dawn went from the hilltop down to the plain to contemplate and adore the rising sun.

Father Maximilian reflected: The Sun is Jesus; the Immaculata is the morning star who announced Jesus! Why not place along the street walked by the Japanese people a beautiful statue of the Immaculata so that on seeing it, they will ask who she is, and in the very asking, they will feel the desire to know her? In this way, the Sun also, whose Mother she is, will be known by them. Soon enough, on the highest and most visible point of the construction, there was raised up a column and upon it was placed a large statue of the Immaculata. Father Maximilian wanted it also illumined at night by a splendid crown of lights. If merchants use lighted signs to advertise their products for material gain, should not the missionaries, with greater reason, use a beacon light in the darkness of night for the spiritual and material good of souls? As a consequence, there arose the mystical beacon light of Mugenzai No Sono, renamed the "city of faith" for those in the darkness of error.

And the beacon light bore its fruits!

In an article prepared for *The Knight* of Poland with the title: "How the Immaculata attracts the non-believers," Father Maximilian related this touching episode:

"A few months or more after the construction of Mugenzai No Sono, we had a large statue of the Immaculata placed on the highest point, which was very visible in the whole pagan district of Nagasaki, Hongonchi.

"The Immaculata has already drawn to herself many pagan souls. Often we notice that people who pass on the busy street stop to look at the Immaculata. The Brothers say that the nonbelievers ask each other what the statue is. They even heard a pagan woman try to explain the meaning of Mugenzai No Sono and the apostolate of the new missionaries. A short time ago, a pagan family came up to view the Immaculata from close range. Since no one could reach the place except through the cloister, it was possible to bring only the father to the feet of the Immaculata, while the mother and the daughters had to be pleased with seeing the chapel and receiving the Miraculous Medal.

"In these last days, a young girl came up. She is probably about twenty years old. She asked to become a Catholic. From interviewing her more at length, we learned that she is a poor unfortunate young woman who never knew her father and was abandoned by her mother. After the death of her tutor, she became a vagabond, sold and sought by those in search of young women. Desperate, she had come up the hill with the intention of throwing herself into the lake, here, near Mugenzai No Sono. But she saw the statue of the Immaculata which attracted her.

"She knocked at the door of Mugenzai No Sono. We offered her supper which she did not want to touch. Only after many words of comfort did she accept a bit of tea with bread. After having consoled her some more and having given her a medal of the Immaculata, we accompanied her to the local pastor and entrusted her to his care.

"But certainly we shall never know all that the Immaculata deigns to do in calling to herself the nonbelievers. Only on the day of universal judgment will we know how much she has inspired the hearts of nonbelievers from the height of this hill.

"To her alone be the glory for everything."

*Father Maximilian*

## Japanese Caramels

For Father Kolbe, "caramels" were every kind of suffering or difficulty accepted for love of the Immaculata. He refers to them in a letter to his Provincial:

"Almost every day of the month of May had its caramel, and then in June, especially during the octave of the most Sacred Heart, I really suffered as never before. But everything has passed and now the Immaculata guides everything in the best of ways."

In another letter, even more explicitly, he states:

"According to the tactics of the Immaculata, Calvary must precede Tabor. To her honor and glory in everything!"

Japan was the crucible in which the sanctity of Father Maximilian was perfected day by day, and reached that fullness from whence flowed forth the final sublime heroism of his life.

The first three years of his stay in Japan numbered a succession of displeasing events and grave trials.

If the foundation of the first "City of the Immaculata" in Poland encountered only initial difficulties and internal ones which were easily overcome with the decisions of the superiors, that of Mugenzai No Sono, besides the very organizational difficulties, experienced many external trials.

Moreover, because of the Japanese climate, so different from that of Poland, more than one Brother who had come with Father Maximilian, and others who came later, had to be sent back to their native land. With his many infirmities, Father Maximilian gave an admirable example of fortitude: not only his lungs progressively worsened, but he also suffered from other ills such as continuous boils, eczema and infections. The condition worsened so that there was fear for his life. How he persevered in that rhythm of work imposed on him by the school, the construction of Mugenzai No Sono and by writing for *Seibo No Kishi* was a marvel to the doctors.

Dr. Paul Nagai Takashi, the heroic radiologist who was a victim of atomic radiation in the bombardment of Nagasaki, candidly testified:

"His life was characterized by a continual heroism. As a physician, I examined him and found out that one of his lungs was in critical condition. Having prescribed complete rest for him, he objected that he would continue to work, since he had been in that state of health for many years. His will to resist was absolutely extraordinary."

The poor health of Father Maximilian and others were the most common "caramels." But by far the greater were the trials to which he refers, although hastily, in his letters to the Polish provincialate.

During the first year, the activity of Father Maximilian was an object of insinuations, suspicion and jealousy on the part of some who resented the success that the new foundation had met. Emphasis was put on the fact that Father Kolbe had arrived in Japan without the prerequisite permission of the Holy See. (Due to the special character of his work Father Maximilian had had first to find a resident bishop to sponsor him. By pre-arranged agreement, the Holy See would then approve his mission with the consent of the sponsoring bishop.)

Although, in fact, the superiors in Rome had completed all of the agreed-on formalities in October, 1930—less than six months after Bishop Hayasaka had given his consent—nevertheless in July, 1931, some instigators succeeded in convincing the new Apostolic Delegate that the foundation was illegal because it lacked due permission from Rome.

The aim of the attack was very clear. It was to make the newly-born Mugenzai No Sono appear in a bad light in the eyes of the highest ecclesiastical authority because plans for a religious house in Tokyo had already been initiated. They thus thought they would succeed in blocking every ulterior development.

The frustration Father Maximilian experienced on this occasion appears from this confession he made:

"When the Apostolic Delegate reproached me, I was about to be overwhelmed by discouragement, but I prostrated myself at the feet of the Immaculata and in prayer I found the strength to remain tranquil and serene."

More serious and painful than accusations coming from outsiders were charges brought against him by the members of his own community. They caused untold suffering to his soul which was childlike and simple, incapable of bitterness and rancor. The nature of this internal trial is made known to us by the Minister Provincial of that time in the following testimony:

"The activity of the Servant of God was beyond common measure. There is nothing strange about its being subject to criticism and discussion on the part of his confreres. On account of this, Father Maximilian was many times opposed although never maliciously. He never became angry with those who made him suffer. Father X, sent to Nagasaki as professor of dogmatic theology, not only was unable to adjust to the different environment, but he was seized by the fear and suspicion that Father Maximilian aimed to found a new order. For this reason, he caused much grief to Father Kolbe. In his letters to the Polish provincialate, he attacked Father Maximilian with firm and decisive blows, and when he was silenced by the Father Provincial, he appealed to the Minister General of the Order in Rome. The Minister General, in his turn, entrusted the case to the Assistant General of Poland who sided with Father X. This situation weighed heavily on Father Maximilian. Being at that time Provincial, I myself went to Father General in Rome to defend the cause of Father Maximilian.

"He [Father Maximilian], however, never mentioned the occurrence. He always justified Father X and continued to show the greatest respect and courtesy for the Assistant General."

This testimony sheds further light on Father Maximilian's patience who, without nourishing resentment for Father X, continued to live with him throughout the time he was in Japan. Although supported by his Provincial, Father Maximilian never asked him to transfer Father X to another place. He limited himself to being vigilant, lest Father X, by his attitude, would do harm to the other confreres, to the new converts and to the apostolate of the M.I.

On April 8, 1933, Father Maximilian left Japan for Poland a second time to participate in the election of the Minister Provincial of the Polish province. He preferred to make the whole journey by sea, since he intended to meet his missionary confreres at Shanghai and to stop in Italy. Most probably, he wanted to go to Rome not only to give a detailed description of Mugenzai No Sono to the Father General, but also to gain the indulgences attached to the jubilee of redemption granted for Easter of that year.

On the departure day, all the religious and residents of Mugenzai No Sono accompanied him to the ship. Father Maximilian, always very sensitive to any form of courtesy, wrote from Shanghai two very affectionate letters to thank his co-workers of Mugenzai. These letters show the depth of his spirituality and his fatherly and loving concern for the spiritual profit of his confreres and subjects.

A characteristic feature of the numerous letters Father Kolbe wrote during his voyage is the absence of any reference to a program for the future, or to his eventual return to Japan and to his varied activities. Everything was left to the care of the Blessed Mother. Although he was the founder of Mugenzai No Sono, for which he untiringly worked for three years, he had only one desire: that everything be in conformity with the wishes of his heavenly Queen.

Father Maximilian remained in Poland three months, until August 31. The temporary stay in his country allowed him to further clarify the characteristics of Niepokalanow.

From the beginning of the apostolate of the M.I., some confreres deemed exaggerated Father Maximilian's stress on Marian devotion; not only in *The Knight* but, above all, in the religious life, first in Grodno and then, even more, in Niepokalanow. Some confreres voiced the opinion that Father Maximilian, with his extravagant Marian devotion, was estranging himself from the spirituality of the Order and was losing sight of the imitation of the founder, St. Francis of Assisi.

On the contrary, Father Maximilian not only faithfully followed in the footsteps of the Seraphic Father in the practice of the religious virtues, but also in what constituted his spiritual physiognomy, that is, his unique Marian devotion. It is commonly known that the chief goals of the Franciscan spirituality are Bethlehem, the Cenacle and Calvary. While the Gospel presents Mary in adoration of Jesus in the crib and near the cross, Christian piety, based on a tradition revived by St. Bonaventure, makes us contemplate her also in the Cenacle. It is no surprise that Father Maximilian, in inculcating in his spiritual sons the practice of the religious virtues at the school of the Immaculata, had continual references to the examples of St. Francis.

On July 23, 1933, during a local meeting of the M.I. in Niepokalanow, some religious referred to the question of the purpose of the Franciscan Order. Their question, somewhat impertinent, echoed the opinions of some confreres concerning the Marian innovations of Father Maximilian. The answers given by participants were at such a variance that the secretary wrote in the report of the meeting that the purpose of the Franciscan Order is the practice of the evangelical counsels according to the Rule, and nothing else.

While this conclusion pleased some, it was not accepted by the majority. Father Maximilian, when asked for his opinion, took advantage of the situation to make these reflections:

"I invite those who oppose us to declare whether at the time of St. Francis the dogma of the Immaculate Conception had already been proclaimed. Granted that we do not have to believe in the Gospel only, but also in Tradition and the teachings of the Church, even if we were to limit ourselves to the Gospel, where does it originate from, if not from the most holy Madonna?

"Who is the Mother of Jesus? Who educated Him?

"The most holy Madonna....

"We must practice the Gospel; that is, imitate Jesus Christ as is written in the Rule. It is true.

"But in the Rule it is not written that we must travel by train, and do we perhaps not travel?

"The Rule does not say to use electricity, and yet we use it!

"With time, God unfolds to mankind truths valid from the beginning of time, but unknown to men.

"A few years ago, the dogma of the Immaculate Conception was defined, and already preparation is being made for the definition of the dogma of the universal mediation of Mary. Perhaps with the passage of time, even other Marian privileges will be more clearly illustrated and more precisely presented.

"As for the rest, the purpose of the Order must be drawn also from its history and its activity; and we know that our Order was found to be in the vanguard of devotion to the most holy Madonna. It is noteworthy that the Franciscans were known for their defense of the dogma of the Immaculate Conception.

"Jesus devoted only three years to teaching and thirty to give us an example of how we must live according to His teaching.

"What was this example?

"The Gospel says that He was *obedient*. He was obedient to His most holy Mother.

"His relation with the Madonna was that of a son with a mother; the Madonna was the best of mothers; Jesus was the best of children. Could there be lacking a cordial love and a sensible attachment between them?

"Nazareth was a little Niepokalanow....

"Paradise and the whole universe are a great Niepokalanow.

"We here at Niepokalanow live according to the example of Jesus, that is, practicing the Gospel. We imitate Him in giving ourselves to the most holy Madonna.

"If God, the Most Holy Trinity, has enriched the most holy Madonna so much in giving her so many graces and privileges that the earth, paradise and the whole universe do not possess, should we not love the Madonna, and should we not love her always more?

*"At no price will we permit that the distinctive characteristic of our devotion of the Immaculata be taken from us.*

"We must only deepen it always more, study it and diffuse it everywhere, but never weaken it....

*"Through the Immaculata* is a distinction of Niepokalanow and at the same time it is a mystery that not all can understand.

"We are reproved as if Niepokalanow were not based on the spirit of St. Francis on account of its accentuated Marian devotion.

"But this means to ignore the history of our Order and how much St. Francis loved the Madonna and how much he urged his first Brothers to venerate her. Isn't this his warning:

"'I command all my friars now and in the ages to come to always venerate the Madonna and to render her the due devotion, in all possible ways and with all the available means, and to turn to her with the greatest veneration and spirit of service.'

"St. Francis therefore clearly, distinctly and firmly has defined the relations our Order has with the most holy Madonna.

"We are familiar also with other words by St. Francis that we can always read on the walls of our friaries and of our cells: 'In every danger, in temptations, in doubts and difficulties, invoke Mary, pray to Mary; may she always be on your lips and in your thoughts.'

"St. Francis wanted his Brothers to be the vassals of the Madonna. And during his time who were the vassals if not the knights who fought for their lords?

"St. Francis, willing his religious to be the vassals of Mary, tells us that we are following his spirit when wishing to be knights who fight for the Immaculata."

*Maria Dabrowska Kolbe,*
*the mother of two Franciscan priests:*
*Father Alphonse and*
*Father Maximilian, the hero*
*of Auschwitz.*

*Maria Kolbe in her later years.*

*The wagons carrying materials for*
*building the* City of the Immaculata
*in 1928.*

*Father Maximilian Kolbe, Father Cornelius Czupryk (Provincial)
and Father Alphonse Kolbe with some of the first students who
joined the newly-established seminary at Niepokalanow in 1929.*

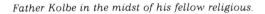

*Father Kolbe in the midst of his fellow religious.*

*Father Kolbe with the seminarians in 1933.*

*Father Kolbe and Brother Kamil Banaszek in Zakopane.*

*Setting type and proofreading for* The Knight of the Immaculata *(Rycerz Niepokalanej).*

*Preparing* The Little Journal *(Maly Dziennik) for mailing.*

*The friars operating the printing presses.*

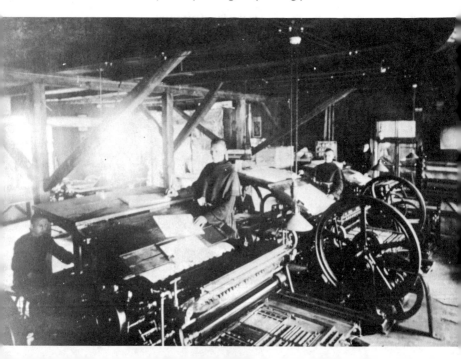

*Father Maximilian, together with four brothers chosen for the foundation of the new "City of the Immaculata" among non-believers, setting out for the Far East on February 26, 1930.*

*Father Kolbe being greeted by the friars on his return from Japan in 1933.*

聖母の騎士

*The front cover of the Japanese edition of* The Knight of the Immaculata *published in January, 1939.*

*Father Kolbe in Mugenzai no Sono (The City of the Immaculata—Japan) discussing religion with some Japanese workers.*

*Several brothers making their religious profession in August, 1938.*

*Father Kolbe with
Cardinal Kakowski,
the Primate of Poland.*

The priests and Brothers of the City of the Immaculata in August, 1939.

Father Kolbe and his friars being led to the Nazi concentration camp in Amtitz on September 19, 1939.

This is the way the workshop in Niepokalanow looked after the Nazi takeover on September 19, 1939. The portrait of the Holy Father thrown on the floor...the statue of the Immaculate Virgin headless.

The Brothers working in the machine shop built in 1940 to repair farm equipment.

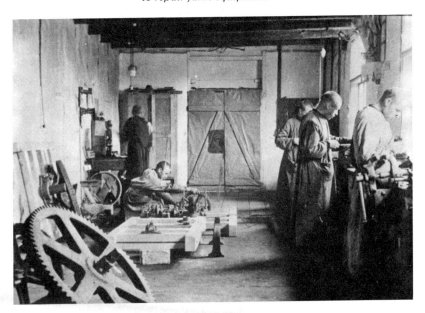

The second arrest of
Father Kolbe on
February 17, 1941.

M. Kościelaniaka

M. Kościelaniaka

Father Kolbe being beaten
by a Nazi officer at the
Pawiak prison in Warsaw
because of his refusal to
denounce his crucifix
and rosary.

*Risking beatings and punishment, Father Kolbe continues to exercise his priestly ministry by hearing confessions and offering spiritual consolation to his fellow prisoners at Auschwitz.*

M. Kościelaniaka

*The meekness and resignation of Father Kolbe enrage Krott, one of the camp chiefs, who vents his anger by viciously beating the priest.*

M. Kościelaniaka

M. Kościelaniak

*Father Kolbe making the heroic offering of his life to take the place of the condemned prisoner, Francis Gajowniczk.*

*Nazi officer injecting Father Kolbe with the poisonous acid that sent him to his death on August 14, 1941—the vigil of the Assumption.*

M. Kościelaniaka

*The last picture known to be taken of Father Kolbe in 1940.*

*Niepokalanow, 1970—A view of the church in the City of the Immaculata taken from the friary.*

*A front view of the church.*

*The interior of the church.*

*The first chapel in the* City of the Immaculata *as it looks today*

*Francis Gajowniczek, the man whose place Father Kolbe took,
visited the American City of the Immaculata (Marytown)
in Kenosha, Wisconsin, in 1977.*

*The American City of the Immaculata (Marytown) as it looks today.
Now located in Libertyville, Illinois, it was moved from Kenosha, Wisconsin,
to these more spacious quarters in June, 1979.*

# Second Stay in Japan—
# Plans for Establishing the M.I.
# on a World Scale

The biography of every saint has at least one chapter which tells of humiliation and suffering generously accepted. It cannot be otherwise. The following of Christ consists not only in the observance of the moral law, not only in a life not at variance with Christ's teaching, but also in conforming oneself to the sufferings of the crucified Lord. "No pupil outranks his teacher, no slave his master. The pupil should be glad to become like his teacher, the slave like his master" (Mt. 10:24f.).

Father Maximilian, raised by the Church to the honors of the altar after rigorous investigations and even more detailed discussions, bore witness to sanctity with his life which was a living expression of the imitation of Christ. His vast works of apostolate are the object of admiration and glorification on the part of the faithful mainly because of all the sacrifices which were involved and which he lovingly embraced in order to promote, through the Immaculata, the glory of God and the salvation of souls.

In his adherence to the incomprehensible will of the Father, in the perfect fulfillment of obedience even when most difficult, in being forced many times to take a direction opposite from what he wished—here lies the source of his spiritual fecundity; a source that is concealed to our computerized world.

This present chapter deals with the three years of Father Maximilian's stay at Mugenzai No Sono in Japan. They were praiseworthy years of daily self-denial. Almost unnoticed, it seems that nothing had changed. As never before, he looked very happy and laborious. Yet, he had cause for discouragement because of the reactions and inactivity related to his work. It was evident that he had a temperament inclined to strong standings and even to obstinacy. But instead, the virtues of self-denial and humility became his habitual, constant and pleasing rule, almost like second nature to him. In these three years, more than in the preceding years, the sanctity of Father Kolbe became always more lofty, almost in remote preparation for the more challenging combats awaiting him.

# A Humble Subject

In July, 1933, under the guidance of the Minister General of the Order, the Chapter was held in Krakow for the election of a new Provincial and other superiors.

Father Kolbe participated as a teacher of theology. Having been nominated by the presiding Father *definitor ex gratia*—a special privilege given to well-deserving priests—he could be present at all the capitular sessions.

After the election of the new Minister Provincial, the Chapter also furthered the organization of the two "Cities of the Immaculata" founded by Father Maximilian. Niepokalanow in Poland—praised by the General Visitator for its editorial activities, and especially for the regularity of the religious life, as well as the spacious buildings—was chosen to become the novitiate house for the entire Polish province. Father Florian Koziura, elected Guardian (superior) of Niepokalanow after the death of Father Alphonse Kolbe in December of 1930, was confirmed in his office.

A new local superior, instead, was appointed for Mugenzai No Sono in Japan, where the seminary and novitiate were beginning to flourish. He was Father Cornelius Czupryk, whose three-year term as Minister Provincial had expired. Father Maximilian received the simple "obedience" to return to Japan as a subject, with the duty of teaching philosophy and theology in the college there and of editing the Japanese edition of *The Knight*.

Why was Father Maximilian not confirmed as superior? From a diligent study of all the "Capitular Acts," several answers emerge. It would seem, first of all, that in the plan of God, Father Maximilian had to give the proof of rare humility united to much self-denial. With the merit that comes from virtue, he was to draw down greater graces on himself and on his work. The unsuccessful confirmation of Father Maximilian as superior cannot be attributed to criticism or remarks referring to the religious and apostolic life as it was lived in the two "Cities of the Immaculata." The obedience of Father Kolbe was well known to everyone. Only a few dispositions from the superiors would have sufficed to soften the voluntary austerity of the "Cities of the Immaculata" so as to be according to the Constitutions of the Order.

Moreover, more criticism had been directed to Niepokalanow, where the same superior was reelected, than to Mugenzai No Sono, the organization of which had not yet been completed.

Most likely, the appointment of the new superior to the Japanese mission was due to the exceptional personality of the priest elected. During his provincialate, Father Cornelius Czupryk supported Mugenzai No Sono. In 1930, he permitted its foundation. He defended the activity of Father Maximilian when the unfounded criticism of his confreres could have been damaging if it would have been believed by the Minister General. Imbued with missionary zeal, Father Czupryk asked to go to the Japanese mission after his term as Provincial was completed. In recognition of his many merits, the capitular Fathers must have considered it appropriate to send him to the mission in the capacity of superior.

This nomination might also be interpreted as grateful praise for what already had been accomplished in Mugenzai No Sono and of hope for the future. At the side of the founder, the new superior would be able to further the development of the work which, in part, because of his constant support, could also be considered his undertaking.

Moreover, the new Provincial, Father Anselm Kubit, was greatly concerned about Father Maximilian's health. He wanted to relieve him of some responsibilities, and also wanted him to assume the duties of world director of the M.I. For this he would need more time and freedom to travel.

Finally the capitular Fathers must have also thought that, because of his humility and docility, Father Maximilian would docilely accept this action and would gladly, under the direct guidance of obedience, intensify the missionary apostolate of the M.I.

And so it was.

However, it was an undeniable fact that the position of Father Maximilian had greatly changed. He had come as leader and founder; he returned as a subject. In the eyes of those who had been the cause of misunderstanding and of the undue charges against him, his failure to be re-elected superior could be interpreted as proof of the grounds for their distrust, and a precaution taken by the capitular Fathers against eventual innovations.

But the virtue of Father Kolbe shone forth even now. Armed with the sound principles dictated by his deep faith, he kept repeating: "As the Immaculata wills." And falling on his knees before the new superior, he pledged his devoted submission in everything.

To him must be applied what is written in the *Imitation of Christ:* "He who works only for the glory of God, he who seeks to fulfill only the divine will and prefers the most humble places, submitting himself to all, he it is who knows how to experience peace of spirit in humiliation."

The Immaculata, however, abundantly rewarded the humble submission of her knight, working out through the instrumentality of the saint, during his brief stay in Poland, a remarkable conversion. He who always considered himself the missionary of the Japanese people wherever he was, was chosen by the Immaculata to be instrumental in the conversion of Dr. Kawai and, in a way, to manifest once more the effectiveness of the Miraculous Medal.

Having come to know that the Japanese plenipotentiary minister lay grievously ill in Otwock, on the outskirts of Warsaw, Father Maximilian put in motion all his material and spiritual resources to prepare him for a Christian death.

From previous contacts with the Japanese diplomatic body, he knew that Dr. Kawai's wife was Catholic and ardently desired her husband, in case of a serious illness, to die a Catholic. Because of some difficulties involved in approaching the dying man, Father Maximilian turned to the Apostolic Nuncio, Mons. Francisco Marmaggi, and asked him to pay a visit to Dr. Kawai in the capacity of dean of the diplomatic body. The zealous prelate willingly consented, but could do nothing for the conversion of Dr. Kawai. Father Maximilian decided, therefore, to approach the sick man himself, and did so much good that he convinced the dying Dr. Kawai to wear the Miraculous Medal. In other visits, Father Kolbe exhorted and instructed the diplomat in the Faith until he was baptized by the well-deserving Nuncio, and then died a holy death.

Soon after, the rest of the family of Dr. Kawai—his wife and daughters were already Catholic—embraced the Catholic Faith. The chronicles of Niepokalanow testify to the zeal displayed by Father Maximilian for the conversion of the two sons, the mother and the servants of the deceased. Although extremely busy in the preparations for his return to Japan, armed with the Japanese catechism, Father Kolbe went every day to Warsaw to carry out his missionary duty.

At the same time he busied himself with the conversion of an Evangelical pastor. But in spite of his unlimited charity, he did not succeed in this task. Faced with the sad reality of the deafness of the minister to the reiterated appeals of grace, Father Kolbe exclaimed: "To convert a pastor or a priest who has lost his faith is more difficult than to convert all men together."

## From Niepokalanow to Mugenzai No Sono

On August 31, 1933, Father Maximilian undertook the return journey to Japan. From Krakow he went to Vienna and from Vienna to Venice where he embarked on board the "Conte Rosso" sailing for the Far East.

At Krakow, he received from the Minister Provincial the departure blessing together with the office of Director General of the M.I. He embraced for the last time Mama Maria who, as we know, had entered the convent of the Felician Sisters. It must have been a most affectionate encounter as we can derive from this news he wrote to Father Florian Koziura during his voyage: "Mama gave me an offering of sixty zloti: please send her some pictures of the groups." At Krakow, Father Cornelius Czupryk joined him and they went together to Venice. Once in Italy they did not want to miss the chance of going to Rome for a short visit. Here the Minister General of the Order ratified Father Maximilian's appointment as Director General of the M.I. and gave him the precise command to further the spreading of the M.I. all over the world, wherever the lawful ecclesiastical authorities would permit it.

We want the reader to note this command because, in obedience to it, Father Maximilian worked indefatigably in the organization of the M.I. during his second stay in Japan.

In the journey from Rome to Venice, he stopped at Assisi. He made a brief pilgrimage to the tomb of the Poverello in order to obtain from that source of Franciscan life a renewed and purified missionary zeal. Finally, on September 9, he set sail from Venice, heading for Nagasaki.

This day began a new story of the Japanese mission founded by Father Maximilian. It is a story that seems like a legend and can well be compared to the missionary apostolate and journeys of the first companions of St. Francis of Assisi who went two by two. The correspondence which began this day was not only from Father Maximilian but also from Father Cornelius. Every letter which arrived at Niepokalanow bore two signatures: that of Father Cornelius and that of Father Maximilian. One was almost not able to differentiate the intensity of love for the Immaculata which burned in their hearts. It is true that it blazed in the heart of Father Maximilian, but whoever approached him was also inflamed.

In the first letter written to Niepokalanow during the voyage from Venice to Brindisi, we read this addition after the signature of Father Maximilian:

"P.S. I never knew how beautiful it is to serve the Immaculata! Why did I not know before? She fills us with graces during the journey toward her second Niepokalanow. Everywhere we receive favors, at times incomprehensible. Father Maximilian is well. We have a separate cabin and we conduct the same life as in the friary."

*Father Cornelius*

On September 20, after the torrid heat of the Red Sea and the monsoons of the Persian Gulf, they arrived at Bombay. Here Father Maximilian was filled with nostalgia. On his shoulders weighed the whole Moslem world which still awaited the true light of the Gospel. At port he wrote to Niepokalanow:

"How sorry I feel because there is not yet a Niepokalanow here. Today I offered Mass for this intention. But may the will of the Immaculata always be done."

At the *Nippon Restaurant,* owned by a Polish man who was married to a Japanese lady, they experienced the sheer delight of meeting a fellow countryman halfway between Poland and Japan. This refreshing feeling was increased by seeing on the table two copies of *The Knight:* one in Polish, the *Ricerz Niepokalanej,* which permitted the owner to remain in touch with his native land; the other in Japanese, the *Seibo No Kishi,* sent from Mugenzai No Sono to the wife. It seemed for an instant as though in that corner of the earth the apostolate of the two Niepokalanows had met. Father Maximilian and Father Cornelius felt right at home. In taking leave of their hosts, they received from the owner the invitation to stop at his restaurant any time they passed by Colombo.

Finally, on October 4, they arrived at Nagasaki. Informed by a telegram, Mugenzai No Sono joyfully welcomed them. Father Cornelius, who during his three-year term as superior had received a monthly report on the status of this mission, could only now realize how inferior was the news to reality.

On that very day, Father Cornelius began his office of superior. The progress made by the Japanese mission in the three years that followed was based on the guidelines given in the beginning by its founder, who was now the most faithful collaborator and affectionate subject of Father Cornelius.

# Apostolate for the Indian People

During his second stay in Japan, having received full authorization from his superiors, Father Maximilian endeavored to extend the ray of action of the apostolate of the M.I. all over the world.

His principal aim was to establish the M.I. in India, to which he had already directed his efforts since June 1932, when, by the will of his Father Provincial, he had set forth for Ernakulam and Tutikorin.

This enterprise had cost him much fatigue at the time, as it appears in a letter to the Polish provincialate:

"After so much traveling [between Nagasaki and Tokyo], I would have willingly remained in Nagasaki to enjoy some rest and regain some health, but for the Immaculata and solely for her I undertake this new trip and this new work."

He had sailed from Nagasaki at the beginning of June, 1932, and had arrived there at the end of the same month.

At that time there were two Catholic bishoprics in India, one of Syrian rite, the other of Latin rite. While Father Maximilian should have directly turned to the Archbishop of the Latin rite, he was prevented from doing so. On his journey toward Ernakulam he had as his companion a Catholic priest, the vicar general of the Syrian rite, who directed him to his bishop. The latter received most kindly the unknown, humble European Franciscan who unfolded the reasons and aim of his journey with such persuasive arguments, fortified by his zeal for the cause of the Immaculata, that the good bishop asked him to establish himself in his diocese.

The solidarity of the Syrian clergy, sympathetic toward the project, and the spontaneous and enthusiastic adherence of a diocesan priest willing even to become a Franciscan and start the work, seemed to assure success to the initiative. The diversity of the rite, however, was so great an impediment that Father Maximilian decided to seek out the Archbishop of the Latin rite although he knew that the prelate was not in favor of the establishment in his diocese. While he was waiting for the audience with the Archbishop, a rose detached itself from a vase of flowers in front of a statue of St. Therese of the Child Jesus. The rose rolled toward Father Kolbe and rested at his feet.

Was this a sign, he thought, launched from the heights of heaven by his patroness, that the Archbishop would be favorable to him? Perhaps yes, because to his great surprise, not only did the Archbishop wholeheartedly welcome his idea, but he himself deigned to drive Father Maximilian to a piece of land just a few miles away from the city, and offered to give it to him along with the house and the church on behalf of his apostolic work.

On December 8, 1932, His Excellency, Mons. Angelo Perez Cecilio, Archbishop of Verapolis, had sent to the Polish provincialate his permission for the foundation of the Indian Niepokalanow. However, Father Cornelius Czupryk, who was then the Provincial, had deemed it prudent to bring the matter of the foundation of the Indian Niepokalanow to the attention of the capitulars of the forthcoming Provincial Chapter and postponed the reply of acceptance to the Archbishop of Verapolis.

New negotiations through Father Maximilian, authorized by his superiors, were resumed in January, 1934. Even this time the good Archbishop ratified the previous invitation. Father Maximilian had accomplished everything in his power. Any other matter would have to be carried out by the superiors of Poland and Rome; nothing else remained for him to do except to wait for eventual new dispositions and to pray until the third Niepokalanow would become a reality.

A letter to the superior of Niepokalanow, containing a plea for all the members of the mystical city, was drafted in these terms:

"I beg to earnestly urge all the confreres of Niepokalanow, priests, brothers, clerics and novices, to take the Immaculata by storm with their prayers for the India affair. May she do her will, not letting her plans be ruined by us and by others."

Yet in spite of all the concern of Father Maximilian, difficulties which arose before and during the Second World War, and the new political order which emerged in India after the war, prevented the implementation of the new foundation not only on the part of Father Kolbe, but even by his Order. Father Maximilian's dream finally became a reality however on May 10, 1981, when the Bishop of Kanjinapally, Kerala, officially opened a

Niepokalanow in India in the town of Chotty. Two friars from Malta made the foundation which is called "Nirmalaram" (the "Garden of the Immaculata").

Having accomplished his mandate for India, while awaiting the approval of higher authorities, Father Maximilian again fixed his gaze over the whole world which he wanted to conquer with the apostolate of the M.I. This ideal is found in many of the letters he wrote over the years. These letters bear witness to the constancy and energy of his action, never motivated by a fleeting enthusiasm but always a mature deliberation, while periods of waiting, imposed upon him by obedience or other factors, served only to make it stronger. To refer only to major statements he made in this regard, we quote what he wrote in 1932 to his Provincial:

"I wanted to omit what I am about to write, but then I decided not to do so because it seems that the Immaculata prefers that I ask you what I should do.... Must I limit myself to the cause of the M.I. only in Japan and answer only the questions that are asked of me from all parts of the world, or should I be concerned with the cause of the M.I. throughout the whole world?

"I am aware that I can never occupy myself with all of this, but in the face of the spread of atheism, I am eager to do so.

"Above all, I desire to know what the Immaculate Virgin wants from me. I feel much fear. I want to always be afraid of myself and of my will, while I want always to desire to know and to carry out only the will of the Immaculata.

"A future program could be the following: 1) To use all the means offered by the M.I. for the propagation of the same in the whole world. 2) To conquer for and to draw to the M.I. the promoters of atheism who are the propagators of the antichrist. 3) I will explain this at the first opportunity by word of mouth: there is time.

"I believe that an outline of organization could be the following: to ask permission of the competent religious authority to begin the M.I. Once permission has been granted, it will be the sign of the divine will and of the will of the Immaculata.

"If the most reverend Father Provincial thinks convenient and urgent what I have explained above, I would desire a reply by telegram, in the event that the Immaculata wants me to pledge myself to her cause and undertake the new work in this her month of May.

"I repeat that I only desire to fulfill the will of the Immaculata; therefore, I beg you to feel free to disregard my words if they do not deserve any consideration. Do not think of hurting my feelings."

To foster a worldwide plan of the apostolate of the M.I., Father Maximilian felt it necessary to captivate the interest of the clergy and seminarians all over the world as a far-reaching force for the penetration of the ideals of the M.I. among the masses. With this in mind, a Latin publication of *The Knight* seemed the most suitable means for implementing such an undertaking. As early as 1932, Father Maximilian outlined the need, the importance and utility of *The Knight* in the Latin language, *Miles Immaculatae,* in a letter to his Provincial:

"It is true that the Immaculata has prepared for herself two cities. It is true that a legion of new vocations burns with love for her, each one desiring to consecrate to her his own life in the future Niepokalanow. It is true that at Niepokalanow, under her loving protection, new knights are formed. However, the enemies work with accelerated rhythm..! Could we not begin to expand this activity throughout the whole world? That is, could we not begin the preparation of artillery while the knights prepare the spears and learn to use them?

"It seems to me that we could begin from *The Knight* in the Latin language for the priests and seminarians throughout the world, attracting mainly the secular clergy and the native clergy in the mission countries. In this way, all the clergy of the whole world and also the candidates for the priesthood would be gathered around *The Knight*. Through *The Knight,* those most devoted to the Immaculata would be strengthened in their love, spreading their ardor all around them. Among these would be those who enroll themselves in the M.I. and would be its propagators among their fellowmen. They would begin to translate *The Knight* into their own language, adding facts of local interest in their countries. In such a way, there would spring forth more Marian magazines of a provisory nature, inspired by *The Knight,* ready, in time, to pass into the hands of the *Militia* of the various Niepokalanows which will be founded.

"But even after the foundation of the local Niepokalanow, our members will always need the natives in order to know their ideas, customs and culture. Meanwhile, not a few natives, spurred by love for the Immaculata, through the provisory editions of *The Knight,* will long for the coming of our members, for one of our religious houses, through which we could also have religious vocations. The useful news to be translated in these temporary Marian magazines, should be taken from *The Knight* in the Latin language which should be like an agency of the press of the different editions of *The Knight* throughout the world.

"The importance of *The Knight* in the Latin language is such as to offer benefits to the Polish and Japanese editions of *The Knight.* These, in fact, will be enriched by the news from all parts of the world and by everything that, in the spirit of the M.I., announces the glory of the Immaculata."

In 1934, however, the *Miles Immaculatae* was still an unfulfilled project. Causes beyond Father Maximilian's control had prevented the publication of this magazine. But now he put renewed emphasis on the program of the *Miles* as the preparatory stage for the world apostolate of the M.I. This ardent desire is reflected in a brief but very effective statement contained in a letter to the Guardian of the Polish "City of the Immaculata":

"Are you thinking there of *The Knight* in Latin for the clergy of the whole world? This is one of my most ardent desires."

Perhaps to his passionate desire for a worldwide apostolate by means of the *Miles Immaculatae* must be connected this plea to all his confreres of the Polish Niepokalanow:

"We must not work only for Japan. What about China, India, Turkey, the Arab world and the whole of Africa? This is arid soil which we must till with missionary work. All peoples must be led to Christ. Is it not a vast field of work? And the harvest will be very large. Will we succeed in this enterprise? Not we. But the Immaculata can and will do it through us. Let us abandon ourselves into her immaculate arms: may she do with us as it pleases her. In this we must put no reservations, and in order to do this we must be of one mind and one heart."

In the designs of Providence, the establishment of the *Miles Immaculatae* was to be directly the work of Father Maximilian himself. More years would pass before its realization. In fact, it was only in 1938, when Father Maximilian was again Guardian of Niepokalanow, that the *Miles* began its publication. Written by Father Kolbe himself, it was sent to all the seminaries throughout the world.

# Organization and Growth of the M.I.

The new developments of the M.I., especially after the foundation of Mugenzai No Sono in Japan where, on a smaller scale, the same editorial and apostolic activities as the Polish "City of the Immaculata" were carried out, exacted a greater coordination of efforts and a more efficient organization of the M.I., not only on a national level for Poland alone, but now on an international scale.

Already in 1931, in a letter to Father Florian Koziura, superior of Niepokalanow, Father Maximilian referred to a certain worldwide organization of the M.I.

"With regard to the M.I., I still do not have all the particulars clear. It seems to me, however, that in every nation there should spring up a Niepokalanow in which and through which the Immaculata must reign over everything, even with the most modern inventions, because the inventions must first serve her, and only then serve commerce, industry, sports and so forth.

"Therefore, the press and now even the radio transmissions and the cinema, and in the future any other invention must be directed to enlighten minds and to revivify hearts. The Niepokalanow itself could invent more modern and suitable means and put them into action.... I think that besides *The Knight* and *The Little Knight* for children, with time there could also be other periodic editions—newspapers, weeklies, monthly and quarterly publications, as well as editions that are not subscriptions, which aim at deepening certain topics. For the different provinces of the same nation, if necessary, appendices or special editions could be printed.

"For this reason, all this preaching with the pen must be adapted to the various classes and social conditions. The character that must inform everything is *through the Immaculata,* while the goal must be the conquest of the whole world and of every soul to the Immaculata, and through the Immaculata to the most Sacred Heart of Jesus....

"Imagine, therefore, that with time, in every place, there will not be a soul who does not wear the Miraculous Medal and who does not belong to the M.I. (in accord with the goals of the membership leaflet). In every place there will rise up a group of the M.I.2. It will not have numerous members but rather zealous ones; or better, there will be various circles, grouped according to the professions, conditions and circumstances of the members, whose purpose will be to accomplish within the limits of their possibilities that which we at Niepokalanow do without limits, because we have consecrated all our lives solely to this cause, while those belonging to the groups have other legitimate goals in their lives. Those belonging to the groups will, above all, strive to conform their wills to the will of the Immaculata, that is, to love her as much as possible. Then they will work to diffuse this fire around them according to their possibilities, not only privately, that is, in particular, but socially, that is, in society; by finding suitable means, studying the results and improving them according to the experience and methods of acting, so that the Immaculata, through their action, may conquer the hearts of all those whom it is possible to reach. Every instruction, directive and help will be prepared by Niepokalanow where there will be many priests, ready to go to the various sections of the country."

But in 1934, during the second stay of Father Maximilian in Japan, the necessity of a more perfect international organization of the M.I. was more keenly felt.

The Brothers of the Polish Niepokalanow asked in their letters the advice of Father Maximilian and submitted to his approval new proposals and new apostolic initiatives. On account of this, from the letters written by Father Maximilian during his second stay in Japan, there emerge precise elements for a more perfect organization of the M.I. It was these details that, after the death of the founder, would be treasured by the superiors for the draft of the general and already definitive bylaws of the M.I.

First of all, the founder made it clear that the division of the M.I. into three degrees should not create confusion among the members.

"The designations M.I.1 and M.I.2 arose from among us, and for that reason we can formulate them as we wish. Nevertheless, following the subdivision used in ecclesiastical legislation, it would be better to consider the M.I.1 as a 'Pious Union' in accord with the law (either juridical or extra-juridical), and the M.I.2 as a 'Sodality,' that is, an association with organization."

The cities of the Immaculata, which are ruled by their own internal statutes, and almost all of whose

members have made a fourth vow of complete dedication to the cause of the Immaculata through obedience,
must be considered M.I. of the third degree. Groups or
secondary centers of the M.I., which have a particular
form of organization for the apostolate according to
local exigencies, can be considered M.I. of the second
degree. But all of them bear the common denominator of
"Pious Union," which is the M.I. of the first degree
properly so called, and as such are canonically
approved by the ecclesiastical authority. But while the
number of the organized groups may be limited, and
even more that of the cities of the Immaculata, every
effort must be directed to the diffusion of the "Pious
Union" and of its essential spirit of perfect consecration
to the Immaculata.

"It is not necessary," wrote Father Maximilian, "to
be anxious over the fact that the M.I. organization has a
small number of members, although every center tends
toward organization. Of greater interest is the conquest
of all souls and of the other Catholic associations for the
Immaculata, rather than the erection of a new association alongside the others. It is not worth the trouble to
be in a hurry to establish organized centers here or
there. What counts is the diffusion of the 'Pious Union,'
that is, of the first degree M.I. That is also easier and
more convenient since the enrollments may be sent
directly to the 'City of the Immaculata.'"

For the conquest of souls for the Immaculata, stress
was laid on the apostolate organized by the single cities
of the Immaculata which Father Kolbe was planning to
establish in every nation, putting them in connection
with each other through an International Center of the
M.I. Each "City of the Immaculata" was to divide its
activity as follows: a) internal organization of the city;
b) organization for the external apostolate in the same
nation; c) organization for relations with others outside
the country, that is, with those members who, although

living in other countries, speak the same language. The guidelines given by Father Maximilian in this regard are crystal clear:

"Even here in Japan we will introduce the division of activities of the M.I.: 1) internal activities of Niepokalanow; 2) external activities in the nation; 3) external activities for [Japanese-speaking persons] outside the nation. Experience shows us how this can be done in practice. Therefore, I desire always to know the projects and the results of the Polish Niepokalanow as it has been established in monthly meetings; thus, we will avoid repeating twice the same experiments.

"The name *Central* or *General Office* has no importance: everything depends on how much activity the Central Office or Management develops, for example, worldwide, national, provincial, local. A certain confusion is caused by the double meaning of *foreign:* one may be referring to emigrants far away from one's country, or to the native inhabitants of a different nation. Every Niepokalanow (Polish, Japanese, Indian, Chinese, etc.) must also provide for its own emigrants in whatever place they live. On the other hand, the local Niepokalanow, if one exists, must provide for the inhabitants of each nation, or [if there is no local Niepokalanow] the International Center must do so directly. The first concern of the International Center will be the foundation of a local Niepokalanow. In this way, the International Center will have direct jurisdiction over all the nations in which there is no local Niepokalanow, but indirect jurisdiction where cities of the Immaculata will have been established. With regard to the International Center, the word *foreign* does not exist, because this center embraces the world. It will seek to coordinate the apostolate of the M.I. and always to improve its organization."

Thus in a few sentences, Father Maximilian outlines the entire organization of the M.I. However, he viewed even the most efficient organization as void of meaning if the members to whom the apostolate is entrusted were to lose the spirit of consecration to the Immaculata. Thus, having launched the grandiose concept of an International Center and of a "City of the Immaculata" in each country of the globe, he again goes back to the source of the apostolate: the love of the Immaculata.

Father Maximilian customarily celebrated his feastday on October 12. In 1935, for his feastday, the Brothers of Niepokalanow sent their best wishes, as usual, on time. On the following day, Father Maximilian answered with a letter revealing his heart on fire with love for the Immaculata which he wished to instill in his confreres:

"Dearest in the Immaculata: Fathers, Brothers, novices, aspirants!

"I received your letter with 180 signatures. May the Immaculata reward the signers and grant to all that which you wished to me, that is, to conquer the greatest number of souls to her.

"I have much trust in your prayers. I have much need of them because I am convinced that I still do too little in regard to what I could do for the cause of the Immaculata, and even that little is done badly. The concern is for souls, and for the greatest glory due to God. We should publish a pamphlet concerning the objectives of the M.I.: the purpose of Niepokalanow, and the reason for so many workers at Niepokalanow, so that the fervor of our activities will not weaken and that the goal of Niepokalanow will be always more precise and more clear.

"We must always develop more fervently and intensely the action of conquering souls for the Immaculata and for the M.I.

"Even in Poland not all belong to the M.I. or even to the Church.... There are many separated brethren, heretics, Protestants, Jews....

"We must strengthen and further ever more the Japanese Niepokalanow because the number of priests is insufficient for the apostolate among the nonbelievers. The few members we have are preparing themselves for the future apostolate.

"It is a pity....

"There is not enough time to study the language in order to draw personally close to the nonbelievers, to take care of the correspondence...(and then there is also my health)....

"We must always remember that Poland and Japan are not the only nations that exist under the sun. An immense number of hearts beat beyond these bound- aries. And so, when will the Knights of the Immaculata go among them? When will they found their Niepokalanows for the whole world? When will they lead all the hearts of men to the most Sacred Heart of Jesus by the white ladder of the Immaculata, that which our holy Father Francis saw?...

"We must think of these Niepokalanows so that we never stop in this holy work as sometimes happens in certain institutions after the passing of the first fervor. We must see to it that each Niepokalanow draws ever closer to the Immaculata and becomes always more hers. May she always act more freely in souls through her *cities.*

"It is necessary to coordinate and to harmonize the activities so that, with one organized effort, these Niepokalanows can reach all souls, even those lost on some small island or among the mountains, and lead them all to the Immaculata.

"We must also see to it that the Immaculata is always better known. We must make known to every soul, through humble prayer and study, the relations of the Immaculata with God the Father, with God the Son, with God the Holy Spirit—with the most Holy Trinity— with Jesus, with the angels and with ourselves.

"It is something that we will never succeed in exhausting. The results of this work will then have to be presented to all and each one in particular through preaching, the press, radio, etc. We still know too little of how much the Immaculata has done for humanity, from the first moment of her existence until today. Every grace has passed through her hands!

"What a marvelous bibliography would be that of the *Acts of the Immaculata in the Whole World*....

"And we will always have to add new volumes.

"All of this must be presented to souls; care must be taken to nourish them with the Immaculata so that they may assimilate and live the life of the Immaculata. Then we will love Jesus with the heart of the Immaculata.

"Every thought, action and suffering of the Immaculata was a most perfect act of love toward God, toward Jesus. We must, therefore, say this to all the souls and to each one in particular, to those who live today on earth and to those who will live. Say it with example, with the living word, the printed word, through the radio, painting, sculpture, etc. Say what and how the Immaculata in concrete circumstances of actual life and in every state had thought, spoken, and did to ignite on earth the most perfect love of her heart toward that most Sacred Heart of God.

"Considering all that I have said above—with my hand on my heart—can I say that I did all that which was in my power to do, so that I neglected nothing and that I did everything in the best possible way? Oh, no!

"Therefore I thank you very much for the prayers and I ask for more prayers so that *sweetly and strongly* I may serve the Immaculata.

"And that all and each one in particular may surpass me a thousand times. And I, that I may surpass them in turn yet a million times, and that they may then surpass me a billion times in a noble race.

"It is not a question that I, this or that one does more, but that the most be done for the Immaculata. She must take possession of every soul as soon as possible in the most perfect way, to live and act in each soul, to love the Divine Heart, the Divine Love, God, in each soul.

"It is a matter of deepening more fervently the love of the creature toward the Creator.

"In the Immaculata, your co-knight, and in our holy Father, St. Francis, your confrere, Maximilian M. Kolbe."

From 1933 on, when he was entrusted with the task of promoting and extending the apostolate of the M.I. everywhere, Father Maximilian strove also to introduce it into the apostolate of his own Order. In 1935, while in Japan, he submitted first to his Minister Provincial, and then to his Minister General, a proposal for consecrating the entire Order to the Immaculata. He requested that this proposal be presented and discussed in the next General Chapter, which was scheduled to be held in Rome in 1936. The wise motives behind his request made their way into the minds of the superiors who were spurred on to efficacious reflections:

"We could point out that the aim of the consecration is the rebirth of the Order.... What some affirm and think of the antiquity of the Order is not true: that it has grown old because of its great age; for the spirit does not experience old age. Only the forgetting of one's ideals on the one hand, and the failure to adapt ourselves immediately to the changed conditions of the times and circumstances on the other hand, bring on the weakening of life and the inevitable process of shriveling up to the point of becoming a dwarf. To achieve the rebirth of the Order, even the wisest prescriptions supported by severe sanctions are not enough. Supernatural grace is needed for the sanctification of the religious. Now the Immaculata is the Mediatrix of all graces and therefore the closer a soul draws to the Immaculata, the stronger will be the life he/she lives. By complete consecration we approach the Immaculata in the most perfect way.

"Therefore, consecration to the Immaculata, not only of the individual religious or of the individual friaries but of the whole Order, will bring about its rebirth. And today the spirit of the Immaculata wonderfully begins to vivify those members who are consecrated to her in a particular way. Let us remember that the vow to approach always more closely to the Immaculata was expressed in the General Chapter of 1719, when it was decreed that devotion to the Immaculata should be fostered and implemented day by day."

The consecration of the entire Order to the Immaculata was favorably viewed by the Fathers present at the General Chapter of 1936. They decreed the requested consecration, and established that it should be annually renewed on the Feast of the Immaculate Conception.

Thus on December 8, 1936, the spirit of the M.I. entered officially into the Order to vivify the entire membership, which did then indeed experience a spiritual revival both in regard to vocations and in regard to various forms of the Marian apostolate, as can be documented from other sources.

# Return to Niepokalanow

On May 26, 1936, Father Maximilian left Japan on board the Italian ship *Vittoria,* and after a very short stop in Italy, he returned to Poland. He had come to Europe for the sole purpose of participating in the Provincial Chapter. Clad with the rare dispositions of perfect obedience, he was ready to go wherever the new Provincial would send him. The Provincial Chapter elected him, after six years of absence, the Guardian of Niepokalanow. He received this obedience without any objection, although the separation from his beloved Mugenzai No Sono must have cost him much grief. Father Maximilian's health was the motivation behind this appointment.

"Between 1935 and 1936, in fact, on account of the hot and humid climate of Japan, he was afflicted again with tuberculosis. He had frequent hemoptyses. Both in the morning and in the afternoon he was obliged to stay in bed."

In the hope of an improvement after a period of rest, his election as Guardian seemed to have been the unanimous desire of the members of the Polish "City of the Immaculata." We are informed by Father Anselm Kubit that "although the other superiors of Niepokalanow had been excellent religious, well prepared for the new form of apostolate, nevertheless the Brothers said of each of them: 'He is not Father Maximilian.'"

Brother Thaddeus Maj stated: "His return from Japan was anxiously awaited. Everywhere he passed, he sowed peace, harmony, reciprocal love; he dispelled doubts, infused courage."

This new commitment, confirmed by the Chapter of 1939, coincided with the last five years of his life. This period is called by one of his Polish biographers, Morcinek, the golden age of Niepokalanow because it marked its greatest splendor and its greatest achievements. Especially *The Knight* with its circulation of nearly a million copies monthly and *The Little Journal* became a dominant factor in the spiritual life of Poland. But what is more important, in this period, a deeper and inner reality underscored the tremendous growth of Niepokalanow. Brother Benvenuto Stryjewski, in his memoirs, paralleled the life of Jesus and Father Maximilian thus:

"As Jesus, Father Maximilian devoted the last three years of his superiorship to the spiritual and religious formation of his subjects. He wanted them to carry out the apostolate thoroughly imbued with his own ideals. As though he foresaw his own passion and death, he endeavored to anticipate the times. The many occupations and preoccupations which weighed upon him as superior did not prevent him from caring for the spiritual direction of his sons. Any occasion offered him the cue to teach us a new truth about the Immaculata, to form and make us ready to withstand the difficulties awaiting us. It seemed as though he was able to unveil the future, and clearly foresaw his own death. As Jesus confided to the Apostles the secrets of the kingdom, so Father Maximilian confided to us the secrets of Niepokalanow."

Forty-two year old Father Maximilian, though young, was a father to his confreres. With St. Paul he could truthfully say: "For although you have ten thousand instructors in Christ, yet you have not many fathers. For in Christ Jesus, through the Gospel, I have begotten you" (1 Cor. 4:15). It is true that even from the

Far East Father Kolbe remained in constant touch with his fellow-religious by exhorting, advising, spurring them on to new apostolic initiatives, but more than ever in these last years he was for Niepokalanow the founder, the director and, above all, the father.

## Spiritual Director

The main topic of the Chapter of 1936 was Niepokalanow. That the "friary-city" during the six years of Father Maximilian's stay in Japan had reached a peak of success under the leadership of Father Koziura who was in turn wisely guided by Father Kolbe, as has been proven by the copious correspondence addressed to him, was an evident fact.

Niepokalanow had also received recognition from both religious and ecclesiastical authorities. These prevailing positive factors, however, had not washed away a residue of criticism still persisting among some confreres. They resented above all the lifestyle of Niepokalanow which was so striking a contrast with that of the other communities where the traditional schemes of the Franciscan Rule were held unchanged.

The testimony of Father Cornelius Czupryk, ex-Provincial, permits some insights into the nature of this opposition:

"During the Provincial Chapter of 1936, Father N. N. expressed himself bitterly and aggressively against the practices of the religious life at Niepokalanow. He threatened a bitter discussion between the supporters and the adversaries of Niepokalanow. The agitation was great. Father Maximilian maintained a balance and a truly heroic calm, despite the fact that such questions mainly regarded him. He just repeated: 'It will be as the Immaculata wills.' He was never unkind toward Father N. N. and never reproved him."

Fortunately, this criticism persisted only sporadically, and it is attested that those present at the Chapter expressed appreciation for Niepokalanow. Their comment, synthesized in these terms: "Niepokalanow is the glory of this Franciscan Province," was the best reward Father Maximilian could receive for all the sufferings he had borne with so much humility and meekness. In reassuming the government of Niepokalanow, its founder, in order to conserve the lofty status reached by the "city," had to lay stress on these objectives:

—to give a perfect spiritual formation to the numerous vocations who daily flocked into Nicpokalanow;

— to further a better organization of the apostolate of the press.

Empowered by the decisions of the Chapter and the lawful superiors, Father Maximilian totally devoted himself to the task of safeguarding the purpose of the Polish "City of the Immaculata"; the sanctification of the members in the spirit of the M.I., and the pursuit of the purpose of the M.I. without limit and with every legitimate means.

In view of this, the most desirable thing to do was to further the consecration to the Immaculate Virgin of all those living within the walls of the mystical city. Without delay, starting from September, 1936, Father Maximilian did not let any occasion go by—religious professions, solemnities, recreations, walks—to instill in his confreres and disciples the true spirit of the M.I. At times, in place of the morning meditation, he would hold particular conferences prompted by the necessity of correcting errors and giving salutary counsels. His leadership met with much satisfaction among superiors and confreres alike and is verified by numerous testimonies. The new Provincial, Father Anselm Kubit, testified:

"In 1936, Father Kolbe returned from Japan to Poland. All the capitular Fathers noticed the failing condition of his health. Therefore, by the will of the capitular Fathers, it was proposed that he remain in the country. He was elected superior of Niepokalanow with the particular task of taking personal care of the formation of the young religious."

Father Cornelius Czupryk brings into clear relief the pedagogical method of Father Maximilian which was entirely based on the necessity and efficacy of divine grace:

"On Saturday, instead of the morning meditations, he gave conferences on Marian topics to the religious. When he spoke of the Immaculata, he never ran short of material. He spoke with such great emotion and in such a disarming way, while at the same time so profoundly and so logically that it was easy to understand, and thus held the attention of his listeners. At Niepokalanow in Poland, he introduced the use of a practice from Japan, that in meeting one another the Brothers should greet each other with the word: 'Maria.' In observing his life, one could see that there was no sacrifice that he would not have been ready to make for Maria.

"In his conversations, he willingly led the participants to subjects of faith. His manner of approaching the others was so delicate that one was not even aware of getting into theological subjects. From these conversations, we inferred that he was wholly penetrated and animated by supernatural principles."

Father Florian Koziura, the immediate predecessor of Father Maximilian, expressed his consensus thus:

"He himself directed the meditations in common of the friary, and in speaking to the Brothers, he said what his heart dictated. He did this twice a week. We took notes on these meditations and a collection of them is conserved in the friary. From his talks flowed forth a singular warmth and affection for the most holy Madonna. He loved the prayers in common and private prayers; he recommended saying the rosary daily."

Brother Kosz, voicing the sentiments of his fellow religious, declared:

"He greatly loved the meditation. Regularly he made meditations in common with the professed of solemn vows, according to the following method:

"He read a passage from a book and then allowed a sufficiently long period of time for reflection. Instead, in the Saturday conferences, in those which preceded the feasts, on feast days and on the vigils of the feasts of the Madonna, as well as on other occasions, he developed at length topics on religious life and, above all, Marian topics....

"He was ready to help his fellow religious to resolve their spiritual doubts. In the afternoon hours, lines of Brothers took their turns speaking to Father Maximilian in his cell. He was particularly concerned about those Brothers who wavered in their religious vocation. He did everything in his power to make them return to the right path so that they might remain in the Order and keep their vows. As an example, I cite the case of Brother G., a perpetually professed Brother, who, despite the efforts of Father Maximilian, left the Order after solemn vows. Father Kolbe was deeply saddened by his situation."

The impact, the effectiveness, the driving force of Father Maximilian's example are beautifully described by Brother Luke Kuszba:

"An expression of his living faith was his Eucharistic and Marian devotion. Often during the course of the day he visited Jesus in the tabernacle. He said that our strength was there, that there was the source of our sanctification. In all the events of life, he saw the will of God. This substantive 'will' he always wrote with a capital letter, at times with red ink among other black letters. An effect of the lively faith of the Servant of God was his unchangeable happiness. I never remember having seen the Servant of God depressed. When the affairs at Niepokalanow were going well, he rejoiced with all his heart and thanked the Immaculata with fervor for the graces received. When things went badly, even then he was happy and said to us: 'Why become sad? Does not the Immaculata know everything?' In fact, the life of Father Maximilian, notwithstanding sufferings and many difficulties, radiated a cloud of happiness. When observing him during adoration of the Most Blessed Sacrament, it was not possible to take one's eyes off him, so fascinating was the sight. During adoration, he was usually seen kneeling before the steps of the altar, not resting himself on anything. More than once I observed Father Maximilian while he celebrated holy Mass. He seemed to me to be radiant with an unearthly light; he was filled with humility and recollection."

Another Brother, Vitaliano Milosz, discloses his impressions with edifying clarity:

"The *principal* idea of the life of the Servant of God was that of winning each soul to the Immaculata. One perceived in him the living image of a most fervent devotee of Mary. Love for her and the deepening of such love must be the purpose of the life of man. Often he spoke of the privileges of Mary, and especially of her Immaculate Conception—the privilege most pleasing to her. He underlined her privilege of being the Mediatrix of all graces, as well as that of her Divine Maternity, privileges inaccessible to our reason. He desired that the Church proclaim as a dogma the privilege of the universal mediation and the Assumption of Mary. Almost all the conferences that he gave us centered around Marian truths and they tended to solidify our devotion to Mary. He stressed the necessity of the apostolate through the Immaculata since this is the shortest, most direct and easiest way to know and love God. To convert and to sanctify oneself, the grace of God is indispensable and the Immaculata is the Mediatrix of grace. Even in the articles published in *Rycerz,* he tended to reawaken trust in the Mother of God. On the occasion of the feast of the most holy Virgin, he organized a religious festival in her honor. Once before the war of 1939, he organized a solemn festival in the Roman Catholic House of Warsaw. The conferences of the Servant of God, which centered on the theme of the Immaculata, never wearied us because he always threw new light on the truths already known from other sources, or proposed new thoughts, new ways of understanding them."

Less detailed, although not less striking, is the information supplied by Reverend Vladimir Obidzinski, pastor of Teresin:

"Father Maximilian was superior at Niepokalanow from 1936 until 1941, when he was arrested. Moreover, he was editor of various publications which were printed at Niepokalanow. The Servant of God fulfilled these duties conscientiously and according to the spirit of God. He also tried to inculcate this spirit into his Brother-collaborators through his little discourses and conferences. At some of these conferences to his religious, I was also present. The Servant of God never spoke to me of the difficulties encountered in the development of his works. I know that he was a man of great initiatives and that he realized them with the help of the Immaculata."

The all-embracing interest of Father Kolbe for the material and spiritual well-being of his religious extended even to the recreational activities. Three playgrounds with facilities for basketball, volleyball, tennis, ping-pong, billiards and especially chess gladdened the recreations of hundreds of religious. Not even a small orchestra was missing. Father Kolbe organized the tournaments between the various groups and sections.

A rich photographic documentation portrays these recreations during which Father Maximilian himself joined in a football game or played chess or participated in a snack with his confreres.

## The Immaculata Is Our Insurer

The years which preceded the outbreak of the German-Polish hostilities were the most rich in spiritual fruits for Niepokalanow and the time of greatest enthusiasm for the City of Mary. The echo of such religious and social activity spread far beyond the boundaries of Poland, although Poland itself was its foremost beneficiary.

On the occasion of an exhibit of the press in Warsaw, the whole editorial production of Niepokalanow
was displayed. Its numerous publications captured the
participants' attention and admiration. Yet the center of
attention was Father Kolbe himself.

The anti-Catholics themselves were spellbound by
the prodigious activity of the humble Franciscan and
even though they did not accept his principles and
ideas, nevertheless they did not hesitate to extol his
genius and extraordinary daring. As a consequonce,
Niepokalanow became the goal of visits on the part of
personalities from near and far. Civil authorities and
diplomats shared their interest for the singular "city"
with members of the Church hierarchy, such as the
primate of Poland, Cardinal Kakowski; his successor,
Cardinal Hlond; and the apostolic nuncios, their Excel-
lencies Bishop Marmaggi and Bishop Cortesi.

Of all the visits, the most momentous was that paid
by the Minister General of the Order, Most Reverend
Bede M. Hess, which took place in the summer of 1936
on the occasion of the Provincial Chapter. Those were
unforgettable days. Finally, having overcome all the
difficulties, the successor of St. Francis, who had
approved in the person of his predecessor the foundation of Niepokalanow, and followed all the stages of its
development, had come now to bless the work and the
workers. The impression he received was beyond compare, as this piece of his testimony gives evidence:

"I first met Father Kolbe on the occasion of the Provincial Chapter of 1936 at which I presided as General.

"In the first session, the Father Guardian of Warsaw
referred to the friary of Niepokalanow in these terms:
'There shines in this friary a truly Franciscan spirit,
fervent devotion to the Immaculata, great zeal, the
greatest poverty and simplicity.'

"At that time I was two times at Niepokalanow and I
immediately saw that I was seeing a work blessed by
the Lord, a city over which Mary Immaculate reigned. It
consisted of fifteen wooden buildings, with only one

brick building in which 700 religious, wearing the Franciscan habit, led a spiritually and materially active life.

"I was able to see with my own eyes how true was the report of the Father Guardian of Warsaw. The spirit of charity among the religious was intense; there reigned a great peace and on their faces shone a serene *Franciscan happiness*.

"They greeted each other with the name of 'Mary'; so much so that it seemed to me that I was in the environment of the true spirit of the primitive days of the seraphic Order. In Niepokalanow there was realized to the fullest the maxim: *ora et labora: pray and work,* because besides perpetual daily and nightly adoration of the most Blessed Sacrament and the other common acts of prayer, there was a double shift of work, day and night.

"The religious spirit of those friars was very intense and in them was unlimited trust in Providence and in the Immaculata...."

At this point in his testimony, Father Hess showed a certain embarrassment recalling a norm of prudence he had suggested to Father Maximilian: after having visited all the pavilions, he urged the dear founder to provide himself with an insurance policy for the protection of the buildings and the equipment. Promptly and with utter simplicity, Father Maximilian answered:

"Our insurance policy is the Immaculata: Niepokalanow arose with the offerings sent to the Immaculata; it realized its growth through the contribution of 'Providence's safe.' For this reason, the best insurance is the protection of the heavenly Queen."

# Anticipation of a Trust

It was January, 1937. Nothing could yet be foreseen of the war of 1939. Relations among European leaders seemed to bespeak peace rather than a forthcoming conflict.

An episode reminiscent of our divine Redeemer on the eve of His passion reveals how the future was also known well enough by Father Maximilian. A Brother tells us:

"It was Sunday, January 10, 1937. The community had planned to see a kind of play or tableau about the nativity of our Savior, called 'Jaselka.' The entertainment was to take place in a suitable hall after supper and was to be staged by the lay brothers and the postulants. It was anxiously awaited by all. During supper Father Maximilian announced the play, while leaving full freedom to the professed in solemn vows who preferred to do so, to stay behind with him in the refectory. The majority went to the play. Several, however—the narrator of this scene, and Brothers Hilary, Camillus, Luke, Emil and others, together with Father Pius Bartosik, stayed in the refectory with Father Maximilian who immediately said: 'Let's sit around the table in the order of profession: we will have a confidential meeting.'

"We did so. To the right of Father Guardian sat Father Pius, and all around the lay brothers in order of religious profession.

"'My dear brothers,' began Father Maximilian, 'for the present I am still with you. You love me and I love you in return. However, you must realize that I will not be here always. I will die, and you will stay. Before departing from this world, I would like to leave you a remembrance. Desiring to do only what the Immaculata wants, I asked that only those who wished to should remain behind of their own choice. This is proof that the Immaculata wants you to be here.

"'You call me Father Guardian, and that is what I am. You call me Father Director, and that is correct, because I am that in the friary and typography. But what am I really? I am your *Father,* really and truly, even more than your carnal fathers who gave you mortal life. But from me you have received the spiritual life, the divine life, your religious vocation that rises above temporal life. Is that not so?'

"'Oh yes, Father, undoubtedly,' said one. 'Without you, without *The Knight,* without Niepokalanow, we would not be in the Order!'

"'Reading *The Knight of the Immaculata,* I came to know the Franciscan apostolate,' said another.

"*The Knight of the Immaculata* made my religious vocation bloom and grow strong,' said a third.

"And each one in turn started to recall his own personal experience. Father Maximilian listened to them with a smile. 'Therefore, I am really your Father. Do not call me guardian or director, but simply Father. This is the reason I address you with the familiar pronouns "thou" and "thee," for you are my children.'

"There was a moment of silence. Father Maximilian seemed now to be worried, as if he were prevented by his humility from communicating something he had at heart. Then he began to speak again very shyly. 'My children, you are well aware that I will not always be with you. That is why I would like to leave you something, to tell you something in remembrance of me.'

"'By all means, Father. Tell us!' they exclaimed, holding their breaths. Visibly moved with emotion, Father Maximilian went on.

"'If you knew, my dear Brothers, how happy I am! My heart overflows with happiness and peace, as much as one is able to be happy on this earth. In spite of the troubles and anxieties of daily life, somewhere at the bottom of my heart there is always this peace, this joy that cannot be expressed in human words.'

"'My Brothers, love the Immaculata, love the Immaculata. She will make you happy. Give her your confidence, without limits. Not everyone is privileged to understand the Immaculata; it is given only to those who ask for this grace through prayer. The Immaculata is the Mother of God. Do you understand what it means to say Mother of God? Really, truly Mother of God! Only the Holy Spirit is able to make known his spouse to whomever and however He wills. I would like to tell you one more thing...but I think this is enough.'

"At this point, Father Maximilian gazed at us all as though he feared something. But we earnestly begged him to speak and to keep nothing from us.

"'I told you, my Brothers, that I am very happy and that my soul is flooded with joy. Do you know why? Because heaven has been promised to me in all certitude. My sons, love the Immaculata, love the Immaculata, as much as you know and can.'

"He spoke with such emotion that tears sprang to his eyes. There followed a momentary silence that no one except Father Maximilian dared to break.

"'There it is, Brothers. That will be sufficient for you....'

"Their entreaties were touching.

"'Speak, Father; perhaps we will never have another *Last Supper* like this one.'

"After a moment's hesitation, he spoke a few words more.

"'Since you ask me with much insistence, I will tell you one more thing. This happened in Japan. Now, I will tell you nothing more, so do not question me further.'

"Some of those present coaxed him in vain to uncover a little more of his secret, but Father Maximilian kept silent, plunged in deep meditation. When we had finished asking him questions, he spoke very paternally.

"'I have disclosed my secret to you in order that it might be a strength and support in the tests that are ahead of you. There will be sufferings, temptations; perhaps you will be haunted by discouragement. Remember then what I have told you and learn to be ready for the greatest sacrifices, ready for all that the Immaculata will ask of you. My sons, do not desire extraordinary things, but simply to perform the will of the Immaculata. May her will be done, not ours.

"'You must tell no one what I have just confided to you. As long as I live, say nothing to anyone.'

"There was so much insistence in his voice that each Brother promised."

The life of Father Maximilian has been enriched with extraordinary supernatural gifts. Among these, two are of paramount importance: first the vision of the two crowns symbolizing sanctity and martyrdom which occurred in his childhood at the beginning of his spiritual life; second, the assurance of his eternal salvation which he received in the fullness of maturity, most probably at the time of the intense spiritual trials of his missionary life in Japan. The Church does not pronounce herself about the supernatural gifts of the saint, especially when it is a matter of private revelations as in the present case. Private revelations are given a rather negative consideration during the investigation of the entire spiritual life of a Servant of God, since they could offer ground for suspecting psychic disorders in the person subject to such phenomena. The alleged case was brought out during the examination of the heroic virtues of Father Maximilian, by the devil's advocate who suggested the hypothesis of "a certain psychological ground of doubtful nature," naturally psychopathic, which could have given rise to the two extraordinary facts.

However, the "psychological ground of doubtful nature" had to be excluded from Father Maximilian's life, since his perfectly sound personality never betrayed spiritual derangement. Among the testimonies scrupulously scrutinized at the processes were those of the doctors in charge of Father Maximilian who were unanimous in recognizing his perfect psychic soundness. Regarding this, Dr. Stanislaus Wasowicz, the doctor in charge of Father Maximilian in Niepokalanow, stated:

"Mentally and physically, he was a most normal person, adequately disposed toward life. I never found in the Servant of God any psychic disorder, related either to the intellect, to the will or to the sentiment."

Dr. James Yasuro Fukahori, the doctor in charge of Father Maximilian in Nagasaki, presented a diagnosis exalting his virtues, the practice of which must have cost him continual self-denial:

"Obviously he had an irascible temperament. In the course of a conversation, he betrayed his nervous and vehement nature, although through self-mastery he was able to overcome himself. It seems to me that he had more a delicate than a scrupulous conscience."

Prince Drucki-Lubecki, the great benefactor of Father Maximilian, describes him in a concise but penetrating manner:

"He was calm, serene, very well-balanced. He was always the same, more or less tired, but of a pleasant disposition. He never gave sign of any hallucinations."

Even the two physicians at the concentration camp of Auschwitz were explicitly interviewed regarding the psychic soundness of Father Maximilian, so as to exclude the possibility that the generous offering of his life on behalf of a father of a family was the result of an uncontrolled act.

Dr. Nicetas Wlodarski testified:

"I became acquainted with the Servant of God in the concentration camp and found him to be a very brave person, psychically sound in the most positive sense. I never noticed in him any nervous symptoms or morbid scruples."

Dr. Rudolph Diem, a doctor of the hospital of Auschwitz, asserted:

"The Servant of God was a man of serene character, well-balanced, of great psychic soundness."

The above testimonies enable us to conclude that the extraordinary phenomena verified in the life of the saint can be considered true supernatural gifts which the Holy Spirit bestows on virtuous and privileged souls. Even if the assent to be given to these supernatural favors is only one of human faith, nevertheless it is supported by the consideration of a life marked by the progressive and constant exercise of Christian virtues, and religious perfection.

The previously-mentioned revelation which Father Maximilian confided to some of his confreres casts light on his firm resolution not to pass over in silence any of Mary's favors, even those experienced and enjoyed in the intimacy of his prayer life, in order to bind to himself those who, after him, would have to continue the "work of the Immaculata."

As Jesus, approaching the hour of His passion, multiplied the revelations of the Father, so to arouse in His disciples the desire to know Him—"show us the Father and that will be enough for us" (Jn. 14:8)—likewise did Father Maximilian do regarding the Immaculata.

Toward the end of May, 1937, Father Maximilian was walking through the walkways of Niepokalanow surrounded by a group of religious. All of a sudden, one of them with utter simplicity asked: "Father, show us the Immaculata!"

Rather surprised, Father Maximilian stopped, and looking at the Brother who had asked this question, replied smiling:

"Do you wish, dear son, that the Immaculata be revealed to you? Here she is. See all this? All these houses, and all the machines which print so many magazines for her glory? And especially so many...many hearts which in Niepokalanow are totally dedicated to her? Here is the Immaculata.

"And what of the Japanese Mugenzai No Sono? Some years ago it did not exist and now it does. Look, look then, my son, at the Immaculata in her works; look how much her mercy has done. And then, my son, after some time, you will contemplate her in heaven."

## The M.I. and Russia

Throughout his priestly life, Father Maximilian cherished the project, so beset with difficulties, of introducing the apostolate of the M.I. in Russia. He felt in his soul a great longing to bring through the Immaculata, Christ—his life, his love, his all—to this country. Already in 1926, when he was still a patient in the sanatorium of Zakopane, in a letter to his brother Alphonse, he expressed his concern for Russia in these terms:

"My dear brother, it would be well to print the membership leaflet of the *Militia* in Russian. Brother Albert knows this language and the typeface can be borrowed from Mr. Redziki."

In October, 1932, Father Maximilian considered the possibility of a journey to Moscow in the company of his Provincial. "If it is possible," he wrote to him, "we could stop several days in Moscow in order to study better the environment and the possibility of beginning the publication of a Russian edition of *The Knight*." The idea of Russia haunted him, too, on his journey from Japan to Poland in 1933. Moreover, he kept spurring on his closest collaborators to do their utmost to prepare suitable material for the eventual purpose of implanting the M.I. in Russia.

For this purpose he had the membership leaflet of the M.I. printed in Lithuanian, Latvian and Russian and began to send the Polish edition of *The Knight* to Lithuania and Latvia. In this way, he intended to lay the groundwork for a seminary in Lithuania for gathering vocations from the Baltic countries in the spirit of the M.I. for the apostolate in Russia.

To publish the magazine in Russian was the burning desire of his life. From a prediction he made shortly before the war broke out, it seems as though the future of Russia was somewhat known to him. In February, 1937, in Rome, the primary center of the Pious Union organized the official commemoration of the twentieth anniversary of the foundation of the M.I. The main speaker was Father Maximilian himself who had come to Rome to study and consider together with the Minister General of the Order, the possibility of organizing an International Center of the M.I. in Rome. In the course of the conference, after having given a report of the apostolate carried out by the M.I. during twenty years, the praiseworthy founder of the M.I., almost on a prophetic note, made this declaration:

"We do not believe the day to be far off, or a mere dream, when the statue of the Immaculata will be enthroned by her Knights in the very heart of Moscow."

These words were spoken to a large audience, but a confidence which was passed over in silence at that commemorative conference was revealed to one of the first seven of the M.I., Father Quiricus Pignalberi. Here is the text of the testimony he made before the judges at the Paduan process:

"Father Maximilian came to see me in the friary of Piglio on February 7 through 9, 1937. From a conversation we had in my room, I came to know all the difficulties of his work in Poland as well as in Japan. He, however, observed that many difficulties had been overcome, that in the center of Moscow a statue of the Immaculata would be set up, but that first we must pass through a trial of blood. I understood that this would occur in the 'City of the Immaculata.' He mentioned this trial of blood again in Rome a few days later. That was on February 11, a feast of the M.I., after a commemorative program in honor of the Immaculata held in the friary of the Twelve Holy Apostles. Not only that: I recall well it was then that he said a trial of blood was actually necessary. This decisive announcement disquieted me, but he kept insisting that things would go well this way; moreover, that it was really necessary."

Was Father Maximilian foretelling the war touched off by the Nazis which would take the lives of many of the friars of Niepokalanow? Or was he foreseeing a more bloody trial in which the mystical "City" would become a place of martyrdom for confessors of the Faith? Not knowing the future, we wish at least to share Father Maximilian's longing that Niepokalanow be always resplendent for its conformity with the will of the Immaculata, and that it be granted the grace of hastening the triumph of the Immaculata over atheism.

# Father Maximilian
# at the Radio at Warsaw

An apostle of the caliber of Father Maximilian could not fail to employ the radio as a means of apostolate. Mention has already been made of his attempts to install a radio transmitter within Niepokalanow. But even before this station began functioning, Father Maximilian endeavored to obtain periodic broadcasts of Niepokalanow news on the government radio. But the presence of Masonic elements among the officials prevented the request from being granted. But in spite of this opposition, the popularity enjoyed by Niepokalanow empowered its founder to broadcast on the tenth anniversary of the foundation of the "Marian City." On December 8, 1937, the founder of the M.I. went on the radio to address the Polish nation for the first time. With words that were simple and humble yet forceful and interesting, he gave an overview of the history of the M.I. and Niepokalanow. The text of his speech, still extant, glows with religious enthusiasm.

"What has Niepokalanow achieved in this decade?" began Father Maximilian. "We are aware that compared with the atheist *Cominform* our work is very little. But in proportion to our possibilities, we have to recognize that with the help of the Immaculata we have carried out our work with zeal, not with a view to personal gain, but only out of love for the Immaculata. Today the members of the M.I. in Poland and among the Polish emigrants are 600,000; *The Knight* has a monthly circulation of 750,000 copies; *The Little Knight* 180,000; *The Little Journal,* with a circulation of 130,000 copies, is inexpensive enough even for the poorest classes.

"Not all, however, know the Immaculata; not all love her. Many look for happiness where it cannot be found and are unable to rise higher. Once some Jews came to Niepokalanow searching for waste paper. The youngest of them asked to visit the 'City.' Having seen and observed our life, he exclaimed: 'I am a communist, but I have to admit that here true communism is lived.' Yes, it is true: at Niepokalanow there exists a real community life. When the spirit of Niepokalanow, the spirit of the M.I., will have penetrated our country and the entire world, when the Immaculata will have become Queen of every heart, then paradise will be found on earth. This will not be the utopian paradise of the communists and socialists, but the true paradise, as far as this is possible on earth, which the inhabitants of Niepokalanow are experiencing today. Niepokalanow is, in fact, a family whose Father is God, whose Mother is the Immaculata, whose older Brother is the divine Prisoner of love in the Eucharist; all the others are not just companions but brothers, younger brothers who tenderly love each other."

This commemorative broadcast brought much favorable comment to radio Warsaw as well as to Niepokalanow. As a consequence, Father Maximilian was granted a second broadcast which was aired on February 2, 1938. The theme of the program was the work accomplished in Niepokalanow during the year 1937. It was a good survey which offered the saint the occasion to urge the audience to collaborate not only with offerings, but with new religious vocations.

# Correspondence Apostolate

Another form of apostolate Father Maximilian carefully encouraged in Niepokalanow was correspondence. He used to say:

"Correspondence is very important, because it is direct contact with souls and spiritual direction. Those who receive our letters do not know personally those who write to them, but they know that the answer comes from Niepokalanow, from a place which belongs to the Immaculata and with which they are in contact. A letter can obtain better results than *The Knight,* because the latter is written for all, while the former is personal."

Letters from people from every walk of life poured into Niepokalanow every day. In 1937 alone, after the return of Father Maximilian from Japan, approximately 750,000 letters came in from Poland, about 9,000 from Polish people outside Poland, and only slightly less from other nations. They not always were conventional letters or donations for *The Knight.* More often they presented true cases of conscience, or asked for advice and prayers. Father Kolbe himself, in a talk aired on radio Warsaw on February 2, 1938, read a rather meaningful letter from a communist which made a deep impression on the audience:

"For some time now I have been receiving *The Knight of the Immaculata.* Last year I wrote to you asking you to stop sending the magazine to me. I openly confessed to you that I am an unbeliever and it has been many years since I went to confession. Today I have to add that I am a member of an organization hostile to the Church, since I am a communist. I am greatly irritated by the persistence with which the magazine keeps coming to my house in spite of the fact that I did not renew it. You keep sending it to me without considering that it may be of no use. In the autumn I wrote you a card begging you to suspend the publication because I was setting out for Russia. On my return, I found all the issues of *The Knight,* the calendar included, awaiting me. Today I received a new issue and again I ask you to remove my name from your file. Perhaps you may send it to some other Catholic family ready to receive it lovingly. Do not think that I despise your magazine. Your Immaculata was once a Mother to me, but it has been long now since I withdrew from her protection. No mercy is available to me any longer. Do not think that I am happy. No! One thousand times no! A sinner is most unhappy; he is ashamed of a soul covered with wounds. Wandering far from God, rejected by his fellowmen, he has no hope of salvation. What he suffers is a real martyrdom. The reading of *The Knight,* which describes the graces received by the faithful through the intercession of the Immaculata, reopens his wounds, reawakens his fear, disperses his tranquillity. I suffer enough. Please spare me more suffering! If in the future God will grant me the grace of conversion, I myself will ask you for *The Knight.* At the present moment God is not necessary to me, nor do I need either the Church or a priest. Perhaps the day will come when I may desire God and a priest, but it may be also that I will not be granted such a grace, since one dies the way he lives. Forgive my frankness. Perhaps you may remember me and my intentions to the Immaculata in your prayers."

As the organization of Niepokalanow grew to meet the needs of the people, it came to include a department charged with the dispatch of correspondence. Abbreviations such as: M.I.P or M.I.M. could be seen on the doors of the various offices, while inside, on the walls, others read: M.I.N. or M.I.I.* Father Maximilian himself highlights their meaning:

"By M.I.P. we mean the Polish *Militia Immaculatae;* by M.I.W., the World *Militia Immaculatae;* by M.I.N, the *Militia Immaculatae* within Niepokalanow. All these divisions are required for organizational purposes and are greatly useful. The most important of all, because of its uniqueness, is the M.I.I. If each one of us endeavors to be the project and property of the Immaculata, he fulfills the most important work of the M.I. The M.I.I. is the essence of Niepokalanow.

"Within the correspondence department the abbreviation M.I.I. had another meaning for the secretaries for whom it was a real password: the addressee receiving the letter had to be able to say: 'This is the Immaculata's own reply since it is she who rules and directs everything in Niepokalanow.'"

---

*The second "I" stands for the personal pronoun "I."

# Franciscan Poverty
# and Expensive Machines

The well-known Jewish philosopher, Henri Bergson, once expressed his deep wonder at the surprising skill with which Catholic mystics could conform themselves to practical life by harmoniously combining action with contemplation. The vivifying unity of these two dimensions permeated every aspect of St. Maximilian's life: he was a man of action, yet an ascetic and mystic; he had a fragile and weak body, yet unlimited spiritual energies; he had the grasp of leadership, while at the same time he was a most docile subject; he possessed a marvelous organizational genius, yet displayed the simplicity of a child; he dedicated all his being to the cause of the Immaculata, while he remained completely abandoned in her hands; he constantly promoted towering projects worth millions of dollars, yet at the same time he remained a most faithful follower of Lady Poverty.

All these outstanding qualifications in Father Kolbe have continually come to the fore in the course of the exposition of his life and through the letters and testimonies which have been referred to. Perhaps the discourse on his living *holy poverty* in relationship to an extremely costly apostolate deserves a longer treatment.

The practice of evangelical poverty was at the root of the reform promoted by St. Francis of Assisi in the thirteenth century; the same spirit of poverty was at the root of the renewal promoted by the M.I. in the twentieth century. In his work for the reform of the lay and ecclesiastical society of his time, the Poverello of Assisi had laid stress on a poverty understood in a radical way as "promoter of humility and root of perfection." This ideal, prior to St. Francis, was advocated by all the heretical movements which arose in opposition to the luxury and worldliness in the Church at that time. But what distinguished the work of the saint of Assisi from that of the heretics was his orthodoxy and total submission to the magisterium of the Church.

St. Francis endeavored to meet the aspirations of the people who sought greater conformity between life and the Gospel, and succeeded in reconciling two aspects which seemed irreconcilable: the practice of poverty and obedience to the Church of Rome. His work for the restoration of Christianity was the chief motive for the dispersion of the heretical movements, which gradually were eliminated.

St. Maximilian, following in the footsteps of the seraphic saint of Assisi, embraced the ideal of evangelical poverty, adapting it, however, to the changed conditions of his time. He saw in holy poverty a two-edged sword: the source of fertile ground allowing for growth in Christian and religious perfection, and the "safeguard" for the costly apostolate of the M.I.

In a letter from Nagasaki, Father Kolbe presents this ideal to Father Florian Koziura in words of fire:

"Our father St. Francis is the model missionary: his example, his Rule is highly missionary and represents the most intense missionary thrust directed to the salvation and sanctification of souls. The fundamental characteristic of such a Rule, holy poverty, is the capital empowering us to measure our possibilities with the great financial power of the Protestants, the sectarians, the atheists, the masons, since holy poverty is the unending cash of Divine Providence. We are experiencing deeply this reality in Japan. If we were to allow ourselves comforts of any kind, we would be hindered from performing our aposolate. Because of our unimpaired poverty, those who can come to help us. At the present moment, our most valid collaborator is Professor Yamaki, a Methodist Japanese minister who preaches in their churches; he is very close to Catholicism and his ideal is our father, St. Francis.

"The Immaculata is our purpose and poverty is our capital: these are two things which Niepokalanow cannot abandon under any pretext. Without this twofold purpose, Niepokalanow would cease to exist and would betray its mission. Without poverty, without abandonment to Divine Providence, one cannot speak of missionary thrust."

In other words, Father Maximilian wanted to make it clear that the conquest of the world for the Immaculata could be achieved solely if Lady Poverty is willingly embraced and loved in an uncompromising way.

This thinking is reflected in the administration of his "Cities of the Immaculata." Regarding this, Prince Drucki-Lubecki gives us this seemingly paradoxical information:

"He went ahead trusting in the Immaculata. I tried to exercise my authority on the point of the administration of Niepokalanow. I did not share his ideas. I questioned him about the accounts, the debts, etc., when Niepokalanow was enlarged. He did not want to hear of accounts. He wanted to trust in the Immaculata."

Not only did Father Kolbe want his apostolate to be inspired by the greatest love for holy poverty, but his whole personal life, even in its most minute expressions, was a reflex of the strictest poverty. Father Florian Koziura offers us this touching testimony:

"In my opinion, the Servant of God observed religious poverty supernaturally. He considered material things not as his own, but only as given to be used. I know from my observation that the Servant of God was content with modest clothes and he took care of them diligently. In doubts, he asked himself how our holy father Francis would have thought in this regard. The religious cell was furnished most modestly. It contained only a bed, a desk, two or three small chairs and a bureau. It had no lavatory but a basin which was kept under the bed on the floor and he washed himself on his knees. With regard to using money, he was very strict in observing what the Rule prescribed about not keeping money on oneself. For example, when he traveled he even desired that one of the confreres should keep the money and spend it for what was needed. I was aware that the Servant of God was not attached to things of this earth, but on the contrary, with all his heart he loved religious poverty and the spirit of poverty. Comparing Niepokalanow directed by the Servant of God to the observance of poverty in the other friaries, it surpassed them and was without doubt an example of poverty in the Order."

Dr. Stanislaus Wasowicz echoes the same reflections:

"One was struck by the magnificent organization at Niepokalanow, of which Father Maximilian was undeniably the animator. At every step it was evident therefore that he knew well and adequately how to draw the greatest benefit from human capabilities. The observance of work on the part of the friars at Niepokalanow, as well as their great zeal, attested explicitly to the fact that on the whole the friary was penetrated with the highest ideal of serving God through the Immaculata. This was the merit of the Servant of God. From what I was able to observe at Niepokalanow, it was striking to see the enormous contrast between the most modern equipment for the single sections of the workshops and the primitive-like poverty of that which concerned the personal needs of the Servant of God and of all the other religious."

Of deep significance is also the testimony of Bro. Zeno Zebrowski, one of the four companions of Father Maximilian on his first journey to Japan:

"He practiced perfectly the virtue of poverty according to the spirit of St. Francis. As a matter of fact, Father Kolbe and I took turns wearing the same pair of shoes when we had to go out."

In 1930, during his three day stay in Rome to take care of his applications for his missions to the Far East, he was a guest of the Seraphic College on the Palatine hill. An eyewitness relates:

"I was in the room of the Father Rector when Father Maximilian knocked at the door. With a smile, he went directly to Father Rector and handed him a billfold, saying:

"'This money, Father, was left over after we bought the ticket for the trip from Poland to Rome.'

"'And don't you have to go back?' asked the rector.

"'Yes, but we will be staying here in Rome for three days and the Holy Constitutions do not permit us to keep money.'

"'I know, but you may hold on to it.'

"Father Maximilian smiled, and since the rector did not want to accept the money, he gently left it there on the chair and went out."

Often in his conferences to the community, he demanded of his confreres to follow his example:

"In our Order, one who keeps money unlawfully, forgetting the vow of poverty, may be condemned to the same fate as Judas. Even a small coin kept by the religious without the permission of the superiors, is an obstacle in the spiritual life and it makes the soul arid. The transgression of the vow of poverty weakens not only the vow of obedience but also that of chastity because the religious who disposes of money, when he crosses the threshold of the friary, usually begins to be concerned about external things and consequently he ends up by losing his vocation and at times even his faith."

In order to remove from his subjects the temptation to illicitly acquire more than the necessary, during his office as superior he wanted common life to be perfectly observed as a means to protect the communities from eventual transgression against this virtue:

"When he returned from Japan and was named superior of Niepokalanow, the Brothers in the sewing room prepared a fur coat for him for the winter. When it was presented to him, he asked:

"'Do the others have a coat like this? Certainly not, and so neither do I want it.'

"He would not accept it for any reason.

"But that year the winter was very cold and Father Maximilian, sick as he was, suffered severe chest pains. A fur-lined jacket was prepared for him which he accepted only after having the assurance that the same jackets were given also to all other sick members."

"One day he went to the barber of Niepokalanow and patiently sat at the end of the line of the other religious waiting their turn. The Brother barber wanted to take him first but he would not hear of this and said:

" 'We all work for the Immaculata and we all are in a hurry.'

"When his turn came, the barber took from the drawer a better towel which was usually reserved for the priests. He protested energetically, saying:

" 'Put away that towel, my brother, and let it be used when the ordinary one is worn out. There should be nothing particular for anyone; we all must be treated the same.'"

Father Dominic Stella recalls this eminently Franciscan conversation he had with Father Maximilian in Assisi:

"With regard to the mission in Japan, he told me: 'Some Fathers have insisted that we acquire the ownership of the land. I told them my contrary opinion. Why ownership? The use of it is enough, as St. Francis said. No ownership. We shall stay here in this place as long as the owner permits. When he tells us that we cannot stay any longer, we shall go elsewhere.' And he stated that with firm conviction. Uppermost in his thoughts was the pure ideal of poverty lived in perfect conformity with the mind of the Seraphic Father.

"He would appear unexpectedly," continued the same religious, "with a simple traveling bag, but it was so flat that he could easily hold it under his arm. From the matter-of-fact way in which he spoke of his trips: 'Now I'm going to Rome, then to Madrid, then to Paris, then to Berlin,...' without any preoccupation as to where he would stay, he revealed that he was a humble pilgrim in the manner prescribed by St. Francis in his Rule."

Even Padua breathed the perfume of his poverty.

"One evening in February, 1937," narrated the master of novices at the friary of St. Francis, "he sat at my table which was surrounded by our sixteen novices. Before beginning to speak, motioning with a finger on the table, he asked, looking at me:

"'Are there ever any ashes here?'

"Thinking that he wanted to play some trick, I replied:

"'No.'

"Then again he asked:

"'I ask, are there ever any ashes on this table?'

"Not understanding what he meant, I replied that if he would like to have some ashes I would get some from the dormitory's stove. Then for the third time he said:

"'No, no!... I ask if there are ever any ashes on the table.'

"'Ah!' I replied. Finally, I understood that in this manner he was asking me whether or not I smoked. I said:

"'No, not here; there are never any ashes on the table.'

"Then he began to speak to the novices about avoiding smoking, exhorting them all to make a promise to the Immaculata to abstain forever from this habit.

"In listening to this exhortation, we all admired his charity toward those who already have had this habit for years. He said that it is almost impossible to free oneself from smoking without the body suffering. Therefore, those who smoke are not to be judged bad. They are to be thought of with compassion, but are not to be imitated.

"So that we might take to heart what he said, he calculated with clear and precise figures how much a smoker spends in a month and he exhorted us for the love of poverty and for love of the missions which have so much need of money for the conversion of the infidels, to abstain from these expenses. Love for the Immaculata would spur us on to make this sacrifice with much joy and generosity, if such could be called a sacrifice rather than a duty of religious profession."

Concerning smoking, Father Lawrence Podwapinski evokes this exhortation, as St. Maximilian's request to the religious living in the "City of the Immaculata":

"My dear Brothers, do me this favor: even after my death do not smoke or drink brandy. Refuse them when these things are offered to you. I warmly recommend and desire that there be no smoking in any of the Niepokalanows, because to permit that would be to relax and weaken the foundation constituted by holy poverty."

Father Kolbe's ideal of evangelical poverty reverberated on the two "Cities of the Immaculata." Although they were distinguished from the other communities of the Order as far as the apostolate was concerned, their government was based on the Constitutions in vigor at the time of Father Kolbe.

From an administrative point of view, the Constitutions established for each community a bursar or an administrator distinct from the superior, and the monthly meetings, called conventual chapters, to be held to discuss the economic situation and other affairs of the entire community. From the acts of these conventual chapters which refer to the superiorship of Father Maximilian, it is seen that he was never a bursar or an administrator, but that he showed the greatest concern to have these chapters monthly, and at times, even more often. The collection of these acts constitutes a most precious historical documentation of Niepokalanow from its beginning to its full development. They even give a detailed account of the purchase of the various machines on particular dates, whether those machines be a rotary press or a simple typewriter; a plow for the fields or a plane to speed up the distribution of the daily *Maly Dziennik* all over Poland.

From these reports, there shines forth the spirit of poverty of Father Maximilian and his confreres in the government of the two cities of the Immaculata which was carried out in a way to deserve the full and complete approval of the superiors.

In one of his letters from Japan, we read:

"Beloved Brothers, here we live poorly, at times even very poorly, but without misery. The Immaculata takes care of us. If anything is lacking to us, let us remember that we are sons of the Seraphic Father who was poorer than we and when everything was lacking to him, he exclaimed with contentment: 'My God and my all!'"

Finally, a most inspiring exhortation of Father Maximilian on the spirit of holy poverty is recalled by Brother Luke Kusba:

"Let our houses be so poor that should St. Francis return, he could choose to live in them. All the money needed for the construction of the most comfortable houses must be used and spent for the sanctification of souls and to attain as soon as possible the goals of the M.I."

# Love for the Sick

Father Maximilian's love for the sick was most admirable. Whoever reads his letters remains astounded at how he, ill with tuberculosis, had such resistance to fulfill the duties and shoulder the concerns of the apostolate. Even the doctors marveled. Father Kolbe wrote much to exhort the superiors and his confreres to have a most tender care for the sick. The sick religious very much appreciated the spiritual maternity of Father Maximilian. This is shown by the unanimous consensus of all who knew him in approving and praising the tenderness that he showed in this mission of mercy which was truly in the spirit of the Franciscan rule.

Every report that we possess, every testimony confirms "the particular love that Father Maximilian had for the sick." This was not a generic affirmation but refers to copious and concrete examples such as the following.

Among the supernatural gifts ascribed to Father Maximilian, Father Isidore Kosbial cites the following fact:

"In the year 1929, at the small seminary of Niepokalanow, one of my companions, Ladislaus Wierzbinski, became seriously ill.... Father Alphonse and Father Maximilian took turns keeping vigil at his bedside. During the night, when it was his turn to stay up, Father Maximilian prayed with fervor and made the sign of the cross on the forehead of the sick religious. Father Alphonse saw this and recorded it in his memoirs. As far as I am concerned, I had seen the young man seriously ill that night, but in the morning of the following day, he was cured and came to school with me."

Brother Taddeus Maj records:

"When I returned from Japan in 1933, I was hospitalized for a serious attack of tuberculosis and was told that I could not communicate with the other Brothers. Nevertheless, every day Father Maximilian succeeded in finding a bit of time among his many duties to pay me a visit."

As soon as he was named superior of Niepokalanow, for three years, from 1936-39, one of Father Kolbe's main concerns was for the sick. Already in January of 1937, he proposed for the approval of his fellow religious the restoration of the infirmary. In May, 1938, he further proposed the construction of a hospital, to be built far from the buildings of the friary-city, in the middle of the forest of Niepokalanow.

The hospital having been built, Brother Lawrence Podwapinski attested:

"Every day he visited the sick Brothers in the hospital. With the seriously ill he was most generous, spending even entire nights at their bedside. I myself was sent one night by bicycle to Sochaczew to buy some special medicine for the very sick. Father Maximilian reminded us often that St. Francis had even sold chalices just to have the means to cure the sick.

The same Brother relates:

"Once in May, late at night, Father Maximilian made me go with a borrowed bicycle to Sochaczew, a distance of eight miles, to look for medicine. When I returned, Father Kolbe was still keeping watch at the side of a sick religious. This manner of acting far outdid that of even the exemplary superiors.

"In another case, since Father Maximilian himself was sick, the Brothers hung a note on the door of his cell, asking that no one should enter or tire him. Coming to know this, the Servant of God had the note immediately taken down saying: 'Brother, take it away; every one can come to me at any hour of the day and the night; I am here for you.'

"This fervent solicitude toward the sick had a mark that was exquisitely supernatural. He saw in the ill the souls who were closest to the Immaculata and the souls most holy because of their suffering."

Another Brother remembers that:

"While one of the Brothers was in the hospital convalescing after an operation, he showed his impatience to Father Maximilian. Father Kolbe went closer to him, embraced him and affectionately whispered in his ear: 'Courage, because even if this suffering were to lead to death you must not even then be frightened. In paradise there is our Mama and many holy Brothers of our Order.'"

What faith must have been his if Father Maximilian was able to infuse into hearts a motive of comfort which was none other than the thought of death itself.

It is related that:

"One time Niepokalanow received the visit of a distinguished person who was brought by Father Maximilian himself to visit all the departments. Having arrived at the general storehouse, he explained to the guest: 'This is the store where one purchases everything gratis.' In fact, there each religious could ask for and receive whatever he needed. Then, turning to the visitor, Father Kolbe added: 'And now let us go to the department where work is most intense and the gain is the greatest.' Curiously, the guest followed Father Maximilian toward the forest. To his great surprise, he saw there a hospital. As they walked in, Father Maximilian explained: 'These sick Brothers, forced into inactivity, are the most useful to us since with their sufferings, they draw the choicest blessings of God upon Niepokalanow and its apostolate.'"

Recalling Father Maximilian's love for his sick religious, and his untiring concern for them, Father Cornelius Czupryk concluded that Father Kolbe's life was a perfect example of charity toward his neighbor. This explains why Father Maximilian would one day be able to willingly and totally lay down his own life for another.

# Deportation and Arrest

Poland's history has been described by historians as beset by tragedy. The developments culminating in World War II and its aftermath were a further confirmation of this reality. The freedom Poland had achieved from prolonged subjection in 1918, was lost in a far more terrible way in 1939. On the morning of September 1, 1939, without formally declaring war, Germany attacked Poland. The Poles fought bravely, but their army was too weak to compare with their enemy's gigantic war machine. The German forces moved relentlessly toward Warsaw. Niepokalanow, located along the highway about twenty-five miles from Warsaw, was soon to be surrounded by the invading army and abandoned to its power.

Father Maximilian's premonitions of approaching catastrophe had become a most sad reality. The hour of trial had already struck for the "City of the Immaculata."

Following the directions previously received by his Provincial in the case of an eventual evacuation, Father Kolbe gathered together the entire community, urging them to take refuge wherever there would be less danger. Some of the religious would find hospitality in other friaries farther away from the danger zone; some would go with their own families. In the course of a few hours, the dispersion of the "mystic city," so many times foretold by Father Maximilian, had taken place.

On that sad afternoon of September 5, 1939, after having blessed the departing Brothers, Father Maxi-

237

milian bade his fatherly farewell in these terms: "Good-bye, my dear sons, I will not survive this war!" Then he rushed by car to Warsaw to ask his Provincial what he should personally do, whether he should leave Niepokalanow or not. From the tone of the conversation, the Fathers who were present understood that Father Maximilian was indifferent although inclined to move to a safer place. But at the request of Father Felix Wilk, superior of the friary of Warsaw, the Provincial ordered Father Maximilian to remain in Niepokalanow without considering the consequences. It was felt that this was necessary for the good of the "City of the Immaculata" itself. Father Maximilian humbly accepted the decision of the Provincial and went back to Niepokalanow. There remained with him about fifty brothers and five priests, who, without consideration for their personal danger, had asked to stay.

After September 5, for those who had remained in Niepokalanow, there began the excruciating days of waiting. Regarding this, we possess information supplied by Brother Mlodozeniec. "Every day," he tells us, "from September 8 through 19, in the morning meditation Father Maximilian reminded us that the present day could be the last of our lives and he prepared us for a holy death."

Continuously, day and night, bombs rained down around Niepokalanow as a preparation for the capture of Warsaw. During these bombardments four bombs of minor caliber struck Niepokalanow, one of which damaged a building, but there were no casualties.

"Father Maximilian was never overcome by fear," continues Brother Mlodozeniec. "He always remained calm, always master of himself, always brave. He exhorted us to renew our total consecration to the Immaculata, for life, death and eternity. He prayed continually while Warsaw was besieged by the German troops, and urged us to pray. He loved his country immensely."

Father Albert Wojtczak, in his biography, portrayed the days preceding the occupation thus:

"While the German troops advanced, terror and tension reigned supreme inside and outside Niepokalanow. Father Maximilian alone, setting aside any fears, was concerned with bringing help to his fellow countrymen. Continuously on the highway there passed by the remainder of the defeated Polish army, wounded men, and thousands of refugees. Those who were stronger continued going along, but those who were exhausted stopped at the door of Niepokalanow.

"Father Maximilian received all within the walls of the 'City of Mary.' He administered first aid to the wounded men, and had meals prepared for the hungry. He helped greatly to calm everyone down and to lift up the spirits of those terrified by the events of the war. He assisted the dying and became the protector of the many wretched people whom the Immaculata had sent to his friary. Even the Jews, who until a few months before had not been sympathetic toward Niepokalanow, now experienced the warmth of Father Kolbe's charity...."

On the morning of September 12, the vanguard of the German army arrived at Niepokalanow. They used its streets to park their cars, but allowed the religious to continue their activity, especially the assistance to the refugees.

In the middle of September, troops of soldiers of the Wermacht raided Niepokalanow, pillaging and destroying everything they could get their hands on: furniture, clothes, tools, especially crucifixes and statues of the Immaculata. They spared only the machines, perhaps with the intention of sending them intact to Germany.

Niepokalanow, which had cost twelve years of sacrifice, the "spiritual Lourdes" of Poland, was jeopardized by the ruthlessness of the new occupants. The founder was there, completely powerless in the midst of massacre and destruction. But not a lament, not a word of hatred toward the irresponsible and cruel invaders could be heard from his lips. Echoing holy Job, he kept repeating:

"The Immaculata has given all. She has taken all away. She knows how things are."

In the supernatural vision and evaluation of the events, his spirit, entirely at peace with God, completely abandoned to His will, knew neither bewilderment nor deviation. Many times he had taught his religious that "restlessness and negligence due to failures come from pride." Now beset by the hardest trial that a teacher and a father could suffer, he offered a rare example of humility and conformity to the will of the Immaculata.

On the morning of September 19, soldiers of the Wehrmacht arrived at Niepokalanow and ordered the religious to assemble in the square. All with the exception of two—who would remain behind for the assistance of the wounded men—were to leave the friary to be deported. If it were not for the intervention of Father Maximilian, no chance would even have been given them to go to their cells to take some clothes and their habits. According to the testimony of Father Jerome Wierzba, "Father Kolbe was given the opportunity of staying in the friary together with another Brother, to offer his service to the wounded Polish soldiers. He chose, instead, the *lager,* to share the common lot of his Brothers."

The Nazis crammed them into trucks and drove west. In the evening, they arrived at the town of Rava Mazowiecka, where they spent the night in the parish church. On the following day, September 20, they were taken to Czestochowa.

During the night, they were thrown into livestock wagons and were driven toward the German frontier. They suffered intensely, locked as they were in those wagons, without knowing what awaited them. Father Maximilian set himself to the task of encouraging all, both the Brothers and the other prisoners who had joined them at Czestochowa. From a report of Brother Mlodozeniec, we know that Father Kolbe urged all with these words: "We do not know what will become of us. Let us be ready to endure anything the Immaculata demands of us. Let us give ourselves totally to her, so that we may be always guided by her will."

On September 21, they arrived at Lamsdorf, Germany. Three days later they were sent to the concentration camp, Amtitz. It was not one of the largest concentration camps which were to become infamous because of the brutal treatment inflicted on the prisoners, but it was similar enough. Suffering was not lacking, especially hunger and cold caused by sleeping outdoors, which was very painful at that latitude even during autumn.

Those who escaped from this camp and the other ones related:

"There every suffering seemed normal and even sweet, because it was accepted with resignation and out of love for the Immaculata. It was enough to look at Father Kolbe to be inspired and to feel capable of enduring any suffering with joy." Those trial-filled days testified to Father Maximilian's full adhesion to the will of the Immaculata in the spirit of total consecration to her.

In the farewell discourse to his religious, Father Maximilian had said:

"Now you are going to the missions. Remember what countless times has been repeated to you: Niepokalanow is not only this place, these premises, these machines; Niepokalanow is wherever one of its members dwells. Niepokalanow must be in your souls, in your hearts."

At Amtitz, the barracks were transformed into a little Niepokalanow. In fact, a statue of the Immaculata shaped out of clay by one of the Brothers was placed in one of the least unbecoming spots they found. This camp, then, was now regarded as the little mission on German soil.

"One day," it is still Brother Mlodozeniec who relates, "three German officers came to our barracks. Surprised, they stopped to look at the statue of the Immaculata while we continued praying. In the evening, Father Maximilian gave us an interesting conference on fidelity in serving the Immaculata. And he added that imprisonment was for us a holy mission allowing us to do the apostolate in Germany...."

Even during those times of trial, his confreres recall, Father Maximilian seemed to be overflowing with peace and joy, intent upon doing things which may be considered the remote preparation for the great holocaust of Auschwitz. On his feast day, October 12, an episode eminently Franciscan, worthy of *The Little Flowers of St. Francis,* took place. The Brothers recalled with nostalgia the celebration of that day in Niepokalanow. Now they could only lovingly surround the revered Father singing a song in honor of the Immaculata. As they finished, Father Maximilian, in his fatherly way, thanked them and added:

"What can I give you, my dear sons? I have nothing. Then, he took his portion of bread, broke it into many little pieces, and gave a piece to each one of the Brothers." Then he continued:

"The Madonna will change into good even these sufferings. We have given ourselves to her; we have promised to conquer souls for her; we have claimed always to be her property. We must be grateful to her if today we are useful here and not in Niepokalanow. We have been brought here gratis. A hut is sheltering us; a piece of bread for each is not lacking. Our fellow prisoners are unable to resign themselves, are disheartened and blaspheme. But looking at us, at our resignation, of necessity they become better persons. If we had wanted to come to this concentration camp to do some apostolate, who knows how many documents would have been necessary and it would not have been granted to us. Let us, therefore, take advantage of the grace the Immaculata is granting us."

Brother Jerome Wierzba provides us with the following:

"When we suffered starvation and cold; when we slept on straw in tents and it was already November, with snow and frost; when we had no water to drink and had not changed our clothes for three months while the insects gave us no rest—the Servant of God endured everything with serenity and joy, because in this way he could show his love for God. Of his admonitions, I remember a sentence I have jotted down: 'Even a fervent soul is overcome by sadness at the thought that in heaven he will not suffer any longer and show thus his love for God.'"

Brother Jerome himself confesses that he was moved to anger any time Father Maximilian showed trust in being freed through the intercession of the Immaculata. But things happened as Father Kolbe had foretold.

"In the concentration camp of Amtitz, the Servant of God repeatedly said that soon we would be set free and that the Immaculata would drive us out of the camp. This greatly irritated me."

We owe to Brother Gabriel Sieminski this moving detail:

"In the camp of Amtitz, Father Maximilian divided his meager ration of bread with the other prisoners. He did so to prevent them from blaspheming."

Brother Herman Juraszek, his eyes brimming with tears, remembered Father Maximilian's care for him when he fell critically ill at the camp. It was at Amtitz that Father Maximilian proposed to his confreres this following singular pact with the Immaculate Virgin:

"'Most holy Mother, for your love I bind myself to remain in this uncomfortable prison, even if others are granted to go home. I will remain here forgotten and despised, without friends and comforts, to suffer for you. I offer myself to you, O Mary, particularly to meet death in this camp among hostile and indifferent men, and to be buried in the forest.'

"If we make this pact with the Immaculata, even if we are set free, we will have the same merit as if we really had endured all this."

The Franciscans remained at Amtitz until November 9, when they were sent to Ostrzesrów in Polish territory. It seems that they owed this transferral to the new commander of the camp of Amtitz, a Catholic officer.

The sympathetic attitude of the new officer toward the Polish Franciscans is evidenced by the following thank you card which Father Maximilian wrote to the officer's mother-in-law in February, 1940, in the hope that she might succeed in forwarding it to him:

Niepokalanow

November 28, 1940

"Dear Madam,

"When I was confined at the camp of Amtitz, I was fortunate enough to become acquainted with your son-in-law. He was there as chief officer. Ten religious and I had been entrusted to him. His high education and his deep sense of justice made a great impression on all of us. I do not know where he is stationed now. I intend, however, to thank him for everything through you, dear Madam, and to let him know that, after a three week stay in Scildberg, we have finally reached our friary.

"May the Immaculata reward him for everything."

*Father Maximilian Kolbe*

# The Hospital of Niepokalanow

Of the sixty religious who had remained in Niepokalanow after the outbreak of the hostilities, a good twenty were absent from the building which constituted the residence of the religious community. Wounded in the bombardment endured by Niepokalanow some weeks before September 19, they were in the infirmary of Niepokalanow which, as we have already seen, was in a separate building. This allowed them to escape deportation.

As the German forces continued moving east, the military authorities turned all the available buildings of Niepokalanow into a hospital. The surviving religious could stay in the "City of the Immaculata" as hospital orderlies. Among them were Brother Vitalis, doctor of the religious community and Father Ceslaus Poltoraczyk, who, knowing German well, could remain disguised as the janitor of the friary. Afterwards, under a more benevolent government, other religious were able to return to Niepokalanow.

However, despite the presence of soldiers and hospital personnel, unwanted persons succeeded in entering Niepokalanow, plundering whatever was still there. The occupants, liberal with what was not rightfully theirs, permitted also the people of the neighborhood, needy of everything, to join the robbers in removing from Niepokalanow whatever they found useful for themselves. Clothing, construction material and paper, which had been stocked up in anticipation of the war, disappeared.

# Father Maximilian
# Goes Back to Niepokalanow

The German campaign in Poland lasted less than a month. The Poles fought valiantly, especially in Warsaw, but they were crushed by German superiority. On September 28, after having suppressed most of the Polish organized resistance, Hitler and Stalin signed an agreement by which Poland was divided between them. Germany took the western and central part of the country, including Warsaw and Krakow, and the Soviet Union took the eastern section. During the winter of 1939-1940, there was little action on the western front. Hitler announced that he had no intention of further aggression now that he had Poland, but the Allies found that difficult to believe. In the following months, even though under the dominion of a foreign power, Polish life began to resume its ordinary rhythm. The intellectuals, churchmen and others who had been deported for preventive measures also took advantage of this time of relative "quiet."

The end of the hostilities found Father Maximilian and his confreres in the concentration camp of Ostrzesrów. Here they had been better off than in Amtitz, since they had been settled in the school building of the Salesian Fathers. They had been granted more freedom to fulfill their religious practices, so much so that they could celebrate the feast of the Immaculata, and hold the annual course of spiritual exercises. It was during this retreat that Father Kolbe foresaw their forthcoming liberation.

On December 8, Feast of the Immaculata, after three months without the holy Eucharist, they had the comfort of receiving holy Communion which was brought to them, with the consent of the commander, by a priest of the nearby town. In the afternoon, almost as a gift of the Immaculata, they had suddenly received the order to leave the camp and to return to their own homes. The joy they experienced at that moment was beyond compare.

"What a joy!" wrote Brother Mlodozeniec. "All night long we traveled the way we could, relying on chance means of transportation, and on the following day we arrived in Warsaw. Here, after the Mass celebrated by Father Maximilian, in small groups, we headed for Niepokalanow where we arrived in the evening of December 9. Father Maximilian remained in Warsaw to confer with the Minister Provincial and arrived in Niepokalanow on December 10."

Upon their arrival at Niepokalanow, there was no longer the motherly figure of the Immaculata on the pillar at the entrance of the "City" to welcome the friars. All over were ruins and disorder. Yet the heavenly Queen, on her feastday, had returned her "City" to her "Knights." They must have thought of replacing her on her throne. On the very day of his arrival, Father Maximilian wanted the chapel to be repaired and perpetual adoration of the Blessed Sacrament resumed. It was not even difficult to find among the things piled up and the rubble a little statue of the heavenly Queen. Although so poor, it was lifted up on an improvised pillar by the entrance of the "City." Her sons could not have done more the same day they arrived from the concentration camp.

Immediately after, they had to begin to work. The Brothers built a garage, a shop for the making and repairing of watches, a carpentry shop and other machine shops. They even began a cheese factory. They carried out all these activities to meet the needs of the people in the neighborhood.

"The Immaculate Virgin does not permit us to miss what is necessary," wrote Father Maximilian to the Brothers who were still in hiding.... In fact, although daily more Brothers kept going back to Niepokalanow so as to reach the number of 300, some could never return because they were sought after by the feared Gestapo. These Brothers, whom Father Maximilian guarded by keeping them as hidden as possible, were, above all, the editors of the numerous magazines.

## Niepokalanow—Refuge of the Jews

Throughout the entire military occupation, at the request of the Polish Red Cross, Niepokalanow was transformed into a hospital. Father Maximilian's charity, however, could not be limited only to the wounded men and to the disabled when, after the battle of Warsaw, the refugees numbered tens of thousands. Already in September, before the deportation, he had ordered the friars to give assistance to whomever knocked at the door of Niepokalanow. A group of Brothers had been appointed to offer a Christian welcome to any kind of fugitives. They were not only given hot food, but also supplied with coal and wood for heating, if they had to stay overnight in improvised barracks.

In the early months of 1940, two thousand men, expelled from Posnania and 1,500 Jews, were given hospitality within the walls of Niepokalanow. The great majority of these unfortunate people were those who had refused to subscribe to the racial declarations of the Nazi laws. Father Maximilian forbade any discrimination and made sure that all received a most charitable treatment. Such Christian charity, given unconditionally to everyone, was not exempt from unpleasant consequences. The presence of those expelled roused the suspicion of the Nazi authorities who began to exert a greater vigilance on Niepokalanow. This situation brought about serious difficulties because of the shortage of food and the insufficient number of rooms. All the religious, however, were pleased, because they were offered the opportunity of performing their apostolate in the spirit of the M.I.

The Brothers were employed in the infirmary and in other duties of common utility, while the priests fulfilled the task of chaplains for the Catholics and of brotherly understanding for the Jews. This new situation reminded Father Maximilian of the days he had spent in the sanatorium of Zakopane. There, too, he had contacts with the Jews for whose conversion he had displayed much zeal. Now it was easy for him to stay with them and to do something to soften their great moral suffering.

Today, among thousands of testimonials of gratitude for the assistance carried out by Father Maximilian in Niepokalanow, there are several from the survivors of the Polish Jewish community. But the most meaningful testimony was written by Prof. Eugene Zolli in the capacity of former rabbi of the Synagogue of Rome, who, in 1949, concluded his praise in honor of Father Kolbe in this meaningful way:

"If I knew how to write a book on Father Kolbe— I am not worthy of so much, otherwise Providence would have given me the capability of doing so—I would entitle it: Father Maximilian Mary Kolbe who died for love."

# For the Brothers Far Away

Although overturned and scattered by the events, the community of Niepokalanow remained spiritually united. Father Kolbe's concern for the religious obliged to remain in hiding was not limited to the concealing of their presence, but resorted to initiatives capable of stirring in them the flame of common Marian ideals. He was the vigilant father concerned with detecting the dangers of his sons to preserve them from material and spiritual harm. First of all, he took steps to organize among them an information network so as to refer to the central office any news each one of them could obtain of the dispersed Brothers. In moving letters, he communicated to those he could contact the list of the living and recommended suffrages for the deceased. He informed them of the present status of Niepokalanow and of the resumption of religious life in the recomposed community.

A few excerpts from these letters suffice to unveil, almost as flashes of living light, the exquisiteness of his love for the "scattered religious" and the zeal he displayed in order to keep high in them the hope of better times. His tenderness could be compared to that of the Apostle of the Gentiles who, even in chains, continued directing, instructing and informing his children and brothers in Christ. He exhorted them not only to be patient, but to keep working for the glory of the Immaculata. Here are given a few examples of these letters:

"The soul consecrated to the Immaculata will work always, wherever it finds another soul. It is May! We recall with nostalgia the sacred functions which cannot be celebrated this year, but when there is love for her, then there is pure internal fervor which is essential.

"Let us apply ourselves in missionary action to conquer other hearts for her. Let us pray for the coming of her reign. Let us offer our sufferings for this end and let it be our care to make her always more content. We will obtain this when our soul is pure. Let us guard purity of soul, and in case there is need, let us purify it as soon as possible. An act of perfect contrition gives life back to the soul; let us often make use of this means, which is not difficult, because the essence of it is the offering of love. Let us be solicitous to be acceptable to her with our sacrifices."

"God is love and since the effect resembles the cause, all creatures live of love. And in regard to our purpose, love must be the principal source and motive of our action. Man, having reached adulthood, seeks a person to whom he offers his heart, and he starts his own family. This love, created by God, has been elevated to the dignity of a Sacrament.

"But there are souls called by God to a more perfect love. Choosing to love only God, these souls do not want their hearts divided. To Him they consecrate themselves totally and solemnly with religious vows. To Him they consecrate all they have and could have, with the vow of poverty; to Him they sacrifice family life, with the vow of chastity; to Him they offer all that man holds most precious, his own will, reason and his whole soul, with the vow of obedience.

"For the faithful observance of the vows, these souls gather together as in a family, in a religious Order, where life in community helps them to detach themselves from all material things. The cloister preserves them from worldly seductions; the rules and orders of the superiors make known to them the divine will in every circumstance of life.

"It is no wonder that the religious soul who lives outside of the cloister becomes tepid in love, except if special graces sustain it; but the soul will certainly be so sustained if the stay outside of the friary does not depend on one's own will, if on one's own part the soul does not leave off prayer and observes the religious vows diligently.

"What will the good God not do for the souls who love him? But if the stay outside of the friary is voluntary, how can the soul hope to have this special grace?

"Since one cannot live in the world without having a bit of money and using it, then it is easy to become attached to it, especially if the earning becomes greater and the family offers conveniences. It is easy then to become attached to other material things, to clothing, to dwellings, in a word, to living comfortably.

"Outside of the cloister...it is very easy to have an affection for persons. In the beginning this will not be strong, but later, without one's becoming aware of it, he will reach the point of harboring in the heart a love that had been sacrificed with the religious vows.

"With regard to the vow of obedience, it is so sublime that people—even though appreciating the excellence of the first two (poverty and chastity)—do not succeed in valuing the worth of obedience. If a religious little by little becomes tepid in recognizing the divine will in the voice of obedience, what will happen to the men of the world who do not have the religious vocation and do not even appreciate it? It will follow that if a religious remains in the world without necessity, he will end up by taking on worldly thoughts according to the proverb: 'Tell me who you go with and I will tell you what you are.'

"People of the world, in whose midst the religious lives, will save themselves by the ordinary way; the religious, instead, who has made the vows and then almost insensibly becomes tepid in his observance will end up by losing his vocation and salvation. Even the enemy of the soul, and to say it more clearly, the devil, will work much to suggest a thousand reasons to delay the return of the religious to the environment which urges him to the observance of the vows. Little by little, as the soul weakens, even the conscience will become less pure and delicate, and as a consequence, the help of divine grace will be less strong, and prayer less fervent, until that which was the ideal of perfection and happiness for this religious will become incomprehensible and hateful.

"Perhaps I have painted religious life in the world in dark colors, but you must believe me, because the news that reaches me from various parts of the world confirms what I have written.

"The Immaculata has drawn our hearts to herself, to consecrate ourselves to her cause without limit, for the conquest of other souls who love her, and through her are drawn closer to the Heart of Jesus which has loved us to the point of the cross and the tabernacle. But how can we carry out this apostolate, when love, instead of burning in our hearts, dies out?

"Let us pray often and with fervor, each one for all and all for each one, so that the Immaculata will preserve us from this danger."

With the steady return of the religious to Niepokalanow, the number soon reached 349. The various duties and offices were resumed and life began to throb again throughout the friary. While perpetual adoration was re-established from the very first day of their arrival, the other practices of religious life were restored gradually, as the Minister Provincial was pleased to notice in his visit of October, 1940. Even more, on December 8, feast of the Immaculata, there took place the religious investiture of a group of Brothers who began their year of novitiate under the direction of Father Pius Bartosik, while another eight pronounced their solemn vows. At the beginning of the school year, the students began to attend their classes regularly, and the Brothers of the printing department, which was temporarily inactive, helped the neighbors to rebuild their houses. All this notwithstanding, there was the care of the thousands of needy people living there, some of whom were invalids. Of course, contact with the Japanese Niepokalanow was also resumed.

With the restoration of religious life, Father Kolbe had a greater possibility of devoting himself to the apostolate of charity. The warmth of his love is thus reflected in this testimony of Father Florian Koziura:

"When the Servant of God was the Guardian at Niepokalanow in the first years of the war, many people came to the friary door and the Servant of God had ordered the friars to help them by giving them food.

"The Servant of God distributed from every oven twenty kilograms of bread to the displaced persons, more than had been ordered by the occupational authorities. The Servant of God often visited the families of the deported and consoled them, not excluding the families of the Jews."

His charity extended also to the German occupants, as Brother Ivo Achtelik manifests:

"In 1940, a garrison of Germans was stationed at Niepokalanow to guard one of the buildings used for storing ammunition. A non-commissioned officer became sick, and Father Maximilian came to know of it from the sick Brothers. He did not hesitate to visit him, giving him and his soldiers the Miraculous Medal. It was later known that the soldiers remained highly edified by the concern of Father Kolbe."

This episode confirms the unanimous attestation of the confreres who were his companions during the first deportation. The sadistic attitude of the Nazis did not arouse in him the slightest sentiment of hatred or rancor. He did not know how to hate. On the contrary, he was always ready to forgive and forget the impoliteness and ill treatment he had received from the soldiers occupying Niepokalanow.

When life resumed as normal, Father Maximilian considered the possibility of beginning again the publication of *The Knight* which he wished to publish in a twofold edition: one in Polish and the other in German for the soldiers stationed in Poland. In January 1940, after repeated trips to Warsaw, Father Maximilian received the permission to publish *The Knight*. With his tactful approach and documentary information he was able to win an officer of the German Propaganda Office of Warsaw who contacted Krakow, thus hastening the granting of the permission which was given on January 20, 1940. Father Maximilian wanted to begin immediately the publication of *The Knight*. Brother Cyprian Grodzki, who was helping him, advised him to ask also the permission of the Gestapo. This delayed its publication. On November 20, 1940, the German Propaganda Office gave the written permission and the Gestapo permitted that the seals should be removed from the printing presses.

The first and only issue came off the press on the feast of the Immaculata. It consisted of a few pages only, reporting the most useful and necessary news prompted by the Polish situation, and an article by Father Maximilian which manifested all the yearnings of his soul. It was his spiritual testament to the "Knights" of all Poland. The founder of the M.I., with renewed passionate insistence, exacted practical fruits from devotion and love for the Blessed Mother. His language, as usual, so simple and unadorned, breathes forth a profound peace that inflames us still.

"December 8," he wrote, "is drawing near, the feast of the Immaculate Conception.

"Let those who can, go to confession. For those to whom this is impossible, because circumstances do not permit it, let them wash their souls with acts of perfect contrition—the sorrow of the loving child who thinks not so much of the punishment and the reward, as of asking forgiveness of the father and mother whom he has displeased.

"It is right, therefore, to have the desire of purifying our souls on the feast of her whose soul was never stained. The souls who have the privilege of knowing her more intimately, love her fervently and seek with the greatest effort to make their consciences pure and delicate to be able to resemble her always more, to become more devoted to her, to please her more.

"But in what does the evil that stains the soul consist?

"If virtue consists in the love of God and in all that which flows from love, evil will be in everything that is opposed to love. Therefore, the soul should always fear this; moreover, it should desire to become always more immaculate after the example of its beloved Lady and spiritual mother.

"On that day, let the souls particularly consecrated to her renew their offering and therefore let also the members of the M.I. renew their act of consecration, with which they gain a plenary indulgence....

"On the day of the Immaculata, after the purification of our consciences, the renewal of the act of consecration, and after having acquired the remission of sin, the soul more easily finds interior peace, and also joy, knowing well that no cross, either internal or external, comes to it without the permission of God, a truly loving Father who permits only that which will lead to the greater good of souls in view of eternity.

"The fruit of this feast, therefore, will be an ever greater purity of conscience, a more profound peace, the peace of resignation to divine Providence, and with it an ever more generous readiness to fulfill, with the greatest possible perfection, one's own duties and thus to give a tangible proof of love for the spiritual Mother and the celestial Father."

During the year 1940, Father Maximilian's speeches had contained allusions to the approach of his fateful hour. He was fully aware that there was a mere step between him and his arrest. Very often, news had arrived from loyal Poles who were employed by the Gestapo that arrangements had been made to arrest him. Despite this, he continued to remain in Niepokalanow.

Yet, if he only had wanted to, he could have avoided arrest and all the sufferings related to it. From the acts of his process for canonization we derive this information:

"During the German occupation, Father Maximilian revealed such uncommon talents and capabilities as to succeed in winning all kinds of persons to himself. The

German police noticed these gifts of his, capable of influencing, especially through the press, the Polish people, for which reason they sought to use him for their own purposes. They tried to win him over, pointing out to him through the distinct authorities of Sochaczew, how pleased the supreme authority would be if he would opt for German citizenship and would be included in the list of those who had German roots, which was possible because of his last name."

Had Father Kolbe consented, what a different direction events would have taken! But the love of one's own country is sacred.

"He rejected the proposal, affirming that he always was and would always remain a son of Poland."

Now his name is glorious all over Poland not only for the sanctity of his life and the heroism of his death, but also for his open confession of loyalty to his country which has raised him to the glory of a national hero.

As the hour of his impending arrest approached, the tenderness of Father Kolbe for his confreres and disciples became always more manifest. On their part, all the religious reciprocated that love. Every evening they surrounded their beloved father, eager to hear his exhortations and recollections. The documentation we possess of these gatherings is the result of personal notes taken by all with the awareness that each speech could be the last one. Even if the contents of these speeches are often repetitious, they are permeated by such a warmth of feeling, by such generous charity that they convince us that his heart was already disposed to the supreme proof of love.

Here are some excerpts:

"Today is the feast of the offering of ourselves to the Madonna. An offering without reserve is the condition for a life full of grace. In order to increase the interior life always more, it is necessary to sacrifice to God the last *but*. Doves can fly to a certain altitude; instead, the soul consecrated to God, if it does not place any *but*, that is 'limits,' can rise always higher and higher, because the love of God always offers new heights."

"Our ideal is filial love for the Immaculata. All of our work must demonstrate this love. Work must not hinder in any way this love. It is our goal that it may burn in our hearts and we may diffuse it. We want the Immaculata to be loved always more and, if possible, we want to increase her glory.

"Our aim is to increase love for her and to inflame the whole world with her love. For this purpose, we work and suffer; for it we want to continue to work even after death. That is most important.

"I...will go away. The goal of Niepokalanow is not the printing plant, nor the realization of other works; these are means. The goal is love for the Immaculata. To stray from this love is to misdirect the aims of Niepokalanow, which instead must be the heart of the M.I. We must sacrifice ourselves for the ideal which is established in the bylaws of the Pious Union. If the Holy See has confirmed the approval of the Pious Union, we must put all our efforts into it, and if necessary give all our lives and being. Yes, even our whole being, because after death we shall be the active members sanctified by the Immaculata, who will glorify her and work to spread love for her."

"Let us strive to draw closer to the Immaculata with prayer and penance. If love for her burns in our hearts, with love will come all good things. God is the supreme Good. If a soul lives for the Immaculata, it is certain that it lives also for God."

"Knowledge puffs up. It is useful, meanwhile, insofar as it serves charity. Satan knows a lot more theology than any of us, but it does him no good. The same could happen in regard to the cause of the Immaculata. The only knowledge that has value is that which proceeds from love.

"Bernadette at Lourdes knelt down; she humbled herself. She asked if the Lady would be so kind as to tell her her name. This must be our method of acquiring knowledge. And we know how much Bernadette loved the Immaculata; she is a saint. It is a matter of humble love that goes in search of knowing always more.

"In practice, our knowledge of the Immaculata must bring forth fruit in sacrifice. The greater the sacrifice, the greater love it proves."

Concerning the last Marian evening, Brother Marcel Pisarek recalls the following detail:

"On the evening of February 16, I had the joy of being able to spend time with Father Maximilian during recreation. I was in the midst of a small group of Brothers who, being the most simple, kept themselves aside. We spoke, above all, of spiritual topics. Among other things, Father Maximilian told us that God satisfies the desires of the soul that sincerely loves Him. Then I asked if this were really possible. He replied affirmatively, citing examples drawn from the lives of the saints, especially from St. Therese of the Child Jesus. Then he continued: 'God can do everything, and He gives Himself willingly to the soul that is consecrated to Him. Between God and the soul there is established a flow and an overflow of love. *What indescribable happiness! What a great grace it is to be able to seal one's ideal with one's life.*'

"These were his last words on the vigil of his arrest."

# The Arrest

After some months of respite during which the German occupation of Poland remained contained within the limits of a certain moderation, there followed the second phase: a period of horror which reached degrees of inhumanity rarely surpassed in human history. The Germans were resorting to extreme measures to strengthen their position, before the invasion of Russia. In the most pitiless way, they transported large numbers of the Polish population to the eastern part of occupied Poland and sent others as slaves to Germany.

This process of mass destruction was especially harsh and systematic in relation to the Polish intellectuals who, insofar as they had not succeeded in leaving the country, had often to go underground to escape the worst. At one stage, the whole academic staff of the ancient Jagellon University in Krakow was put into concentration camps where many perished, and all institutions of higher learning were closed "for all times." Poles, if they deserved to live at all, could at best claim an existence as slaving robots.

No such claim, however, could be made by those three million Jews of Poland, the largest Jewish population in any European country. For them, and for millions of other European Jews, the Nazis built the gas chambers of Auschwitz (Oswieceim), and many other less famous extermination camps, where hundreds of thousands were put to death.

The basic criterion governing that process of mass destruction was to eliminate those who were undesirable and those who were influential, the leaders. Father Maximilian was certainly one of them. On February 17, 1941, at 9:45 a.m., two cars, which from the color and license plate were immediately recognized as being the Gestapo, entered the enclosure of Niepokalanow. Five Nazi officials got out—four in uniform, one in civilian clothes—and immediately headed toward the residence of the religious. As the car had approached, the doorkeeper had hastened to telephone Father Maximilian who had already been informed from Warsaw of the arrival of some authorities.

Brother Ivo Achtelik, who was in the cell of Father Maximilian when he received the call, related that the saint uttered on the phone a trembling "yes," but, immediately controlling himself, added: "All right, my son. Mary!"

He went down to meet the officials and courteously greeted them. Instead of responding to his greeting, the Nazis roughly began to question his educational methods employed in teaching the young vocations.

Father Maximilian replied: "Since the beginning of the war, the acceptance of new students has been suspended. The present students are only those who entered before September, 1939, and who returned after the military operations ceased."

Dissatisfied with this answer, the Nazis arrogantly made their way to the inside of the monastery, where they carefully searched all the rooms. At that time, there were stationed in Niepokalanow nearly three hundred and fifty religious and seven Fathers: Father Maximilian, superior, Father Pius Bartosik, novice master; Father Anthony Bujewki, Father Justin Nazim, Father Florian Koziura, Father Urban Cieslak and Father George Wierdak, master of clerics.

A fortunate occurrence saved the former superior of Niepokalanow, Father Florian Koziura, from imprisonment. Although he was explicitly requested and sought after by the Gestapo, he succeeded in escaping the Nazis because unanimously all the religious asserted his absence. All, in fact, were sure that he had gone to Warsaw to shop, although at the last moment something had prevented him from going. Another fortunate one was Father George Wierdak who, according to the usual procedure, was entrusted with the direction of the friary.

At 11:50, the head of the Gestapo called the names of the other five priests and ordered them to get into the car. Father Urban Cieslak recalled that the official pronouncing the name of Father Kolbe called attention to the fact that it was a German name. Once again, Father Kolbe protested, saying:

"Perhaps some of my grandparents may have come from Germany, but I was born in Poland and therefore I am Polish."

Brother Pelagius Poplawski added this detail:

"At about 12:00, the Gestapo, leading Father Maximilian, went toward the car. We all knew that the Servant of God had been arrested. I had the possibility of being able to give him at that moment a bag containing a piece of bread and butter. Father Kolbe conducted himself with calm and seriousness; I observed him the whole time while I followed him from the house to the car and I saw how, before leaving, with a nod of the head, he greeted us who remained standing on the square."

Brother Ivo Achtelik described the serenity of the saint while the automobile drove away with him who knew that he would never return:

"His comportment betrayed not the least apprehension. Thus, serene and tranquil as always, he left his dear Niepokalanow, his beloved enclosure of the Immaculata, never again to return."

Father Kolbe and the other priests were taken to Warsaw and kept in the historical Pawiak prison. That very moment marked the beginning of his ascent to his sorrowful Calvary.

Justification for Father Kolbe's arrest had to be given by the Nazi authorities. Because of the fame of the arrested priest and his great achievements, it was foreseeable that the ecclesiastical authorities would intervene, as in reality they did. Even more, Father Kolbe's Minister Provincial and confreres had recourse to every possible means to obtain his release from prison. They turned also to influential persons in the hope of succeeding in their holy cause. In particular, a nun, who had been obliged to give her service at the principal command of the Gestapo, took the Kolbe case to heart. But despite her generous efforts, a few days later she had sad news to communicate to the Provincial. The acts of the arrest of the five religious of Niepokalanow contained a denunciation against Kolbe brought forth, as it was maintained, by a certain Rembisz, a former religious Brother of Niepokalanow. The well detailed accusation, clothed in legal language, referred to a plot against the occupational authorities and as such rendered utterly impossible any step on behalf of the imprisoned religious. The striking news made a great impression on all the members of the community of Niepokalanow, to whom such a falsification seemed incredible.

Father Maximilian, utterly concerned with "the work of the Immaculata," never referred in his conferences to political arguments. Secret agents of the police sent to spy on him were never able to hear from his lips words deserving denunciation and condemnation. This charge, if it had really been made against Kolbe, as it had been asserted, could only have been, at worst, the result of an irresponsible act of revenge on the part of the former Brother Rembisz, who had been expelled by Father Kolbe for disciplinary reasons.

Since any way of proving the innocence of the convicted seemed impossible, the religious of Niepokalanow had recourse to an extreme measure which proved to be a most moving attestation of love for their "father."

On February 26, 1941, twenty Brothers presented to the Police Command of Warsaw the following petition:

"We, the undersigned, turn to you, the Command of Police, with the present letter, to beg you courteously to imprison us in exchange for our Fathers. We declare that no one has ordered us or obliged us to do this; but we take this important step of our own spontaneous will. We declare also that we are ready to take upon ourselves all the accusations as well as all the final consequences."

That very same day, a copy of the petition was also sent to the Minister Provincial with a communication drafted in these terms:

"Most Reverend Father Provincial,

"Since Providence has permitted so sorrowful a trial, mindful of all our dear Fathers have given us, we have decided unanimously to explain to our superiors what follows. Desiring to come to the aid of our Fathers, we offer ourselves to go to prison and to accept all the further consequences. We pray wholeheartedly that our

Father Provincial will support this desire before the authorities. We add that we are perfectly aware of the seriousness of our decision, but we are ready for everything. We trust that you will accept our request favorably."

The petition of the twenty generous Brothers was refused, while the Provincial, who continued working for the release of Father Kolbe and his confreres, was given by the Gestapo a copy of the denunciation of Rembisz, with the reply that such a crime rendered utterly impossible the liberation of the five religious.

At this point of the narration, it is necessary, in the name of truth and justice, to vindicate the honor of poor Rembisz, who was only the instrument of a deceitful maneuver of the police. After the arrest of Father Kolbe, he was summoned twice by the police of Rzeszow, his native town.

"I was asked," he said at the process, "what Father Maximilian had said against the Germans. I denied that he had said anything in my presence on this subject.

"There was given me a paper to sign. But not knowing the German language, I was not able to know the message, so I signed it unawares."

In good faith he had signed the grave denunciation. Time however brought forth the truth and proved that the accusation submitted by the Gestapo of Warsaw to the Minister Provincial was only a forgery made with the very purpose of frustrating any attempt for the release of Father Kolbe.

# In the Pawiak of Warsaw

During the German occupation, Father Maximilian repeatedly spoke of martyrdom for the faith. Brother Vitalianus Milosz, former secretary in the editorial department of *The Knight,* once made this objection to Father Kolbe:

"You, Father, speak of martyrdom for the faith, while there are many people who are in concentration camps perishing; this is not for the faith but for the country."

Father Kolbe replied: "Son, I tell you that if it is thus, the martyrdom is certainly for the faith."

And he continued to explain: "As soon as the German administrative authorities took possession, I went to the District Head at Sochaczew, to present to him our small statute. I told him the purpose for which we were reunited at Niepokalanow, the purpose for which we worked—that the program of our work was what was prescribed by the statutes and that we are ready to give our lives for our ideals. Therefore, my son, the German authorities are informed of the reason for which we are here. If they move against us, their steps would be directed not only against the country but also against the faith."

With the awareness of performing his civic duty toward his country, but even more of making a public profession of faith by enduring any kind of suffering with Christian resignation, Father Maximilian crossed the threshold of the terrible prison of Warsaw, called Pawiak. This hellish place was the gathering center of civilian prisoners, who after a stay of two or three months were transferred to various concentration camps.

Father Maximilian was to stay there longer than his Franciscan confreres since, stricken by pneumonia, he had to be confined to the infirmary. He remained in jail from February to the end of May, 1941, while his four confreres were taken to the concentration camp of Auschwitz during the first days of April. For a month, however, they remained together, all of them being assigned to the same cell, as the letters of Father Maximilian bear evidence. In fact, he wrote on February 21, 1941:

"Send for each of us a sweater, underclothes, two pairs of stockings, two towels, two handkerchiefs, a toothbrush and toothpaste. Send the five packages separately for each one and add the name of the sender. Send by mail ten zloti."                              *Raymond Kolbe*

On March 13, 1941:

"...May all the Brothers pray much and well. May they work with fervor and not be too concerned about us because without the permission and the will of God and of the Immaculata, nothing can happen to us."

Later on, a card contained only the date:

"Warsaw—Temporary prison infirmary—April 2, 1941."

Thus, in the impossibility of providing information about his confreres, because of the strict censorship, Father Maximilian succeeded in letting his community know that he was in the prison infirmary, that is, already separated from his confreres of whom he no longer had any news.

It is hard to exaggerate when speaking of the sadistic brutality of the Nazi jailers toward their victims, a cruelty which did not stop even at the sight of the sacred. Religious persons and objects seemed rather to aggravate their fury. Father Maximilian was not spared any form of outrage during his confinement in the prison at Pawiak, and then at Auschwitz. He, however, knew no fear and could not be intimidated in dealing with his ruthless persecutors. When God's honor was endangered and exposed, to him all other things were considered nothing. Threats, insults, beatings, instruments of torture seemed wished for by him as delights more than horrors. His intrepidness and resoluteness, if it served to increase the hatred of the Nazis, made, instead, a great impression on his prison companions. He had been just a short time at Pawiak when he was called to give an admirable example of an heroic profession of faith, which an eyewitness, Mr. Gniadek, has recorded for us:

"At the beginning of March, 1941, I found myself in Pawiak prison at Warsaw in cell 103, Section III. Together with me there was a Jew by the name of Singer. After some days, Father Kolbe was transferred to the same cell. He was dressed in his religious habit and was shaved although before the war he had had a beard. The presence of Kolbe calmed me. I had the sensation from one moment to another, however, that they would take him away. God knows where.

"Five days after his transferral to our cell, we received an inspection from the head of the section, a Nazi. When he saw Father Kolbe with the religious habit, it seemed to me that he was going to have a stroke. That man's hatred was not only for the religious garb, but also and above all for the crucifix and the rosary which hung from the cincture of the Franciscan. After the report made by Mr. Singer who was the oldest one in the cell, the section officer seized the crucifix of Father Kolbe and, pulling it violently, he yelled: 'And do you believe in this?' To which Father Kolbe answered with the greatest calm: 'I believe, and how!'

"The German raged in fury. He immediately struck Father Kolbe on the face. Three times he repeated the question; three times he received the same reply, and three times he struck him. I wanted to strike out at the Nazi, but certain of making things worse, I hid my anger. Otherwise, the guard would have become even more infuriated against Father Kolbe and would have taken revenge on us.

"Nonetheless, Father Kolbe remained totally calm and the only indication of the incident was the livid color of his face. A Polish guard was also present, standing at the doorway.

"After the section officer left, Father Kolbe started to walk up and down in the cell, praying. We two were more irritated than he was, which is most explainable. In certain moments, even the strongest nerves give way.

"It was precisely Father Kolbe who sought to calm us saying: 'There is no reason for getting so upset; you already have grave personal motives for concern. This is a small thing; everything is for the Immaculata.' After some time, the Polish guard brought prison clothes to Father Kolbe to avoid causing further annoyance to the head officer by wearing that habit and crucifix.

"The news of the event spread throughout the whole prison and in a short time, because of this and because he now had pneumonia, the doctors facilitated the passage of Father Kolbe to the infirmary."

The heroic faith and conduct of Father Maximilian at Pawiak are recalled by another of his prison companions, Mr. Thaddeus Lucian Chroscicki, who shared his cell with him for a one to two month period:

"...When Father Kolbe was brought to Pawiak prison, where I was already a prisoner, he told us that he had been arrested at Niepokalanow together with his fellow priests, but I do not remember if he spoke of the reasons for the arrest. It was the second time that he had been arrested by the Germans. While we were in the cell, we often held conversations on various topics: political, social or religious. And since I was quite young, being hardly 22 years of age, together with others, I listened to these conversations and discussions. Father Kolbe had a calming influence upon me and my other prison companions, and that was for us very precious because of the difficult prison conditions. All of the prisoners in the cell had in him the best of spiritual protectors and fathers. He enjoyed much respect from the prisoners, thanks to his simple way of holding the discussions and of reacting to the often hard conditions of life in the prison. His whole being inspired calm, so much so, that we all gathered around him. I remember that even the prisoners who at times were skeptical found words of approval and respect for Father Kolbe after the discussions. He defended us against spiritual discouragement and encouraged us to be strong and to persevere. In every suffering he understood us and knew how to give counsel, consolation and encouragement.

"From the conversations of the priests arrested with him, there appeared much preoccupation for Niepokalanow. Father Kolbe, instead, placed all things in the hands of God and the Immaculata. The Servant of God endured the hard conditions of the prison most generously and with fortitude, so as to be for all of us a model and an example. With calm and dignity he endured the oppression of the SS, provoked mainly by his religious habit. I never heard him complain about the beatings or the oppression."

# Toward Auschwitz

At Pawiak, Father Maximilian won the love and affection of everybody for his goodness. The Polish personnel, knowing him by reputation, attempted every available means to prevent his departure for the death camp, but after having postponed it several times, in the end they did not succeed.

Three cards written by Father Maximilian from Pawiak permit us to have some idea of his life in jail before he was transferred to Auschwitz. The first is dated May 1, 1941:

"They have permitted me to receive packages of food (5 kilograms) twice a month. These may be picked up and received on the fifth and the twentieth of each month through the Police Commissary."

The second, written the same day, indicating that they were not able to mail the letters, once again reveals the depth of his soul, already raised to the contemplation of the divine, resigned and inspired to the most holy ideals:

"I received the Easter packages. I received also the card of Brothers Felix, Ivo and Arnold. The Immaculata, our most loving Mother, now and in the future will watch over her sons. I was confined for some time in the infirmary and I still receive the food given to the patients. At the present moment I am working in the prison library. Today marks the beginning of the beautiful month of May, a month consecrated to the Madonna. I trust in your prayers for me. I invoke the blessings of the Immaculata on all the Brothers and cordially send greetings to everyone."

*Father Maximilian Raymond Kolbe*

His last card, dated May 12, ended with these words:

"Let us be ever more entirely guided by her, wherever and in whatever may be pleasing to her, so that doing our utmost to perform our duty, we may, through love, save all souls. Greetings to all and each one of you."

*Raymond Kolbe*

A few days after this solemn promise and generous offering of himself, the Immaculata was to lead him to the camp of his martyrdom to gird his head with the red crown he had been shown in his far distant childhood.

# Auschwitz

Auschwitz, a name which arouses a pervading sense of horror, unfolds in all its terrifying dimension the excesses to which human wickedness can fall when man fails to follow the way traced by reason and morality, and fails at the same time to call upon God, whose mystery and love transcends reason and morality.

The concentration camp at Auschwitz was brought into existence toward the end of 1939, by the order of Heinrich Himmler, chief of all the German Police. It was organized the following spring by Rudolf Hoess, its first commandant, assisted by fellow members of the SS Death's Head Division. The hatred of these pitiless and unscrupulous men for the doomed prisoners sent there inspired them to degrade, humiliate and reduce the prisoners to a state worse than slavery before finally exterminating them in accord with Hitler's demonic command.

Auschwitz was commonly called a "death camp" for the millions of victims who died there. Originally, the place was a small, unimportant town named Oswiecim. The Germans called it Auschwitz, but it had always been Polish. The concentration camp lay in the province of Krakow at the junction of the Sola and Vistula Rivers, and was established on the site of an old Polish army garrison. It's purpose was the extermination of Jews, Poles and other persons and groups Hitler and the Nazis considered threatening or undesirable. Indeed, not only Poles were imprisoned and died in this Golgotha of the modern world, but people of many nationalities: Danish, French, Greek, Jewish and Yiddish, Spanish, Flemish, Serbo-Croat, German, Norwegian, Russian, Rumanian, Hungarian and Italian.

The other concentration camps of Dachau, Treblinka, Buchenwald, Mathausen, Maidanek and Orannienburg were also arenas of unspeakable atrocities where millions of defenseless people met death. Yet, none of the death camps could compare with Auschwitz. The efficiency and vastness of its operation made it a "death factory" beyond compare.

The inscription "ARBEIT MACHT FREI" ("Work makes one free"), which still stands above the entrance gate, could not have had a more sardonic meaning considering what took place within.

When Father Maximilian was there, Auschwitz was a single camp where the Pawiak prison periodically poured out its "surplus" victims. The single gas chamber crematorium at the northwest corner of the camp soon became too small for the mass exterminations decreed by Hitler; so, at the end of 1941, a second camp known as Auschwitz II or Birkenau was built a mile and a half west of Auschwitz. It was the largest and most efficient of the extermination centers established on Polish soil by the Nazis. Gas chambers and crematoria eventually reached a capacity for disposing of 3500 persons in 24 hours. Most prisoners then were killed on arrival, though many were saved for slave labor.

Among the latter, hunger, fear and killing labor were the rule. Those who were stronger, so to speak, were better off, but the weak, incapable of carrying out the amount of work expected of them, received blows and slaps and all kinds of ill treatment. The sick in the hospital, covered by dirt and filth, lacked almost all care. The dead were found in their own excrement. There was no end to suffering. For some, there was a special horror of all horrors: the starvation bunker, in which prisoners received neither food nor water until death.

In this place, Father Maximilian was to fill up the measure of all his sufferings and crown them with the greatest, the most sublime and heroic of actions—the total immolation of himself.

# Witnesses and Documentation

Father Kolbe's confinement in Auschwitz lasted from May 28, 1941, the day which marked his arrival at the camp, until August 14, the day of the consummation of his holocaust. Usually, his imprisonment is divided by his biographers into two periods, the first of which goes from his arrival at the "Death Camp" to the first days of August, and the second, from the first days of August to his martyrdom.

Among the fortunate survivors of Auschwitz, there were found witnesses of both periods who have enabled us to reconstruct, even though not completely, Father Kolbe's last days on this earth.

Eyewitnesses to the facts which characterized the first phase are the following:

1. Prof. Mieceslaus Koscielniak, a professional artist, who arrived at Auschwitz on May 2, 1941, a month before Father Kolbe, whom he met several times.

2. Dr. Joseph Stemler, a school superintendent, who had made his acquaintance with Father Kolbe in 1937, during the Congress of editors. He was in Auschwitz from April 4, 1941, to March 19, 1942. In July, 1941, he was confined to the camp infirmary where Father Kolbe also was an inmate.

3. Mr. Alexander Dziuba, a tailor by profession, who was imprisoned in Auschwitz in September, 1940. He had frequent contact with Father Maximilian between June and July, 1941. Once he also received the Sacrament of Penance from him.

4. Father Corrado Szweda, prisoner in Auschwitz from December, 1940 to June 3, 1942, when he was transferred to the camp of Dachau. On April 29, 1945, he was set free. From June, 1941, he had continual contact with

Father Maximilian. After Kolbe's segregation in the starvation bunker, he ceased being an eyewitness to the events of his life. Acting, however, in the capacity of a male nurse, he was able to draw reliable information about the moving details of his passion and death.

Besides the testimonies given at the canonical process of Warsaw and at the apostolic process of Krakow, Father Szweda has left a written report of the holy life of Father Kolbe at Auschwitz. In 1945, he published his recollections of Auschwitz which were related to Father Kolbe. They appeared in installments in the *Rycrz Niepokalanej.*

5. Father John Lipski from Lublin. An admirer of Father Kolbe's apostolate, Father Lipski had been corresponding with Father Maximilian since he was pastor at Zamch in the diocese of Lublin. He met Father Kolbe personally at Auschwitz, where he remained until June 9, 1941, after which he was transferred to Dachau. He was informed of the holy death of Father Kolbe by some prisoners dispatched from Auschwitz to Dachau.

6. Dr. Ladislaus Lewkovicz, a veterinarian who in 1937 had been a postulant in Niepokalanow. He was present at the tragic roll call, but being out of ear reach, he failed to hear the dialogue between Kolbe and the chief officer, Fritsch.

7. Dr. Thaddeus Lucian Chroscicki, architect. He was Father Kolbe's cell companion at Pawiak, and was transferred to Auschwitz with the same convoy as Father Maximilian. At Auschwitz, he had the opportunity of meeting Father Maximilian until the vigil of the priest's departure for the starvation bunker.

8. Mr. Henry Sienkievicz, professional forester. He himself has described the occasions of his meetings with Father at Auschwitz:

"In the period before the war, I heard much about the Servant of God, as founder of Niepokalanow. However, I personally met the Servant of God for the first time toward the end of May, 1941, in the concentration camp of Auschwitz, where I was a prisoner and where

Father Maximilian also arrived. For about five weeks we remained together in the same block, in block 18, and we slept next to each other on the straw mattresses. During this time my relations with Father Maximilian were very restricted. After those five weeks, the Servant of God was sent to the camp hospital for a period of about two weeks. And after the hospital stay, they assigned him to block 14. But even then, until the moment when he was enclosed in the starvation bunker, toward the end of July or the beginning of August, 1941, there was not a single day that I did not see him."

9. Dr. Rudolph Diem, doctor in charge of the camp hospital of Auschwitz. He was the only non-Catholic witness present at the canonical processes. His testimony gives us a glimpse into the very heart of the saint and reveals such a thorough religious commitment that an indelible impression is left on the readers.

The second period of imprisonment, from the first days of August to August 14, comprises two moments: Father Kolbe's offering of his life and his two week confinement in the starvation block.

Eyewitnesses of his generous offering are:

10. First, among all, Mr. Francis Gajowniczek, the man whose life was spared. He served in the war of 1939 as a sergeant of the Polish army. On September 28 of the same year, during the surrender of the fort of Modlin, he was taken prisoner by the Germans. He escaped, but near the Slovak border he was captured and imprisoned in Zakopane. On November 8, 1940, he was shipped to the concentration camp of Auschwitz, where at the end of July, 1941, he was condemned to capital punishment, but saved by the heroic intervention of Father Kolbe; he remained in the camp until October 25, 1944.

He gave his testimony in the canonical process of Warsaw after having put into writing a detailed report on the facts of July, 1941, which were enclosed in the acts of the process. He repeated his testimony in the apostolic process of Warsaw, during which he was more deeply interviewed on his encounters with Father Kolbe. His testimony will be given later.

11.  Father Sigismund Ruszczak, inmate in the camp of Auschwitz from February 2, 1941 to July 1, 1942, when with other priests he was transferred to the camp of Dachau. He himself has described the details of his encounter with the venerated Father:

"I was never in the same block with Father Maximilian. However, I had the singular fortune of going to confession to him. I met Father Kolbe on the square and, after an exchange of cordial words, I asked him to hear my confession. After he did so, Father Kolbe said to me: 'Now I also want you to hear my confession.' Thus, we revealed our consciences to each other. My confession to Father Kolbe was for me a great experience. I had the pleasure of confiding my sins and my difficulties to a *saint* and to receive absolution and comfort from his lips."

12.  Brother Ladislaus Swies, religious of the Pious Society for the Catholic Apostolate (Pallotines). He was transferred from the Pawiak prison to Auschwitz with the same convoy as Father Kolbe. Upon arrival they were separated. It happened, however, that he was present when Father Kolbe went to the death bunker at the end of July.

13.  Dr. Joseph Sobolewski, a lawyer, was incarcerated in the "Death Camp" in July, 1941. His testimony is of great value because it refers to the final episode of Father Kolbe's offering of his own life. In his testimony at the apostolic process at Warsaw, he has declared:

"I was in the last line of block 8. Directly behind me were the prisoners of block 2, from whom were chosen the ten prisoners. I saw perfectly the whole action take place."

14.  Dr. Nicetas Francis Wlodarski, physician, prisoner in the camp of Auschwitz from August 15, 1940. In July, 1941, he was stationed in the same block as Father Maximilian. He is a very important witness, after

Mr. Gajowniczek, because, as he affirms, in the evening of the tragic roll call, between him and Kolbe there were only three or four prisoners. He has given a detailed account, sealed by oath, of the short conversation between Father Maximilian and the camp commander, Fritsch.

At the apostolic process of Warsaw he testified:

"In the camp, I was the doctor for the section in blocks 17, 21 and in others. At that time, since I had given some help to the sick prisoners, I was withdrawn from the district and assigned to Bavhof Command at block 14, where I found the Servant of God. This happened in the spring of the year 1941. I met the Servant of God during work in the block.

"We took walks together and I assisted at the prayers organized by the Servant of God. I went to confession to him, and I was an eyewitness to the 'choice' of the prisoners of block 14, which was carried out because toward the end of July or the beginning of August a prisoner had fled, I believe, from the Gartnerei command. Since the man who fled had not been found, the camp authorities gave the order that in block 14 ten prisoners should be chosen. During the selection, I stood about three or four persons distant from the Servant of God."

15. Mr. George Bielecki, technician, inmate at Auschwitz since October, 1940. He met Father Maximilian three times in the "Death Camp." The third encounter fell on the day Father Kolbe offered his life:

"I saw Father Kolbe from a distance. I was about twenty meters away from him. I was not able to hear but I accurately saw the whole action take place.... I saw everything together with my companions from the window of the block which faced us on the square. I saw Fritsch the Lagerfuhrer personally choose the men who were to be condemned."

16. Finally, the only and providential eyewitness of Kolbe's confinement and death at the starvation bunker was Mr. Bruno Borgowiec. He was one of the oldest

inmates of Auschwitz. Together with other Poles, he had laid the foundation of the camp through hard work interspersed with blows. With the passing of time, his health failed and his companions, wishing to save him, succeeded in finding a less heavy job. Being from Silesia, he spoke the German language perfectly and became the interpreter at the death block. His task required much prudence, since Nazi authorities liquidated the witnesses of their crimes. But Borgowiec must have known how to handle his position tactfully if he succeeded in remaining there until they were set free. He died in March, 1947, as a consequence of the infirmities he had contracted in the camp. Foreseeing his imminent death, he spontaneously went to the rectory of the church of St. Hedwig in Chorzow, where before the pastor, Father John Gajda, and three witnesses he testified on oath to all that he knew about Father Maximilian's imprisonment at the starvation bunker and about his holy death. The testimony of Mr. Borgowiec is of inestimable worth, because without it the details of Father Kolbe's martyrdom would be unknown to us.

The documentation consists of four records of great importance, two of which are preserved in the historical archives of the National Museum of Auschwitz:

1. The first document reports the list of 305 prisoners who were transferred from the Pawiak prison to the concentration camp of Auschwitz with the same convoy as Father Kolbe. Each one is listed in the progressive order of the number which had been assigned to him and described with a few biographical notes. Father Kolbe was the twenty-seventh and corresponded to # 16670.

2. ,The daily register of the x-rays taken at the camp hospital. The photocopies of this register concerning Father Maximilian go from March 2, 1941 to September 27, 1941. On page twenty-three, the medical visit marked with # 927 indicates that Father Kolbe underwent a first x-ray on July 2, 1941, and, being found with a lung disease, was kept in the block hospital. Page

twenty-three of the second volume reveals that Father Kolbe underwent a second x-ray on July 28, 1941, with the diagnosis of bronchitis.

The other two documents are kept in the archives of the friary of Niepokalanow. They are:

3. A card written in German by Kolbe to his mother on June 15, 1941:

"My dear Mama,

"At the end of the month of May I was transferred to the camp of Auschwitz. Everything is well in my regard. Be tranquil about me and about my health because the good God is everywhere and provides for everything with love.

"It would be well that you do not write to me until you will have received other news from me, because I do not know how long I will stay here.

"Cordial greetings and kisses, affectionately."

*Raymond Kolbe*

4. The death certificate of Father Kolbe sent from the central office of the concentration camp of Auschwitz to the friary of Niepokalanow on January 28, 1942.

# Arrival at Auschwitz

Father Maximilian arrived at the concentration camp of Auschwitz on the evening of Wednesday, May 28, 1941, from the Pawiak prison with a convoy of 320 prisoners, among whom were some clergymen. Early in the morning they had been brought to the station of Warsaw and loaded on freight trucks. Information, which was recorded by Father Ladislaus Swies, portrays the sad journey:

"As soon as the escort guards had piled us into the freight cars, bolting the doors from the outside, the silence of a tomb enveloped us. But as soon as the train started to move, someone intoned religious and national songs. The chant was taken up by all and began to ring throughout the train car.

"I was interested in the person who had started those songs and I understood that it was Father Maximilian Kolbe, founder of Niepokalanow. Since I like to sing, and was the first to follow his singing, Father Maximilian also took an interest in me. The crowded condition and the lack of air in the freight car produced a suffocating and frightening atmosphere. The certainty of being taken to a concentration camp weighed upon us in a depressing way. Despite that, under the influence of the songs and the discourse of Father Maximilian, we took heart, almost forgetting our sad lot."

When the deportation train carrying the 305 prisoners reached its destination, the deportees still had to walk a mile and a half to arrive at the camp. Watched not only by the guards with their rifles at the ready, but also by attack dogs, they had to cover the rest of the way at a run, in the continual fear of being seized by the teeth of the dogs or of being struck by the blows inflicted by the SS men with their riflestock on the weak prisoners or the late-comers. Father Maximilian, who had just been released from the Pawiak infirmary and had not yet perfectly recovered from pneumonia, had to keep pace with his companions to avoid the worst.

On their arrival at the great courtyard of the camp, they had to submit themselves to the norms regulating the coming of each new contingent of deportees, that is, to the roll call and to a temporary settlement. The roll call was performed in a most brutal and at the same time grotesque way, aimed perhaps at giving to the newly arrived a foretaste of the kind of life awaiting them in their new quarters.

After their names were called aloud, the prisoners had to leave one column and hastily go to join the ranks of those who had already been called. Moreover, in the rapid transit from one line to the other, prisoners were hit with ropes reinforced by pieces of lead, which obliged the inmates to jump and stumble, and aroused coarse laughter and insults from their warders. Jews and priests were especially subjected to this brutal treatment. The former were easily identifiable by the physical characteristics of their race, and the latter by their dignified posture and their instinctive reaction to repulsive measures. The long-awaited sleep did not bring any blandishment to their physical and moral sufferings. They were, in fact, brought to spend the night in a hall twenty-five by one hundred feet, with all doors and windows closed.

Those who in the morning had not fainted or had not been half-suffocated due to lack of air and the stench thoroughly permeating the environment were dazed and exhausted.

To their greater consternation and innermost humiliation, before being allowed to leave the gloomy hall, they were ordered tersely to remove their clothes and were subjected to a common bath consisting of violent jets of ice-cold water sprayed on all of them in groups. Then vexed, beaten and mocked with obscene words because of their nakedness, they were given old, worn-out coats to wear, many of which were stained with blood. A number marked on each coat was destined to be the label earmarking each one of them in the camp. Father Maximilian became number 16670.

Assembled anew in the courtyard, the priests and the Jews were ordered to break ranks so as to be granted the "privilege" of receiving particular and more refined tortures. The Jews, without any exceptions, were destined to become fodder for the gas chambers. Entrusted to the "Punishment Company" in the death block, within two or three weeks they would all be slaughtered. The priests, instead, were condemned to penal servitude. Father Maximilian and his fellow priests were assigned to the block of penal servitude, No. 17. As evidence of the brutal treatment reserved to priests and Jews, there is an inscription which today is preserved at block 6 of the State Museum of Auschwitz. The director of this museum, Casimir Smolen, has explained that the words recorded in the inscription were addressed to the prisoners at the arrival of each convoy, a fact that has been established by the testimony of many eyewitnesses:

"You have not come to a sanatorium but to a Nazi concentration camp from which there is no other exit except the crematorium.

"If this does not please anyone, he can throw himself into the barbed wire immediately.

"If there are any Jews in the convoy, they do not have a right to live more than two weeks. If there are priests, they can live a month; the others, three months."

This horrifying inscription is confirmed by another document, the SS act of faith, which was found on the grounds of the Auschwitz camp in 1945 by Prof. John Sehen from Krakow. Its text is as follows:

"Prayer books are objects for women, also for those women who wear pants. We hate the smell of incense; this ruins the soul of the German, like the Jew ruins the race.

"We believe in God, but we do not believe in His representatives. This would be idolatry and paganism.

"We believe in our Fuhrer and in our great country.

"For this and for no other reason do we fight; then when it comes time for us to die, it will not be with the words: 'Mary, pray for us.'

"We live free and we want to die free.

"Our last breath: Adolph Hitler!"

*Eiche, SS.—Group-Head,*
April 30, 1940

# Father Maximilian
# at the Penal Servitude

On the third day, the newly arrived of block 17 were visited by the camp commander, Colonel Fritsch, who, having assembled the prisoners, ordered: "Out priests! Come with me!"

Full of fear they were obliged to follow him to a barracks which housed the block kitchen and the military command for penal servitude, in a place called *Babice*, located two and one half miles away from block 17. Here, after a long wait further tormented by gnawing hunger, the priests were entrusted to a certain Krott, the department chief, a man notorious for his refined methods of cruelty, with this order: "Take these useless beings, parasites of society, and teach them how one must work." The bloody chief received the new victims into his custody and answered with a mocking smile: "Leave it to me!"

During the first days, Father Maximilian worked as a bricklayer with the task of pulling carts of gravel and stones for the construction of a wall around the crematorium. It was one of the heaviest works, since those who were assigned to this work had to pull their load at a quick trot, and each time they slowed down, blows rained down on their backs from guards who were stationed every thirty feet.

Other work at Babice consisted in cutting and transporting bundles of sticks and tree trunks which were used to enclose the humid, boggy lands. Here also the same work discipline was in force, that is, beating and blows with riflestocks when they were not moving fast enough. Here Father Maximilian lived a true way of the cross which lasted two weeks.

He had to carry on his shoulders a load two or three times as much as the other prisoners, walking on a road full of stones and holes. Anytime he stopped a few minutes to regain strength, he was assailed by blows imparted with guns or sticks. His companion priests, seeing him bleeding and stumbling under the weight, offered themselves to help him, but he, calm and smiling as always, answered: "Do not risk a beating. The Immaculata is helping me; I will make it!"

Details about the life of Father Maximilian during the first fifteen days of June are supplied by Mr. Miecislaus Koscielniak, from whose report we select the following episode:

"It was the day of Corpus Christi (June 12, 1941). On this day, the camp breathed a few hours of tranquillity because the guards had received permission to go to the city. After the so-called mess, my friend Sigismund Kolodziejski invited me to go with him to blocks 18 and 19 where he knew there could be found friends and civil companions of our transport, so that we could speak with them a little about things that did not regard the camp. Here I met a quiet, modest prisoner full of seriousness and peace, whose name I did not understand well in the act of presentation. But Sigismund intervened saying to me: 'This is Father Maximilian Kolbe, founder of the Cities of the Immaculata near Sochaczew and in Japan.'

"I looked at him with attention and also with a bit of curiosity, but without amazement. We were tanned by the sun, black with dirt, covered with rags, deprived, I would say, of every human trace of dignity, of liberty.

"We walked about with caution not to be noticed by the other prisoners; then we sat down on the posts and the bricks of the block in construction (block 17).

"Father Kolbe began to talk softly about the feast of Corpus Christi, of the great and omnipotent God, of the sufferings with which God tries us to prepare us for a better life, exhorting us to perseverance and courage because the trial would pass. There exists, he continued to say, divine justice, and being certain of its manifestation, there was no need to yield morally.

"We listened to him with devotion, forgetting for the moment hunger and humiliations. And he continued:

"'No, no, they will not kill our souls because we prisoners are something different from our persecutors, who cannot kill in us the dignity of being Catholic and Polish. No, we shall not yield; we shall persevere, and they will never succeed in killing with fear the soul of the Polish people. And, if we die, we will die pure and tranquil, resigned to the divine plans.'

"Thus he spoke to us—Father Maximilian Kolbe, Franciscan, a great priest, later, a hero and voluntary martyr who offered his life for a prison companion. We returned to our block spiritually comforted."

We owe to Prof. Koscielniak, who as we know was a painter, this testimonial:

"Upon the request of Father Maximilian, I had designed with pencil two images: one of Christ and the other of the most holy Madonna which the Servant of God always carried with himself, putting himself in great danger of receiving maximum punishments on the part of the head-officer if he ever became aware of it. When the Servant of God lost the images, he asked me to make others and I did.

"His conferences not only sustained us in spirit, but they were also for us an admirable revelation of his faith. We said that he was truly a heroic confessor of Christ. Even the unbelievers looked with admiration and approval at Father Kolbe's calm and balanced spirit."

Of another opinion however were the camp chiefs, who were amused at the panic of the prisoners. Perhaps for this reason, the meekness and resignation of Father Maximilian, instead of appeasing, rather increased the rage of the ruthless Krott, who, as a reaction, had chosen him to be the particular victim of his cruelty as it is revealed by the following episode narrated by Mr. Francis Gajowniczek:

"One day, with other prison companions, I was digging dung from a ditch to carry into the field. One of my companions standing above received the dung and then threw it out. All of a sudden a guard came by with a dog and asked the prisoner who received the dung the reason why he took so little at a time. After a moment, he began to strike him and to incite the dog against him. The dog began to attack and bite him. The poor prisoner conserved a surprising calm; he did not even let out one complaint. My other companions heard the conversation with the German. The prisoner said openly that he was a priest. It was then that the guard became even more enraged. Only after the death of Father Kolbe did I learn that that poor prisoner was precisely he."

The infamous conduct of Krott becomes even more hateful in the following account of Father Szweda:

"There was another day particularly hard for Father. The bloody officer chose him for his victim and tormented him with openly wild joy like a rapacious bird on his defenseless prey.

"He himself loaded pieces of heavy wood which he had particularly chosen on the shoulders of Father Kolbe and then he ordered him to run. When Father Kolbe fell to the ground, he kicked him in the face and stomach and struck him with a stick, yelling: 'You don't want to work, you faker. I'll show you what it means to work!...' During the interval of the afternoon, between the derision and the blasphemies, he ordered him to stretch out on a tree trunk. Then he chose one of his strongest cut-throats and commanded him to inflict fifty blows on his victim.

"Father Maximilian moved no more. He was thrown into the mud and covered with sticks. After that and the work of the whole day, there followed a debilitating march to the camp. Father Kolbe was so exhausted that they had to transport him, and the following day he was not able to go to work.

"They took him then to the hospital. He was taken to the internal section and was diagnosed thus: 'pneumonia with general exhaustion.'"

More details are provided by another eyewitness, Mr. Henry Sienkiewicz:

"Father Maximilian and I shared the same room. During some months we slept near each other, until the day that he was taken to the camp hospital. I saw how he made the sign of the cross and prayed on his knees, and I even pointed out to him that he should not expose himself to punishments by the block officer or the SS. His answer to my advice was: 'Sleep, son, because hard work awaits you and you must rest, and I, already old, will pray for you. I came here to share your sad lot of the camp.'

"In the first days of his stay in the camp, Father Kolbe was assigned to the section in which the priests and the Jews worked. They were building the crematory. Once the Servant of God was pushing a cart full of gravel. The cart was big while the wheel was small, and this increased the difficulty of the work. I wanted to help him, since the work was greater than human strength. I proposed that he remain still for a moment while I would make some trips with the cart for him.

"By misfortune the head-officer noticed it and, because we had spoken to each other, we each received ten blows with a billy club. And to make us even more ridiculous in the eyes of the others, Father Kolbe had to push the cart full of gravel with me seated on top of it to the place where the cart was emptied and then bring me back in the empty cart to where we loaded the gravel. With the cart full of gravel, I had to push him once and he had to push me twice. We thus worked with the gravel until the evening call. To console me, the Servant of God told me: 'Henry, all that we suffer is for the Immaculata.' In June of 1941, the Servant of God was assigned to the *Babice* command, where the infamous prison warden, Krott, was in charge. Once he was strongly beaten during work by Krott and then sent back to the district, that is, to the hospital of the camp."

Another episode which once more sheds vivid light on the supernatural fortitude of Father Maximilian and on his conformity to the divine will has been recorded by Dr. Joseph Stemler:

"I don't remember well," said Dr. Stemler, "whether it was at the end of June or in the beginning of July of 1941. After the usual call of the evening, such an electrifying thing happened that even to this day I remember it with chills down my spine.

"I returned dead tired and hungry to my block (number 8), when suddenly there appeared before me one of the guards who shouted something and threatened me with a stick. He made me hurry to the side of the building where two lines of prisoners were waiting. They chased us to block 28, that is, to the hospital, and they made us take the dead bodies to the crematory.

"I have lived through many springs, and even though I was a soldier in the First World War, it never happened that I had to touch the dead. That night, instead, another prisoner and I were ordered to lift two dead bodies on a kind of trough, which reminded me of the kind used by butchers for killing pigs.

"I found myself in front of the first dead body. He was young, nude, with a ripped stomach, bloody legs, hands contorted behind him, a swollen neck, and a face that clearly showed signs of his painful agony. I was unable to move.

"The guard let out a yell, to which a calm voice made an echo:

"'Let us take him, brother.'

"For the fraction of a second, it seemed to me that I knew that voice.

"With repugnance, I took the dead corpse by the bloody legs while my companion lifted him by the shoulders and we placed it in the trough; then we took the second corpse and placed it next to the first and we went to the crematory site near the camp command.

"I was terribly disturbed. My arms were weak; my wooden shoes fell off my feet. I thought it would have been far better if I had been the one to be transported in that horrible trough.

"Suddenly, behind me I heard the calm and moving voice of my companion: 'Holy Mary...pray for us!...'

"Almost as though a current of electricity had passed through my body, I suddenly felt strong.

"Now I held that kind of a bier with strength.

"We reached the crematory, a low construction with a flat roof and a high chimney from which the wind blew away the pestilential smoke.

"There we had to stack up the corpses after having given to the guard the number marked with a marking pencil on the chest of the dead person. A mistake would have provoked fatal results. Some family would have received news of the death of a relative while he was still alive.

"Then we had to watch the burning of the gruesome catafalque made of a large, mobile grate on which were cremated the bodies of the poor prisoners who died in the camp.

"I was seized with delirium, dazed.... We turned away, my companion and I. Meanwhile, I trembled all over. My legs again became rigid; it was my companion who pushed the trough slowly and me with it.

"We had hardly passed the door of the crematory when I heard the same clear and humble voice.

"'Eternal rest...grant unto them, O Lord.'

"Again it was a familiar voice.

"He turned to whisper:

"'And *the Word was made flesh!'*

"Who was it?

"It was the Franciscan of Niepokalanow, Father Maximilian Kolbe."

About Father Kolbe's stay in the camp hospital, we are told about this moving episode by Father Szweda:

"I was then a nurse at the camp hospital, in the section for the contagious. When I knew that Father Kolbe was in the hospital, I went immediately to visit him. He was not delirious. His face was livid; his eyes were languid. The high fever burned in his body to the point that he was unable to move his tongue, and his voice died in his throat.

"Because of the difficulty of being moved from one section to another, I recommended Father Kolbe to another nurse so that he would take special care of him. After some days, Father Kolbe was somewhat rested, but the pneumonia had not cleared up and the fever continued.

"In the face of his suffering, his conduct amazed the doctors and nurses. He conducted himself manfully and with complete resignation to the will of God, and often repeated: 'For Jesus Christ I am ready to suffer even more. The Immaculata is with me, and helps me.'

"For an inexplicable reason, the fever did not cease even after the crisis of pneumonia had been resolved! They then transferred Father Kolbe to the section for the contagious and placed him in the room of those suspected of typhoid fever. Here contact with him was easier. He was assigned to the bed near the main entrance of the large room.

"Every dead person whom they took away received from him a blessing and conditional absolution. In the midst of the sick and suffering brothers, he carried out his mission as pastor of souls. Often he related episodes, taking them from the rich treasure of his experience, listened to confessions, said prayers in common, lifted spirits and gave conferences on the Immaculate Virgin, whom he loved with the simplicity of a child. When the rooms were dark, the imprisoned came to him, asking him to hear their confessions or for words of comfort.

"When after the day's work I went to him, he pressed me to his heart like a mother her child, consoling me; and pointing out the Immaculata as a model, he told me: *She is the true consolatrix of the afflicted; she hears everyone; she helps everyone!* I always went away consoled and peaceful.

"Once I took him a cup of tea I had saved, but how surprised I was when he did not accept it, saying: 'Why should I make an exception? The others do not have any.'

"He had become popular among the sick and everyone called him *our little Father.*"

In spite of the strict vigilance exercised by the SS men and the extreme measures adopted for any action against "camp rules," Father Kolbe, as we have seen, was able to exercise extensively his priestly ministry among his comrades. He resorted to preaching and counseling; he exhorted his fellow-prisoners to bear lovingly and patiently their infirmities. He especially availed himself of his priestly power for calming, through the Sacrament of Reconciliation, souls whom the persecutors' inhuman treatment had filled with hatred.

Did Father Kolbe ever attempt to celebrate the Holy Sacrifice of the Mass in some hiding place of the camp? Notwithstanding much investigation for a long time, his biographer did not succeed in filling the gap until a testimony supplied by an eyewitness, Henry Sienkiewicz, at the process for his beatification shed a most welcome light on the object of this research.

Celebrating the Mass or administering the sacraments in the "death camp" was a most daring action. A priest who had been caught in performing this act of cult deserved the frightful punishment of the "steinbunker" or execution by shooting. Father Maximilian, however, brave as always, did not consider the fate awaiting him if he would have been discovered. In secret he celebrated the sacrifice of the Cross on that Calvary of the twentieth century. Here are the details as they are found in the acts of the beatification process.

"I went often to the hospital to visit Father Maximilian. From the other prisoners I came to know that he had won the hearts of all. He shared his meager ration with the prisoners; he prayed and said words of comfort to everyone.

"Father Kolbe himself said that he was grateful to the Immaculata for being in the hospital because the patients needed prayers and comfort. At that time I worked at the Bunawerke command. Since I had obtained the trust of the civic workers of Auschwitz, I received from them bread and money. Once I brought into the camp four hundred marks and thirty medals. The Servant of God divided the money among the prisoners and also the medals after he had blessed them. Once I was given some hosts by Mrs. Kania. Father Maximilian took advantage of the gift and secretly celebrated two holy Masses. They were attended by thirty of us who also received Communion from his hands. He gave us sermons also, exhorting us to pray and to trust in the Immaculata. At Bunawerke, I received food supplies from the civilians. Bringing them into the camp was quite a problem because of the strict inspection at the gate. Fearful and at the same time eager to bring food to my fellow-prisoners, I asked advice of Father Kolbe who answered: 'Put yourself under the protection of the Immaculata; she will help you.' Moved by faith in the help of the Mother of God, I succeeded in bringing food into the camp. Once I carried bread and some bacon around each leg under my coat. At the gate the SS men searched me without realizing anything. When I told this to the Servant of God, he said: 'Trust in the Immaculata; she will show you her favors more than once.'

"Then the day came when I saw him for the last time. A general 'cleaning out' of the hospital was in progress. The hospital block chief was overtaken, as it often happened, by a raging fury. With a cynical smile, he moved from bed to bed as though he were a physician, taking temperatures while never really looking at the thermometer. Instead, he scrutinized the faces of the prisoners. He searched for the faces of intellectuals, because that 'dwarf' hated those who looked as if they were educated. That very day he threw out Father Kolbe and myself.

"While we were waiting for clothes and an assignment to a new block, we remained outside between blocks 21 and 22. I was standing on one side of the wall and Father Kolbe on the other side. He kept looking at me as if he wished to tell me something. Taking advantage of the guard's distraction, I went near him. He pressed my hand and said with a clear voice: 'I entrust you to the protection of the Immaculata.'

"He had just finished saying these words when a yell from the guard sent me back to my place.

"I kept looking at Father Kolbe. It was to be for the last time, and I still remember him thus today: his head slightly bent, his shaved crown,...eyes like profound orbits of burning coals, regular nose, cheeks looking even more sunken because the beard had not been shaved for some weeks, and lips slightly formed into a smile of forgiveness. From the short blue coat came his thin arms and his extremely thin legs.

"They called my number.... I had to leave.

"'Goodbye!' I shouted to Father Maximilian.

"And he continued to follow me with his gaze and his smile."

The preceding testimonials are confirmed by the following of Dr. Stemler:

"Near the end of July, 1941, I again met Father Kolbe at block 20 where both of us were patients. Father Maximilian occupied a bed near the door, I, the bed in front, next to that of the famous socialist writer, Humbert Barlicki. In the hall I was informed of the presence of Father Kolbe by the lawyer, John Pozaryski, judicial counsellor of the Society of the Authors. After the example of many other prisoners, during the night, I also approached Father Maximilian, crawling on the floor.

"Our greeting was most moving. We exchanged some impressions about the terrible crematories. Then we remained in silence. I looked at his emaciated face, beardless, difficult to recognize. Only the eyes, gleaming more than ever, betrayed the fever. I did not wish to tire him, yet I wanted to tell him so many things!...

"It was he who encouraged me, and I ended up going to confession. I was dominated by sentiments of sorrow and despair. I wanted to live!...

"His words instead were deep and at the same time simple. He exhorted me to have faith in the triumph of good.

"'Hatred is not a creative force. Love alone creates,' he whispered, pressing my hand in his burning one. 'These sufferings will not bend us, but they must help us become ever stronger. They are necessary together with other sacrifices so that those who will come after us may be happy....'

"He kept pressing my hand, and his references to the mercy of God infused a renewed strength in me. Only his words exhorting me to forgive the oppressors, to render good for evil, caused in me a rebellious reaction.

"During the following nights I again approached his bed. Without uttering any words, we understood each other. During the night I sent to him other prisoners who wished to receive the comforts of our Faith."

# In the Block of the Invalids

As was previously mentioned, according to the x-ray register of the hospital of Auschwitz, Father Maximilian was first x-rayed on July 2, 1941, and a second time on July 28, 1941. From the two dates, however, we cannot infer that Father Maximilian was in the block hospital during the entire month of July, but most probably from July 2 to July 20 as it may be deduced from the available testimony.

Information provided by Father Szweda records that Father Kolbe was released from the hospital still feverish and assigned to block number 12, called the block of the invalids. In this block, the inmates were dispensed from work, but "the privilege" did not make life any easier for the prisoners. In fact, the only "advantage" it presented over block number 11, the starvation bunker, was a longer agony. The invalids received only half of the already insufficient food ration reserved to the other prisoners and no treatment whatsoever. The mortality rate among them was excessively high because the greater majority of them, full of sores, died of infection.

Despite his extreme weakness, in this block Father Maximilian continued secretly his priestly apostolate on behalf of the many dying. He remained there until July 29, when he was considered improved enough to be assigned to block number 14, which was to put the seal on his holocaust.

The testimony we possess about this point is provided by Mr. Sienkiewicz and is very important for the determination of the dates and also as a witness to the constant spiritual ascent of Father Maximilian:

"Released from the hospital, he was assigned to block 14*...with those who peeled potatoes in the camp kitchen. Even at this command Father Kolbe captivated the affection of all and became very popular. Everyone drew around him for advice and prayers. I remember how in July of that year, on a Sunday afternoon, he gathered us near him, recited the litany of the Blessed Virgin, and gave us an inspiring sermon. I did not foresee that this was to be his last."

The foregoing citation from the testimony of Mr. Sienkiewicz offers the following clues for consideration:

Undoubtedly, "the Sunday afternoon of July" must have been that of the last of the month which in 1941 fell on July 27. Since on Monday, July 28, Father Maximilian went to the camp hospital for an x-ray checkup, the transferring of Father Maximilian from the block of the invalids to that of the potato-peelers spoken of by Father Szweda must have occurred after this date. Moreover, the allusion made by Sienkiewicz to "his last teaching" obliges us to consider July 27, 1941, not too far distant from the date marking Father Kolbe's supreme proof of love, which, with the convergence of all the events, points to the week between July 28 and August 3.

## Priestly Service Means To Reign

Maximilian Kolbe was a man made of flesh and blood like us, yet he had risen above the claims of

---

*The testimonies do not agree about the numeration of the blocks. For example, the block of the invalids was for Father Szweda block 12; for Sienkiewicz, it was block 14. It is certain that in the camp the block numbers were not steady but were often changed. This explains the confusion of the witnesses who recalled facts and circumstances after a length of time.

human nature until it seemed as though he had been released from the very passions that are an integral part of our existence. A true priest of God, he had not been merely content with preaching fine homilies, but he had given himself totally in fidelity to his priestly vocation. He wanted to be found similar to his Master, because the priest is another Christ, who is and remains both priest and victim. As a consequence, self-sacrifice had become so much a part of Father Kolbe that it was second nature to him. His death, then, was a logical consequence of the way he had lived his life. A man who corresponded to the grace of the Spirit, he stands out for all time as a splendid exemplification of priestly and religious consecration.

All his witnesses were unanimous in asserting his modesty, meekness and humility:

"He never spoke of himself or of his sufferings.

"He never made a show of himself in front of others. He did not seek the glory of men. Exteriorly, he gave the impression of being a meek, humble and pious man.

"He always placed himself last. I never noticed that he ever put himself above others. In his manner of treating with others, in his conversations with us, one perceived in him simplicity and humility. He told of his previous life and spoke to us of his work in Japan, of his studies, of Niepokalanow, but he never boasted about what he had accomplished and took no credit for himself. He did not cling to his opinion and had regard for the opinion of others. I can affirm that in general he never sought an easier work for himself in the camp.... On the contrary, when he was able to do so, he chose the heaviest work for himself so that the other prisoners would be less burdened."

Father Kolbe's only boast, one which he never passed over in silence, was that of being a Catholic priest.

The fortunate survivors of Auschwitz who personally experienced the warmth of his zeal and charity have rendered him their tribute of gratitude and love, and have greatly contributed to the glory of the Church and the edification of the People of God.

These testimonies remain the best proof of the luminous spiritual maturity he had achieved by the eve of his heroic death.

Brother Ladislaus testified:

"In the camp of Auschwitz, we all had the impression that he submitted himself perfectly to the divine will and that he loved the Immaculate Mother supremely In talking, he always directed us toward the most holy Virgin Often, after the evening call, I met him, and his words strengthened me with the hope of being able to bear those pains and gave me great and deep satisfaction and joy. He knew how to speak so well that after having listened to him I felt full of courage and unafraid of death, even though this was always a threat. He gathered the prisoners about himself, encouraging us and uplifting us spiritually....

"When on one occasion I showed Father my deep compassion because the head officer had beaten him mercilessly, he answered that he was happy to be able to suffer and that everything comes from God. Even then, he did not show himself resentful toward the inhuman Germans. This was a characteristic trait in Father Kolbe's life: while other priests and religious spoke of hunger and of how to obtain a piece of bread to satisfy their hunger, and of the fear and uncertainty of each day, the Servant of God never spoke of these things. He lived as though he were in another world, prayerfully immersed in God. One saw in him only humility and peace and total submission to the designs of God and to the Immaculata and a great compassion for the prisoners. One saw in him, above all, the spirit of prayer....

"Sometimes I made some inquiries regarding his interior life and at the end I had to confess that his life was different from ours; that in him there had to be a special grace of God, since he was always serene and tranquil in spirit. This was not seen in others. When all of us waited impatiently for freedom and our return home, he abandoned everything in the hands of God and the Immaculata. He never said that he wanted to return to Niepokalanow. Instead he said: 'The best thing is that which is disposed by God and the Immaculata....'

"In the concentration camp, he was very happy to be able to do some spiritual or material good to anyone. He gathered us together, made us feel secure and elevated our hearts to God. When he underwent cruel beatings from the German boss in command, he bore them tranquilly as a mortification. Sometimes I wanted to lend him some money so that he could get a little bit of soup at the canteen, but he never wanted it so as not to decrease my savings. Yet he was disposed to give his own to others."

The moral stature of the saint led to this most beautiful appraisal by Dr. Lucian Thaddeus Chrosicki:

"From meetings with him, we were always uplifted in soul and became stronger in our will to resist and not to become discouraged. He often recommended that we trust in God and abandon ourselves to the protection of the Immaculata. From other prison companions I often heard that the influence of the Servant of God came to be generally defined as a kind of 'reign' over the prisoners. Thus was interpreted the blessed influence which he had over his prison companions. He was always calm and ready to be of help."

Rich in simple but touching episodes is the witness of Mr. Alexander Dziuba:

"He loved the Lord and the most holy Madonna above everything, and with this love he conquered us all. When he spoke to us of God, we had the impression that it was not a man of this world speaking. When it happened that some prisoner conducted himself badly in the camp, he suffered and sought to lead him back on the right path. When the prisoners fought with each other, he pacified them. He asked them to forgive each other and said that he would pray for them. He desired to draw everyone to God. He saw the will and the finger of God in everything.

"In the camp of Mathausen-Guzen I heard one of the priests say: 'O God, if You truly exist, punish these criminals.' I never heard such words from the mouth of Father Kolbe....

"He would have given anything to be able to help his neighbor. I remember the following incident:

"Once in front of the block, I saw how he gave his own dinner and a portion of soup to one of the youngest prisoners in the block of the young ones, saying: 'Take it and eat. You are younger; you must live.' Another time he would have wanted to do the same but we would not permit him to, obliging him to eat his portion.

"Sometimes, after confession to Father Maximilian, we desired to receive Holy Communion, but that was not possible, since at that time Mass could not be celebrated in the camp. Then, wanting to symbolize the Eucharist for us in some way, he would take his own bread, bless it and give a piece to each one of us. Then he would not want to accept anything from our rations.

"Once he was kicked by the block chief. Father Kolbe's only reaction was the words: 'May God forgive you.' I heard these words because I was seated right next to him. He consoled us, cared for our souls and helped us to write our letters home in German. He did this for me twice.

"Personally, I owe to his counsels and to his instruction the fact that I got rid of thoughts of suicide. Each time that I had gone to confession to him, I felt renewed in my spirit and I saw a different world before me.

"Never in the life of the camp did I ever see Father Kolbe become angry or strike anyone. On the contrary, he did everything with profound reflection. We saw the supernatural in everything that he did or said. It was not a matter of wisdom or cleverness or human interest.

"We prisoners perceived in him a superior strength. He was ready to do everything for God. I saw myself that the Servant of God, before eating, made the sign of the cross with seriousness and devotion, unmindful of the fact that he could have been seen and beaten by the chief. He was not afraid of work in the command. Neither did he seek work that was less heavy. He always went where he was sent. Once, one of the prisoners stole a pair of slippers from another. The one from whom they were stolen immediately marked the number of the 'thief,' wanting to report the affair to the head of the block. The guilty one would have received for this a strong punishment of at least twenty-five blows with a club. Wanting to avoid such a punishment, the Servant of God took the slippers, restored them to the owner, and begged him not to make the report."

Testified Henry Sienkiewicz:

"During the stay of the Servant of God in the camp, I never noticed that he nourished any hatred for the Germans. On the contrary, not only did he pray for them, but he also exhorted us to pray for their conversion. We were all amazed at the extraordinary virtue that we saw in that man: faith, the constant spirit of prayer, great humility and the spirit of fellowship pushed to the point of sharing his own food rations with the other prisoners.

"He lived every day only for God. He drew us to God and desired that we live well and that we put up with the life of the camp. He really had within himself a kind of magnet which drew us to him, to God and to the most holy Mother. Often he spoke to us of God and inculcated in us the truth that God is good and merciful. The Servant of God desired to convert the whole camp....

"Father Maximilian Kolbe prayed for sinners.... He suffered because the prisoners cursed and swore at each other. I saw how he accepted the will of God in everything. I know that he discussed religious topics with an ex-socialist deputy....

"I also know that he shared his food rations with other prisoners. I myself once received from him a quarter of a loaf of bread. He gave his own good wooden shoes to another prisoner in exchange for a quite worn-out pair.

"Once a prisoner was beaten by the chief because he had washed his tin bowl badly. Father took care of the prisoner and washed the bowl for him because he had been severely beaten on his hands. Father Kolbe treated each prisoner as his own brother."

Dr. Rudolph Diem, doctor in charge of Auschwitz, presents Father Maximilian as having already arrived at the summit of charity, ready for the supreme sacrifice:

"I knew Father Kolbe as a man of serene character, balanced, psychologically healthy. He arrived at the district with a fever and chest pains, but despite his sufferings he was very tranquil. Patiently, he awaited his own turn since from two hundred to as many as a thousand persons a day were waiting. He caught my attention particularly when, on my recommendation that he come to the hospital, because being sick he needed attention, he answered that he could wait some more, *that I take instead, in his place, a prisoner whom he pointed out to me.*

"Since I had desired at different times to place him in the hospital because I saw that his health required treatment, he always pointed out to me another more in need. Captivated and amazed, I asked him: 'Who are you?' He answered that he was a *Catholic priest.* Against the background of the general animal instinct of self-preservation, seeing such abnegation and a desire to sacrifice oneself for others was surprising for me, and I saw in Father Kolbe an uncommon man. When I asked him if he still believed that God watched over us, he sought to persuade me with all his fervor that God effectively watches over us. And he proposed that I talk with him in the Birkenalei in free moments.

"In these conversations, we touched upon questions relating to faith. I told him that I no longer believed because I found myself at that time in a state of discouragement. In our conversations, he never manifested hate or anger against the invader....

"I noticed in him the virtue of faith. At my words that I did not believe, the Servant of God assured me that I still believed in the existence of God and he proposed that I go to confession. Then I admitted to him that I was of the evangelical faith.... I must underline that against the background of the general fight for life and the instinct of self-preservation, to be able to resist and to come out of the camp—a thing that was a motive in the actions of almost every prisoner—Father Kolbe with his moral attitude, that is, with his lively faith in God and in Providence, with Christian hope and, above all, with love of God and neighbor, surpassed everyone and distinguished himself from everyone. In the camp of Auschwitz there was no man like him and I never knew anyone like him, even though every day I met hundreds of prisoners, among whom were priests, religious, professors, princes, artists—men of every kind of social sphere.

"I was also struck by the virtues of justice and gratitude in him, when after giving him medical care, he told me: 'You, Doctor, have done much for me, very much, and I would wish to repay you with something.' And when, in fact, I was spiritually and religiously discouraged, the Servant of God proposed that I go to confession to him and thus draw closer to God....

"According to my opinion, the virtues of faith, love of God and neighbor, of hope, justice and fortitude were not a thing of momentary impulse in Father Kolbe, as one often sees in others, but they were constant in him, deeply rooted in his being. Among other things, he told me that every man has a purpose in life. He, Father Kolbe, had consecrated his own life for the good of every man, and therefore he believed irrevocably that what happened to him was what God had destined."

## The Escape of a Prisoner

Father Maximilian had been at block 14 only a few days when an incident occurred which was to shock and frighten the entire camp of Auschwitz. A prisoner escaped. According to a law which had been enacted in the camp and of which everyone was fully aware, as punishment and as a lesson, ten men of his block would be condemned to die by starvation in the horrible underground bunker. The inmates of the camp were terrified. They were assembled in the marching field, and, in unrelenting July heat, all had to stand at attention for three endless hours, until 9 o'clock P.M., when the order was given to break ranks and to distribute the meager evening meals. Everyone ate except block 14. Instead, they were forced to watch as their food ration was dumped into the canal. Then, tormented by hunger and sick with fear, they were sent to bed. Lying sleepless on their filthy bunks, they were vexed by a torment which was similar to death itself.

On the following day, after the morning roll call, the other blocks were sent to work as usual, except block 14. They stood lined up in the square, exposed to the burning rays of that scorching July sun, where they were to remain all day long. Distraught with grief, burnt by thirst, exhausted by weariness, many collapsed. When, despite the blows of the wardens, they failed to regain consciousness, they were dragged out of the lines and piled one on top of the other. They were permitted nothing to drink, nor any refreshment while the unbearable heat caused their faces to become swollen and their sight to grow dim.

Around three o'clock in the afternoon, they were given a half hour break to receive the delayed noon meal. Afterwards, they again lined up, standing at attention. In the meantime, the number of those who were fainting increased uninterruptedly.

Despite his infirmities and extreme weakness, Father Maximilian, instead, did not collapse, nor did he fall. Was he so deeply immersed in the thought of offering his life that he became insensitive to that accumulation of torments, or was he enraptured by the contemplation of his heavenly Queen?

Toward evening the other inmates, coming back from work, formed lines in the large square in front of their panic-stricken brethren. Tears shown in many eyes as they stared at the dismal company from cell block 14, the "semi-condemned." The rest of the camp had the great pain of feeling powerless to do anything to mitigate the agony of the pitiful group. After night roll call was over, the infamous Colonel Fritsch, accompanied by Palitsch, officer in charge of the report, and by a group of armed guards, approached the men of block 14 and ordered them to stand at attention. The men stood rigid with fear. There was a deep and penetrating silence. It was broken only after a moment, which seemed an eternity, by the sharp voice of Commander Fritsch who announced: "Since the fugitive has not been found, ten of you will be condemned to death."

The frantic men began to whisper: "Who will be chosen? Will it be me?"

Delighted by the spectacle, Commander Fritsch carefully weighed his every word and gesture. Finally, staring at the prisoners, he passed along the front row and pointed to the first victim, who was immediately removed from the ranks and put to one side, while his number was carefully written down. After the first, then the second row, then the third...and so forth until the fateful number was completed.

At the end of the gruesome procedure, those who had been spared could breathe again. Auschwitz, in fact, had become such a terrible place that the struggle for survival was for most prisoners the sole priority.

All hope of being spared vanished in the ten men destined for the starvation bunker. Sick, terrified, exhausted, their imaginations and memories flashed the events of their entire lives. They longed for their families, their parents, their wives, their children. Some began to cry; others to call "goodbye!"

"Goodbye, friends; we will meet again where there is justice," said one.

"Long live Poland!" sobbed another.

"Goodbye! Goodbye, my dear wife; goodbye, my dear children, already orphans of your father," cried an inconsolable Sergeant Francis Gajowniczek.

Suddenly, the unexpected happened. In fact, it was more than unexpected. It was almost unbelievable. A prisoner, stepping out of the ranks, walked calmly toward Commander Fritsch. Quick as lightning, voices spread from rank to rank:

"It is Father Maximilian! It is Father Kolbe!"

Clad with the splendid armor of his immense faith and his inextinguishable love, Father Kolbe approached the fierce commander.

Closer and closer the priest came until he stood in front of Fritsch. Every eye was on the two of them—the burly Nazi Colonel and the emaciated priest dressed in his striped prison coat, number 16670. As they stood there for what seemed to be an eternity, the total contrast between the two was something those eyewitnesses would never forget. Basically, it was the contrast between the man who rejected God and the man who dared to love Him totally.

At this point of the narration, we endeavor to reconstruct faithfully, based on the testimonies of eyewitnesses, the most heroic action which the human mind can conceive in the name of love for one's neighbor. The testimonies are brief, as they only could be, in that particular moment, because those present must have been seized by such a tremendous emotion as to remain dumbfounded.

The following is the testimony of Francis Gajowniczek, the most brief of the entire canonical process due to his little acquaintance with Father Kolbe. This fact, however, contributes to increase the heroism of Father Maximilian's action, insofar as it was not accomplished for a friend or a confrere but for an unknown "brother" whom Father Kolbe loved in Christ and in the Immaculata.

"I knew Father Kolbe personally only during the summer of 1941, the day that he offered his life for me.

"I knew him in the following circumstances. Some weeks previously, before the condemnation of Father Kolbe, I heard that in our same block there was a priest who raised the spirits of those who were at the point of despair, and he instructed them. At that time, I did not know that it was Father Kolbe; I found this out only after his condemnation and death.

"The circumstance which accompanied Father Kolbe's condemnation and death were the following:

"After the escape of a prisoner from our block, we were lined up in ten rows during the night roll call. I was in the same row as Father Kolbe; we were about three or four prisoners away from each other. The *Lagerfuhrer,* Fritsch, [deputy] commandant of the camp, surrounded by guards, approached and from the rows began to choose ten prisoners to send to death. The Fuhrer also pointed with his finger at me. I stepped out of the row and cried that I desired to see my children again. After an instant, a prisoner stepped out of the line, offering himself in my place. The Lagerfuhrer came closer and began to say something to him. A guard led him to the group of those condemned to death and made me get back in line.

"This had happened after roll call. The second or third day after, I heard that the ten were in a bunker and that they were condemned to die by starvation. From my prison companions I knew that he who offered himself in my place was Father Kolbe. It was also said later that of the ten, he lived the longest. My prison companions had great admiration for Father Kolbe."

In his testimony, Gajowniczek did not report the words spoken by Father Maximilian to Deputy Commandant Fritsch. Filled with deep emotion, most probably he did not hear anything or, if Father Maximilian made his request in German, he would not have understood.

Another eyewitness, instead, Dr. Nicetas Francis Wlodarski, who was close enough to hear the whole conversation, listened to it attentively and noted the words down, not on paper, but in his heart. Continually he must have recalled them exactly to mind. Let us listen to him:

"After the choice of the ten prisoners, Father Maximilian stepped out of line and, taking off his cap, he stood at attention before the Commandant. Surprised, and directing himself to Father Maximilian, he said: 'What does this Polish pig want?'

"Pointing his finger toward Francis Gajowniczek, already chosen for death, Father Maximilian replied:

"'I am a Polish Catholic priest; I am old; I want to take his place because he has a wife and children....'

"It appeared that the amazed officer could find no strength to say anything. After a moment, with a hand gesture, accompanied by only one word: out, he ordered Gajowniczek to return to the line he had stepped out of. In this way, Father Maximilian took the place of the condemned.

"The distance between me and Fritsch and Father Maximilian was not more than three meters. A short time later, the ten condemned men were closed up in block number 11, at that time number 13, since the numbers had been changed.

"It seemed incredible that Commandant Fritsch had taken Gajowniczek from the group of the condemned and had accepted the offer of Father Kolbe, instead of condemning both of them to the starvation bunker. With such a monster that would have been possible.

"Those chosen were of different ages, but they were, above all, physically weak, even though Fritsch did not usually have a criteria for making the choice."

At the apostolic process of Warsaw, Dr. Wlodarski completed his testimony with further details which make it clear that Father Kolbe's offer of his own life was not the result of a psychic imbalance, but arose from a heart filled with love for God and his fellowmen:

"Father Kolbe had offered his life voluntarily for Gajowniczek, desiring to save him for his family. Undoubtedly, he did it moved by love of God and of neighbor. I consider the act of the Servant of God as one of supreme heroism. It excludes any imprudence or rashness.... He had many persons devoted to him and a good possibility of resisting and of getting out of the camp. On the basis of the knowledge that I have of the Servant of God, I affirm that he offered himself out of supernatural motives, eminently religious, to take the place of Gajowniczek."

The general astonishment that this event produced in those present is even more clearly put in relief by the testimony of Dr. Stemler:

"...I felt his influence with far greater strength after the event which shook the camp, that is, after he offered his own life for that of another prisoner. The news of the episode was spread throughout the entire camp that same night. I am profoundly convinced that the commandant of the camp agreed that the prisoner chosen by him should be substituted by Father Kolbe only because Father Kolbe was a priest. He had clearly asked: 'Who are you?'

"Having obtained the answer, he repeated to his companion:

"'He is a *Pfaffe*' (a poor little priest).

"And it was only then that Commandant Fritsch said:

"'I accept.'

"I formed this conviction immediately after, in the camp, when the event was told to me. The sacrifice of Father Kolbe evoked a great impression on the minds of the prisoners since in the camp there was almost no manifestation of love of neighbor. One prisoner refused to give a piece of bread to another, and here was the example that one had offered his own life for the life of a prisoner whom he did not even know."

Another testimony, that of Mr. Sobolewski, underlined a particular passed over in silence by the others: the impression that the event made on camp authorities.

"...After the choice was made of the ten unfortunates, behold, all of a sudden there stepped out from the ranks of block number 14 Father Maximilian Kolbe, Franciscan of Niepokalanow, who went directly toward Commandant Fritsch. He stopped before the commandant, straight as a stretched cord, with his arms at his sides, and he made his request, that is of wanting to go to die in the bunker in the place of one of the prisoners, whom he pointed out with his hand. The commandant agreed and Father Kolbe took the place of the condemned, Francis Gajowniczek. This man returned to his own place in the ranks of block 14, while Father Kolbe remained near the left wing, among the condemned.

"The fact that Father Maximilian sacrificed himself for another prisoner aroused the admiration and the respect of the prisoners while it provoked consternation among the authorities of the camp. In the history of the camp of Auschwitz, this was the first case in which a prisoner sacrificed himself voluntarily for another.

"When the selection had ended, the condemned were led by an escort to the bunker to die of starvation."

•

Interpreting the event literally, the witnesses laid stress on the fact that Father Kolbe gave his own life to save the life of a fellow-prisoner. But we would fail to grasp the full implication of Kolbe's act, if we were to restrict it to this sole motive. At the core of his offer, there was a further motivation. His task was not merely to save one; he realized the grave need to save the nine others from abandonment and despair. He had to help them and he would help them to die as Christians. As soon as the great door swung shut behind the condemned men, he took charge of them all, and not of them only, but also of the others dying of hunger in the neighboring bunkers. Their hoarse groans, fierce yells, and loud wailing had spread far and wide, terrifying all who had heard them.

Father Maximilian went voluntarily to this most evil place ever erected by man, conquering its confines with a heart full of love. Thus hatred was replaced by love, injury by pardon, cursing by prayer. The guards themselves were amazed and exclaimed: "We have never seen the like." With his self-immolation, Father Kolbe, who had become a mere number, won the hardest of all victories—the victory of love, which forgives and pardons.

All the survivors of Auschwitz are unanimous in testifying that from the feast of the Assumption, 1941, the camp became a somewhat less hellish place.

# The Death Block

This underground room was on the basement level of block 13, which was therefore called death block or bunker. Those condemned to this most atrocious death knew beforehand that they would come out as corpses to be directly taken to the crematorium.

The starvation bunker was encircled by a solidly constructed wall, twenty-one feet high, which no one could approach without the risk of being immediately shot. There was no communication from the outside. Only the jailers had access to the cells for their daily inspection. Divested of the slightest human sentiment, the jailers mocked their victims without compassion, without mercy.

Any attempt to ask information about one of the condemned meant to risk sharing the same lot. Father Szweda who, on account of his office, enjoyed a certain freedom, received this answer for having dared to ask news of Father Maximilian: "Would you like to go with him? Do you not know that it is forbidden to take interest in them?"

Only a few Poles who were assigned to render service in that bunker would be able to provide us with priceless information. It was through one of them, Mr. Bruno Borgowiec, that we are in possession of the details shedding light on the last days on earth of Father Kolbe and his companions. One cannot read his most impressive report without being filled with contrasting sentiments of deepest horror and highest edification.

"Having read the article: 'Memoirs of the last moments in the life of Father Maximilian Kolbe' in

Rycerz Niepokalanej," began Mr. Borgowiec, "I would like to describe his last days in the starvation bunker of Auschwitz.

"I was then a secretary and interpreter in the so-called subterranean area, and thinking over this heroic man's sublime conduct in the face of death, which amazed even the guards of the Gestapo, I still remember with all preciseness the last days of his life.

"Block number 13, situated on the left side of the camp, was surrounded by a wall twenty-one feet high. There were cells on the ground floor where the company of discipline had rooms. Some cells had little windows and folding beds. Others were without windows and dark.

"To one of these cells in July, 1941, after the evening call, ten prisoners were led from block number 14. After having ordered the poor condemned men to strip, they were pushed into the place where there were already about twenty other victims from the last process. The newly-arrived were accompanied to a separate cell. Closing them in, the sneering guards said: *We will dry you up like tulips!* From that day on, the unhappy men were given no more food.

"Each day, the guards, making their routine check, ordered that the bodies of those who died in the course of the night be taken away. During these visits I was always present, because I had to write the names in the register, or translate (into German from Polish) the conversations and requests of the prisoners.

"From the cells of the condemned men, every day there were heard prayers in a loud voice, the rosary and religious hymns, in which even the prisoners of the other cells joined. In the moments when the guards were absent, I descended into the subterranean cell to talk with and to console my companions. The ardent prayers and hymns to the most holy Virgin resounded through the whole subterranean area. It seemed to me that I was in church. Father Maximilian Kolbe started, and all the others responded. Sometimes they were so immersed in prayers that they were not aware of the arrival of the guards for their usual visit. Finally, at the shouts of the guards, the voices died out.

"When the cells were opened, the poor, condemned, crying prisoners pleaded for a piece of bread and some water. This was denied them. If any of the stronger ones got close to the door, he was immediately kicked in the stomach by the guards, and when he fell, he died or he was shot on the spot.

"The martyrdom that the condemned prisoners had to endure by such an atrocious death is attested to by the fact that the pails were always empty and dry. From this it was deduced that the unfortunate prisoners, because of thirst, drank their own urine.

"Father Maximilian Kolbe conducted himself heroically, asking nothing and complaining about nothing. He encouraged the others and persuaded the prisoners to hope that the escaped prisoner would be found and they would be freed.

"Because they were already so weak, they said the prayers in a whisper. During each visit of the guards, when they were already almost all stretched out on the pavement, Father Maximilian Kolbe could be seen standing, or kneeling in their midst, looking serenely at the visitors. The guards knew of his offering. They also knew that all those who were together with him were dying innocently. For this reason, having respect for Father Kolbe, they said among themselves: 'This priest is a real gentleman. Up until now we have never had anyone like him.'"

This delayed recognition of Father Kolbe's merits on the part of the SS is confirmed by the process deposition of Dr. Nicetas Wlodarski:

"How Father Maximilian lived the last moments in block 11 I know in part from the report of the chief, a German of that bunker. I took care of that office, and he told me about it because he knew the facts, having had to go into the bunker every day. Unfortunately, I do not remember the last name of this officer. He told me that in the bunker the Servant of God lived longer than the others, and that he sustained them in spirit, and prayed with the prisoners. The chief called Father Kolbe an extraordinarily courageous man, a hero. He also underlined the character of Father Kolbe and his calmness and said that he made a great impression on the SS men who would go to look into that bunker. He said that for the SS it was absolutely shocking."

# Death

"Thus two weeks passed," Borgowiec's testimony continues. "Meanwhile, the prisoners died one after the other, so much so that at the end of the third week only four remained, among whom was Father Kolbe. To the authorities it seemed that they lived on too long. The cell was needed for other victims.

"For this reason, on August 14, the criminal Boch, a German and the director of the hall of the sick, was brought in. He gave everyone an injection of poisonous acid in the left arm. With a prayer on his lips, Father Kolbe held out his arm to the killer. Being unable to stand what my eyes beheld, under the pretext of having to work in the office, I went away.

"After the guard and the executioner left, I returned to the cell, where I found Father Maximilian Kolbe sitting down, leaning against the wall, with eyes opened and his head bent to the left side. (It was his usual position.) His serene face was beautifully radiant.

"Together with the barber of the block, Mr. Chlebik from Karwina, I took the body of the hero to the bath. Here it was placed in a box and taken to the mortuary cell of the prison.

"Thus died the priest, the hero of the camp of Auschwitz, offering himself voluntarily for the father of a family, quiet and tranquil, praying until the last moment.

"This heroic act of the priest was remembered in the camp for months. The name of Father Maximilian Kolbe was remembered at every execution.

"The impression which I reported from this and other similar facts will always remain carved in my memory."

## In the Light of the Immaculata

Father Maximilian died on August 14, 1941, the vigil of Our Lady's Assumption into heaven. The Immaculata, who had been the ideal of his life, the burning fire of his zeal, the inspiration of his leadership, the ecstasy of his prayers, the Queen of Niepokalanow and Mugenzai No Sono, had come in the light of her glory to bring him into paradise.

His emaciated body—tortured, consumed and even desecrated by nakedness which was, in the last days of his imprisonment, imposed upon him and his companions—that poor body, on the day of death, appeared almost as if transfigured and clothed with light.

This information is available because of the serene and objective testimony of Mr. Borgowiec, who twice and almost with identical expression referred to the radiance of Father Kolbe's countenance after his death.

In fact, in the oral report given to Father Szweda, he related:

"When I opened the iron door, he lived no more. But he looked to me as though he were alive. His face was unusually radiant. The eyes, wide open, were fixed on one point. His figure was as if in ecstasy. I will never forget that sight."

Later on, in the written report, he retold the story thus:

"After the guard and the executioner left, I went back into the cell where I found Father Maximilian Kolbe leaning against the wall, with his head tilted to one side. His face, serene and beautiful, was radiant."

The note dominating this description is the radiance of his face: "His eyes, wide open, were fixed on a point. His figure was as if in ectasy."

It is not difficult to believe that the Immaculata, wanting to reward her most devoted son and zealous apostle in the hour of his death, would appear to him, inviting him to her maternal enraptured embrace. And while receiving his spirit, she would also want to let shine through his motionless body a reflection of the luminous candor of his soul, and to give in the fixity of his eyes a sensible sign that she had appeared, and a further indication of the eternal and immutable vision of God which Father Maximilian had found.

According to the testimony of Father Isidor Kosbial, Father Maximilian, more than once during his life, expressed the desire of dying on a day consecrated to the Virgin.

It seemed that the Virgin, the Madonna, answered the prayer of her "Knight." He was killed on the vigil of the Assumption so that the holocaust could be consummated on the solemnity of the Assumption.

On Assumption day, Friday, August 15, his body, placed in a box, was taken to one of the ovens which, at Auschwitz, burned day and night. A longing he had often expressed: "I would like my ashes to be scattered to the four winds," was thus granted by his heavenly Queen. But the second part of his longing: to disappear "without a trace," was not to be part of God's plan. Instead that humble desire was to draw upon him the attention of the whole Church which now rejoices in invoking him as St. Maximilian Kolbe.

## NATIONAL CENTERS OF THE *MILITIA IMMACULATAE* THROUGHOUT THE WORLD

ITALY, Centro Internazionale M.I., Casa Padre Kolbe, Via San Teodoro, 42, 00186 Roma

AUSTRALIA, National Center of the M.I., Mt. St. Francis, 69 New Windsor Road, Kellyville, N.S.W. 2153

AUSTRIA, Marianische Aktion Kolbe, Minoritenkonvent Zur Allerheiligsten Dreifaltigkeit, Alserstrasse, 17, 1080 Wien

BELGIUM, Ridderschap der Onbevlekte, Minderbroeders Konventuelen, Tiensestraat 78, B-3000 Leuven

BRAZIL, Jardim da Imaculada, Frades Franciscanos Conventuais, 77-220 Cidade Ocidental, (Goias-Brasil)

ENGLAND, National Crusade Center, Franciscan Friary, 2 Redclyffe Road, Urmston, Manchester M31 2LE

FRANCE, Centre National M.I., 5, Rue des Petits-Fossés, 65100 Lourdes

HOLLAND, Ridderschap der Onbevlekte, Convent St. Lambertus, Driessensstraat 24, 6015 AG Neeritter

ITALY, Centro Nazionale M.I., Casa Padre Kolbe, Via San Teodoro, 42, 00186 Roma

ITALY, Centro M.I. per I Polacchi Emigrati, Convento dell'Immacolata, Via Giunone Lucina, 75, 00050 Santa Severa

JAPAN, Seibo no Kishi Shudoin, 196 Hongochi, Nagasaki, 850 Nagasaki-ken

MALTA, Milizzja Ta'l Immakulata, St. Francis Friary, Tower Road, St. Paul's Bay

MEXICO, Sede Nacional de la M.I., Av. San Fernando No. 54, (ésquina con Morelos), Tlalpan México 22, DF

POLAND, Niepokalanow, 00. Franciszkanie, 96-515 Teresin k-Sochaczewa

PORTUGAL, Cidade da Imaculada, Avenida Camilo, 240, Porto

SOUTH KOREA, National Center of the M.I., Franciscan Mission, 782 Beom-Eo-Dong, 500 Seong Ku, 634 Daegu

SPAIN, Sede Nacional de la M.I., Padres Franciscanos Menores Conventuales, Grupo, Alferez Rojas 26, 3'izqda Zaragoza

SWITZERLAND, Mission de L'Immaculée, Couvent des Cordeliers, C. H.-1700, Fribourg 2

U.S.A., Knights of the Immaculata National Center, 1600 W. Park Avenue, Libertyville, IL 60048

W. GERMANY, Kreuzzug der Unbefleckten Jungfrau Maria (M.I.), Franziskanerkloster, Postfach 35, D-8700 Würzburg 11

ZAMBIA, National Center of the M.I., Franciscan Center, P.O. Box 70992, Ndola

## REGIONAL CENTERS AND HOUSES OF THE IMMACULATA

ARGENTINA, Misioneras de la Immaculada, Vicente López 1862, 7400 Olavarria (Buenos Aires)

INDIA, Nirmalaram, Franciscan Center, Chotty-Chittady, P.O. 686524, Kottayam DT, Kerala (S. India)

ITALY, Casa dell'Immacolata, 40044 Borgonuovo di Pontecchio Marconi (Bologna)

ITALY, Casa dell'Immacolata, Via del Pasero, 2, 95121 Catania

ITALY, Casa Mariana, Piana della Croce, 83040 Frigento (Avellino)

ITALY, Piccola Citta dell'Immacolata, Via Monte Fasce, 81, 16133 Genova-Apparizione

JAPAN, Misakae no Sono, Konagai-cho, 859-01 Nagasaki-ken

PHILIPPINES, Knights of the Immaculata Center, Franciscan Conventual Friars, St. Quiteria Church, Caloocan City, Metro-Manila 3108

U.S.A., Knights of the Immaculata Movement, St. Hyacinth College-Seminary, Granby, MA 01033

**Pauline** *BOOKS & MEDIA*

**ALASKA**
750 West 5th Ave., Anchorage, AK 99501; 907-272-8183

**CALIFORNIA**
3908 Sepulveda Blvd., Culver City, CA 90230; 310-397-8676
5945 Balboa Ave., San Diego, CA 92111; 619-565-9181
46 Geary Street, San Francisco, CA 94108; 415-781-5180

**FLORIDA**
145 S.W. 107th Ave., Miami, FL 33174; 305-559-6715

**HAWAII**
1143 Bishop Street, Honolulu, HI 96813; 808-521-2731

**ILLINOIS**
172 North Michigan Ave., Chicago, IL 60601; 312-346-4228

**LOUISIANA**
4403 Veterans Memorial Blvd., Metairie, LA 70006; 504-887-7631

**MASSACHUSETTS**
50 St. Paul's Ave., Jamaica Plain, Boston, MA 02130; 617-522-8911
Rte. 1, 885 Providence Hwy., Dedham, MA 02026; 617-326-5385

**MISSOURI**
9804 Watson Rd., St. Louis, MO 63126; 314-965-3512

**NEW JERSEY**
561 U.S. Route 1, Wick Plaza, Edison, NJ 08817; 908-572-1200

**NEW YORK**
150 East 52nd Street, New York, NY 10022; 212-754-1110
78 Fort Place, Staten Island, NY 10301; 718-447-5071

**OHIO**
2105 Ontario Street, Cleveland, OH 44115; 216-621-9427

**PENNSYLVANIA**
Northeast Shopping Center, 9171-A Roosevelt Blvd. (between Grant Ave. & Welsh Rd.), Philadelphia, PA 19114; 215-676-9494

**SOUTH CAROLINA**
243 King Street, Charleston, SC 29401; 803-577-0175

**TENNESSEE**
4811 Poplar Ave., Memphis, TN 38117; 901-761-2987

**TEXAS**
114 Main Plaza, San Antonio, TX 78205; 210-224-8101

**VIRGINIA**
1025 King Street, Alexandria, VA 22314; 703-549-3806

**CANADA**
3022 Dufferin Street, Toronto, Ontario, Canada M6B 3T5; 416-781-9131